WHO'S WHO
IN
HOCKEY

Harry C. Kariher

ARLINGTON HOUSE   New Rochelle, New York

Library of Congress Catalog Card Number 73-11868

MANUFACTURED IN THE UNITED STATES OF AMERICA

Library of Congress Cataloging in Publication Data

Kariher, Harry C   1932-
   Who's who in hockey.

   1. Hockey—Biography. I. Title.
GV848.5.A1K37   796.9'62'0922 [B]   73-11868
ISBN 0-87000-221-X

ACKNOWLEDGMENTS

In the research on this book, the author wishes to thank the staff of the Hockey Hall of Fame in Toronto—Lefty Reid, curator, and Bonnie Low and Paul Kitchen—for letting him spend time going through their reference material and archives.

Frank Selke, Sr., retired general manager of the Montreal Canadiens, also was most gracious in combing his memory for the whereabouts of many retired players.

EDITOR'S NOTE

As every sports buff knows, the records of athletes and coaches are sometimes in dispute. Add to this the possibility of human error and you can see why the author is asking every reader of this work to pass on any corrections he might discover.

Beyond that, can you think of any significant omissions? These will normally fall into the gray "matter of opinion" area. But if sentiment does build for including a particular athlete or official in a revised edition, the author will want to.

If you have any suggestions or corrections, please write to the author in care of Arlington House, New Rochelle, N. Y. 10801. Since this volume is likely to become one of the established sources, you will be making a significant contribution to sports research. Everyone who helps will be given a credit line in the revised, enlarged, updated edition we hope to bring out in the later 1970s.

ABBREVIATIONS OF HOCKEY ORGANIZATIONS USED

AHL—American Hockey League

CAHA—Canadian Amateur Hockey Association

CHL—Central Hockey League

CPHL—Central Professional Hockey League

EAL—Eastern Amateur League

ECL—Eastern Canada League

EHL—Eastern Hockey League

EPHL—Eastern Professional Hockey League

IHL—International Hockey League

JAHA—Junior Amateur Hockey Association

NHA—National Hockey Association

NHL—National Hockey League

NOHA—Northern Ontario Hockey Association

OHA—Ontario Hockey Association

PCHL—Pacific Coast Hockey League

QAHA—Quebec Amateur Hockey Association

QHL—Quebec Hockey League

USHL—United States Hockey League

WCL—Western Canada League

WHA—World Hockey Association

WHL—Western Hockey League

ABEL, CLARENCE JOHN (Taffy) B. 5/28/1900, Sault Ste. Marie, Mich. D. 8/1/64. Defenseman. 250 lbs. Played eight years in NHL, three with N.Y. Rangers, five with Chi. Black Hawks. Played as amateur with Fields Nationals, who won McNaughton Cup in 1919. Joined St. Paul as "amateur," enabling him to represent U.S. in 1924 Olympics in Paris. Returned to play in 1925–26 with Ching Johnson on Minneapolis Millers. Joined Rangers following season. Sold to Black Hawks after 1928–29 season. Retired 1934. Made abortive comeback in 1935; plans fell through when Abel and Chicago management could not resolve salary dispute, which amounted to $88.33. Victim of hoax in 1935 when fake telegram caused him to play in amateur game in Britt, Ont. Thinking he had permission, he endangered amateur status of 23 other players before situation resolved.

NHL record: 18 goals, 18 assists in 8 seasons; 1 goal, 1 assist in 38 playoff games.

ABEL, SIDNEY GERALD (Sid) B. 2/22/18, Melville, Sask. Forward. Hall of Famer. Starred as center before making bigger name at management level. Started with Det. Red Wings in 1938. With them through 1952–53 season with two years out during World War II. Finished career as player-manager of Chi. Black Hawks, 1952–53. Remained as manager one more season. Red Wing coach mid-1957–58; GM 1962. Stepped down as coach after 1967–68; quit as GM 1/71, in squabble over direction of club. Named St. L. Blues' coach in May 1971 and became

GM before season was over.

NHL record: 189 goals, 283 assists in 610 games; 28 goals, 30 assists in 97 playoff games.

ADAMS, CHARLES FRANCIS B. 10/18/76, Newport, Vt. D. 1947. Hall of Fame builder. Bought Western Canada League from Patrick brothers in 1926 for $300,000; major step in turning NHL into top pro organization. Started as handyman in grocery and made fortune as head of grocery chain. Secured NHL franchise for Boston in 1924, forming team with Art Ross after seeing Stanley Cup final in Montreal. Purchase of Western League brought such players as Eddie Shore, Harry Oliver, and Duke Keats to Bruins, with other Patrick stars going to other American NHL teams. Guaranteed $500,000 in 1927 over five years for Bruins' home games, and Boston Garden was built.

ADAMS, JOHN JAMES (Jack) B. 6/14/95, Fort William, Ont. D. 5/1/68. Made way into Hall of Fame as executive, although outstanding player in younger days. Turned pro 1918 with Toronto Arenas. Joined Vancouver 1919, won PCL scoring title. Played with Toronto St. Pats and Ottawa Senators. Joined Det. Red Wings as coach in 1927, remaining until 1947, then served as GM until 1962. Team won seven straight league titles. Named president of Central Pro League.

NHL record: 82 goals, 29 assists in 7 seasons; 11 goals, 1 assist in playoffs.

ADAMS, WESTON W., SR. B. 8/9/04, Springfield, Mass. D. 3/19/73, Brookline, Mass. President of Boston Bruins 1936–51 and 1964–69, following father, Charles F., who brought team into league in 1924. Adams, stockbroker, served as traveling secretary for old Boston Braves. Had horse racing interests. Was governor of Boston Braves, Bruins' franchise in American League, and chairman of board of Bruins until death. Made home in Brookline.

AHEARN, T. FRANKLYN B. 5/10/86, Ottawa, Ont. D. 11/17/62. Hall of Fame builder. Molded Ottawa Senators into NHL power after buying controlling interest in club in 1924. Stocked team with future Hall of Famers such as Alex Connell, Hooley Smith, Frank Nighbor, Syd Howe. Depression reverses forced him to sell players and finally rink holdings, hockey eventually costing him $200,000.

ALLAN, SIR MONTAGU B. 10/13/60, Montreal, Que. D. 9/26/51. Hall of Fame. At urging of William Northey, Sir Montagu donated Allan Cup, signifying Canadian amateur hockey supremacy, in 1908, when Stanley Cup became trophy for professionals. Queen's University won first cup, valued between $300 and $500. Allan Cup was donatéd to Canadian Amateur Hockey Assn. in 1928 after having been controlled by board of trustees. Financier.

ALLEN, COURTNEY KEITH (Bingo) B. 8/21/23, Saskatoon, Sask. GM Phila. Flyers. Had brief NHL career as player with Det. Red Wings, playing 28 games 1953–55 without scoring. Became Seattle coach 1956, GM 1965. Joined Flyers as coach 1966, guiding team to West Division title. Asst. GM, then GM during 1969–70 season. Lives in Bryn Mawr, Pa.

   NHL record: no goals, 4 assists in 28 games; no goals, no assists in 5 playoff games.

ANDERSON, RONALD CHESTER (Goings) B. 7/29/45, Red Deer, Alta. Forward. 6', 180. Turned pro in 1965–66 with Memphis of CPHL. Played there two seasons. Had minor league service with Fort Worth, Buffalo of AHL and Salt Lake City of WHL, as well as major league stays at Det., L.A., and St. L. Went to Buffalo in 1970 in trade for Craig Cameron, then to Salt Lake.

   NHL record: 28 goals, 30 assists in 251 games.

ANGOTTI, LOUIS FREDERICK (Lou) B. 1/16/38, Toronto, Ont. Forward. 5'8", 170. Spot player used by Chi. Black Hawks in special situations. Survived goalpost crash 3/4/72 in Minnesota with dislocated shoulder and gashed head. Played at Michigan Tech. Turned pro in 1962–63 with Rochester, making N.Y. Rangers two years later. Played briefly at St. Louis of CPHL, then went to Hawks in 1965–66. Taken by Philadelphia in 1967–68, went to Pittsburgh next season and drafted back to Hawks in June 1968, after going to St. L. in trade. Served as vice president of Players Assn. Became hockey rarity in 1968 when he announced he still had all his teeth.

   NHL record: 91 goals, 163 assists in 602 games.

APPS, JOSEPH SYLVANUS (Syl) B. 1/18/15, Paris, Ont. Forward. Hall of Famer. Averaged 20 goals a season for 10 years with Tor. Maple Leafs. Attended McMaster U. in Hamilton, Ont. Was hockey, football, track star, winning one British Empire and two Canadian championships in pole vaulting; also sixth in 1936 Olympics. Joined Leafs in 1936 and won Calder Trophy as Rookie of Year. Missed 1943–44 and 1944–45 while serving in armed forces. Then returned to play until retirement in 1948. Won Lady Byng Trophy 1942, was first-team All-Star center twice and second-team three times. Lives in Kingston, Ont., is member of Canadian parliament.

NHL record: 201 goals, 231 assists in 10 seasons; 25 goals and 28 assists in 69 playoff games.

APPS, SYLVANUS MARSHALL, JR. (Syl)   B. 8/1/47, Toronto, Ont. Forward. 6′, 185. Son of Tor. Maple Leafs' Hall of Famer Syl Apps, Sr. Pitt Penguins' center; led club in scoring 1971–72 in second NHL year, 15 goals, 44 assists in 72 games. Turned pro 8/12/69. With Buffalo (in N.Y. Ranger organization), Omaha. Split 1970–71 season between Rangers and Penguins, going to Pittsburgh in trade for Glen Sather, 1/27/71. "Best deal ever made," said Penguin coach Red Kelly. Scored 10 goals, 9 assists in CHL playoffs, 1970. On 2/13/71 scored 2 power-play goals against Black Hawks in 20 seconds. Lives in Kingston, Ont.

NHL record: 54 goals, 118 assists in 211 games.

ARBOUR, ALGER (Al)   B. 11/1/32, Sudbury, Ont. Defenseman. Wore spectacles during his 14-year NHL career, which started in 1953 with Det. Red Wings and continued through 1971 with St. L. Blues, and included stops in Chicago and Montreal. Played 19 years of hockey. NHL career broken three times by stays in minors. Named Blues' coach in May 1970. Stepped down in Feb. 1971 to become player again. Named asst. GM at end of season, but 12/25/71 became Blues' third coach of season, replacing Bill McCreary. Replaced as coach by Jean-Guy Talbot in Oct. 1972. Fight in Philadelphia 1/6/72 involving 10 Blues, numerous Philadelphia fans, and police, ended with Arbour charged with assault. Suit was ripped from his back in melee. Later cleared.

NHL record: 12 goals, 58 assists in 624 games; 1 goal, 8 assists in 80 playoff games.

ARMSTRONG, GEORGE EDWARD (Chief)   B. 7/6/30 in Skead, Ont. Forward. Spent 20 years with Tor. Maple Leafs. Finally quit as active player 10/20/72 after four previous attempts to retire. Retains post in Toronto front office with some scouting duties. Played as amateur with Toronto Marlboros before joining Leafs in 1949, serving 12 years as captain. Led team to four Stanley Cups. Called "Chief" because his mother was Indian. First winner of Charlie Conacher citizenship award (1969) for work with retarded children. Entertained teammates with war dances, whoops, chants, and turned off clubhouse television set during westerns while Indians were ahead.

NHL record: 296 goals, 417 assists in 1187 games; 26 goals, 32 assists in 110 playoff games.

ARMSTONG, MURRAY ALEXANDER B. 1/1/16, Manor, Sask. Forward. Hockey coach at U. of Denver, spent seven years in NHL with three clubs. Son of blacksmith. Played as amateur with Regina Pats. Joined Tor. Maple Leafs in 1938–39, went next year to N.Y. Americans, spending three seasons, then finished career in 1945–46 after three seasons with Det. Red Wings. Coached at Regina before taking Denver job. Always insisted his players further their educations. Believes "old, crude" approach to hockey has gone out of date.

NHL record: 67 goals, 121 assists in 7 seasons; 4 goals, 6 assists in 27 playoff games.

ARMSTRONG, ROBERT RICHARD B. 4/7/31, Toronto, Ont. Defenseman. Spent 11 seasons with Bos. Bruins. Played as junior with Stratford Kroehlers, got into two games for Bruins in 1950–51, then made team next season and stayed until retirement, 1961–62. After retirement took job as teacher at Grove Prep Schools, Lakefield, near Peterborough, Ont.

NHL record: 13 goals and 86 assists in 542 games; 1 goal, 7 assists in 42 playoff games.

ASHBEE, WILLIAM BARRY B. 7/28/39, Weston, Ont. Defenseman. 5'10", 180. Played second full NHL season in 1971–72 in pro career which began in 1959. Started as junior with Barrie Flyers, then turned pro with Kingston (Ont.) of EPHL. Spent 1962–70 with Hershey Bears of AHL, playing 14 games in 1965–66 with Bruins. Made Phila. Flyers when acquired at age 31 in 1970.

NHL record: 11 goals, 57 assists in 215 games.

AURIE, HARRY LAWRENCE B. 2/8/05, Sudbury, Ont. D. 12/11/52. Forward. 5'6", 145. Spent 12 seasons with Det. Red Wings and his No. 6 was retired when he stepped down after 1938–39 season. Coached in Det. farm system at Pittsburgh and Oshawa after retirement.

NHL record: 150 goals, 129 assists in 12 seasons.

AWREY, DONALD WILLIAM (Don) B. 7/18/43, Kitchener, Ont. Defenseman-forward. 6', 195. Broke ankle in Nov. 1971, allowing him to get into only 34 games in 1971–72 season after four straight seasons as regular with Bos. Bruins. Played as junior with Niagara Falls, turned pro in Boston organization in 1963, played at Minneapolis most of that year. Split 1964–65 between Bruins and Hershey. Made Bruins in 1965–66, then sent to Hershey for 1966–67 season to learn to play rough. He did, racking up 153 penalty minutes. Returned to Bruins 1967–68. With exception of broken-ankle year, penalty minutes have totaled more than

100 each season. Team Canada 1972. Operates hockey camp in off-season.

NHL record: 21 goals, 87 assists in 543 games; no goals, 11 assists in 54 playoff games.

BACKSTROM, RALPH GERALD B. 9/18/37, Kirkland Lake, Ont. Forward. 5'10", 170. Retired in Nov. 1970, in his 13th year with Canadiens, but unretired in Dec. when he told Montreal club he would be amenable to trade to West Coast club. Sent to L.A. Kings 1/26/71, then traded to Chi. Black Hawks 2/25/72 for Danny Maloney. Captained Junior Canadiens 1956–58, and played total of three games in minors (Montreal Royals and Rochester) before joining Canadiens for good in 1958. Won Calder Trophy as Rookie of Year.

NHL record: 278 goals, 361 assists in 1032 games; 27 goals, 32 assists in 116 playoff games.

BAILEY, GARNET EDWARD (Ace) B. 6/13/48, Lloydminster, Sask. Forward. 5'11", 192. Reduced penalty minutes in 1971–72 from 136 to 64, then apparently took out excess hostility after regular season, being arrested 5/15/72 as drunk and disorderly after fight in club owned by teammate Ed Johnston. Lives in Lloydminster. Played as amateur with Edmonton Oil Kings. Turned pro in 1967 at Oklahoma City, then moved to Hershey and made Bos. Bruins in 1969. Sent down for 11 games at Oklahoma City in 1970–71 before rejoining Bruins. Traded to Det. Red Wings for Gary Doak 3/1/73.

NHL record: 33 goals and 57 assists in 245 games; no goals or assists in 2 playoff games.

BAILEY, IRVINE WALLACE (Ace) B. 7/3/03, Bracebridge, Ont. Forward. Tor. Maple Leafs. Career cut short 12/12/33 when Eddie Shore knocked him on his head in Boston. Bailey almost died and never played again. Joined Leafs in 1926. Led NHL in scoring in 1928–29 with 32 points, 22 of which were goals. His No. 6 was retired by Leafs after injury, but he requested it be given to Ron Ellis. Now in insurance business in Willowdale, Ont.

NHL record: 111 goals, 82 assists in 8 seasons; 3 goals, 4 assists in 4 playoffs.

BAIN, DONALD H. (Dan) B. 1874, Belleville, Ont. D. 8/15/62. Hall of Famer. Starred in many sports, winning championships in roller skating, gymnastics, bicycle racing, shooting, speed skating, figure skating, lacrosse, and golf in career lasting 35 years. Played on two Stanley Cup champions as amateur with Winnipeg Victorias in 1896 and 1901. Spent most of life in Winnipeg.

BAKER, HOBART AMERY HARE (Hobey) B. Jan. 1892, Wissahickon, Pa. D. 12/21/18, France, in air crash as member of Lafayette Escadrille in World War I. Hall of Famer. Never played pro hockey. Made reputation in athletics at Princeton U. Also starred in football, golf, track, swimming at Princeton, which he entered in 1910, graduating in 1914. Played rover in days of seven-man hockey. Princeton team known as "Baker and six other players." Skated for St. Nicholas team after graduation, winning praise of Montreal observers as first-class player, though American.

BALFOUR, MURRAY B. 8/24/36, Regina, Sask. D. 5/30/65, of cancer. Forward. Member of Chi. Black Hawks' "Million Dollar Line" of 1960s with Bobby Hull and Bill Hay. Joined Mont. Canadiens in 1956, was traded to Hawks in 1959, and finished NHL career with Bos. Bruins in 1964. Was playing with Hershey Bears, where he had been sent by Bruins, when stricken by cancer.

NHL record: 67 goals, 90 assists in 306 games; 9 goals, 10 assists in 40 playoff games.

BALON, DAVID ALEXANDER (Dave) B. 8/2/38, Wakaw, Sask. Forward. 5'11", 180. Played no hockey until 10. Turned pro in Ranger organization with Saskatoon in 1958. Played at Three Rivers and Kitchener with occasional visits to New York before making Rangers at end of 1961–62. Traded to Mont. Canadiens 6/4/63 in deal involving Gump Worsley, Jacques Plante, Donnie Marshall, Phil Goyette, others. Sent by Canadiens to Minn. North Stars in 1967 expansion draft, then traded back to Rangers 6/13/68 for Wayne Hillman, Joe Johnson, and

Dan Seguin. Rangers sent him to Van. Canucks in Nov. 1971 for Gary Doak and Jim Wiste. Noted for accuracy of shot, and in first half of 1970–71 was credited with scoring on 27.7 percent of attempts.

NHL record: 192 goals, 222 assists in 876 games.

BARILKO, WILLIAM (Bill)   B. 3/25/27, Timmins, Ont. D. 8/26/51. Defenseman. Played only five seasons for Tor. Maple Leafs, from 1946 to 1951, then was killed in off-season plane crash in which body was not found for 11 years. Just 19 when called up from Hollywood Wolves. Scored winning goal in 1951 Stanley Cup finals at 2:53 of overtime. Then 8/26/51 left on plane trip with friend, Dr. Henry Hudson, and never returned. Wreckage of plane and bodies was found 6/6/62 near Cochrane, Ont.

NHL career record: 26 goals, 36 assists in 252 games; 5 goals, 7 assists in 47 playoff games.

BARKLEY, DOUGLAS (Doug)   B. 1/6/37, Lethbridge, Alta. Ex–Red Wing coach was outstanding defenseman before injury ended playing career. Played with Calgary and Buffalo in minors before NHL, 1957, with Chi. Black Hawks, playing three games in 1957–58 and three in 1959–60. Made league to stay in 1962, with Det. Red Wings, to whom he was traded in 1962 for Len Londe and John McKenzie. Missed Rookie of Year award by just two-tenths of point. Suffered eye injury 1/30/66; specialists in Detroit and Boston unable to save eye. Moved into front office, helping with scouting, and in 1969 took over Fort Worth, Wings' farm in Central League. Took over for Ned Harkness as Wings' coach in mid-1970–71. Replaced by Johnny Wilson in mid-1971–72. Lives in Calgary.

NHL record: 24 goals, 80 assists in 253 games; no goals, 9 assists in 30 playoff games.

BARRIE, DOUGLAS ROBERT (Doug)   B. 10/2/46, Edmonton, Alta. Defenseman. 5'9", 175. Turned pro with Memphis of CPHL in 1966–67. Played minor league hockey at Pittsburgh, Kansas City, Omaha, Tulsa, Amarillo, Baltimore; eight-game appearance with Pitt. Penguins 1968–69 before making it with Buffalo Sabres. Traded to L.A. Kings 12/16/71. Went to Alberta Oilers of WHA after 1971–72.

NHL record: 10 goals, 42 assists in 158 games.

BARRY, MARTIN (Marty)   B. 12/8/04, St. Gabriel, Que. Forward. Hall of Famer. Played 12 years in NHL, although did not play regularly there until he was 25. Started in Montreal amateur leagues, then joined N.Y. Americans in 1927. Played just one game, then went to Philadelphia and

17

New Haven in minors before returning to NHL with Bos. Bruins in 1929–30. Traded to Det. Red Wings in 1935. Finished career in 1939–40 with Mont. Canadiens. Lives in Halifax, N.S. Played on Stanley Cup winner with Red Wings in 1935–36. Won Lady Byng Trophy in 1936–37, and made first All-Star team that season.

NHL record: 195 goals, 192 assists in 12 years; 15 goals, 18 assists in 7 playoffs.

BATHGATE, ANDREW JAMES (Andy) B. 8/28/32, Winnipeg, Man. Forward. Called it quits in 1971 after 19 years in NHL. Captained Guelph to Memorial Cup in 1952, and joined N.Y. Rangers for 18 games in 1952–53. Spent 10 more years in New York before going to Tor. Maple Leafs with Don McKenney for five players, in mid-1963–64. Went to Red Wings in 1965. Grabbed by Pitt. Penguins in 1967 draft, and ended NHL career there after 1970–71 season. Almost always among top scorers. Tied Bobby Hull for scoring title in 1962 with 84 points, and in 1962–63 scored goals for Rangers in 10 consecutive games. Has performed as pro golfer. In 1971 sought to regain amateur status after offer to play in Switzerland.

NHL record: 349 goals, 624 assists in 1069 games; 21 goals, 14 assists in 54 playoff games.

BAUER, ROBERT THEODORE B. 2/16/15, Waterloo, Ont. D. 9/16/64, Kitchener, Ont. Forward. Was member of Bruins' Kraut Line with Milt Schmidt and Woody Dumart, all of whom lived as boys in Kitchener area. Played for St. Michael's juniors, then Boston Cubs, moved up to Bruins in 1936 with Dumart and Schmidt, and stayed until 1952, with time out in 1942–45 for RCAF. All members of line joined service at same time, and were carried off ice by teammates before leaving for military duty. Won Lady Byng Trophy in 1940, 1941, 1947. Coached Canada Olympic team twice after retirement. His brother, a clergyman, also served as Olympic coach. Later, operated business in Kitchener.

NHL record: 123 goals, 137 assists in 9 seasons; 11 goals, 8 assists in 47 playoff games.

BAUN, ROBERT NEIL (Bob) B. 9/9/36, Lanigan, Sask. Defenseman. 5′9″, 182. Considered one of league's roughest body checkers. Played as amateur with Toronto Marlboros. Turned pro with Rochester in 1956. Joined Tor. Maple Leafs same season and stayed until 1967, when he was drafted by Calif Seals. Went to Det. Red Wings for two seasons, then sold to Buffalo in 1970. Sabres traded him to St. L. Blues. Never played at either Buffalo or St. Louis because of contract dispute; sent back to Toronto 11/14/70. Once played through playoffs on broken foot. Lives on farm on outskirts of Toronto with wife and five children.

NHL record: 37 goals, 187 assists in 964 games; 3 goals, 12 assists in 96 playoff games.

BEATTIE, JOHN (Red) B. 1907, Ibstock, England. Forward. Played eight seasons as forward in NHL, six with Bos. Bruins. Joined Edmonton Superiors after moving to Canada, went to Bruins in 1930. Broke leg playing baseball in summer of 1931 and missed 1931–32 season, returning in 1932 and staying in Boston until 1937, when he went to Det. Red Wings, who sent him to N.Y. Americans in midseason. Finished career with Americans in 1938–39.

NHL record: 62 goals, 85 assists in 8 seasons; 4 goals and 2 assists in 5 playoffs.

BELIVEAU, JEAN B. 8/31/31, Three Rivers, Que. Forward. Spent 19 years with Mont. Canadiens, from 1950–51 to 1969–70. In order to get him, Canadiens purchased entire Quebec Senior League, where Beliveau was playing as an "amateur" for $20,000 a year. Canadiens had attempted to lure him away earlier, but were reluctant to do so for "political" reasons, some observers claiming Quebec lawmakers had threatened Forum with loss of liquor license if Beliveau left Quebec Aces. A big man at 6'3" and 210, he was criticized at first for having too placid a disposition, but learned to hit and later went on to win the Hart MVP Trophy in 1956 and 1964, and was named 10 times to All-Star teams. There was a flurry of concern in 1962 when Beliveau experienced minor heart difficulty, but he continued to play for seven more years. Now vice president of Canadiens in charge of corporate relations.

NHL record: 482 goals, 661 assists in 1055 games; 73 goals, 81 assists in 142 playoff games.

BENEDICT, CLINT (Benny) B. 1894, Ottawa, Ont. Goalie. Hall of Fame. In 1929–30 was one of first to wear mask, after shot by Howie Morenz splintered his nose. However, soon discarded, saying nosepiece obscured vision. Spent 13 years in NHL, starting in 1917 with Ottawa Senators, then going to Montreal Maroons in 1924. Retired 1930, forced by second shot from Morenz that season, this one injuring throat. Benedict known for falling on puck in net, which was illegal. Said he could get away with it "if you did it sneakily and made it look accidental." Rule later was changed. Lives in retirement in Ottawa.

NHL record: allowed 874 goals in 364 games for 2.37 average, 57 shutouts; gave up 87 goals in 49 playoff games for 1.78 average, 15 shutouts.

BENTLEY, DOUGLAS WAGNER (Doug) B. 9/3/16, Delisle, Sask. D. 11/24/72, Saskatoon, Sask. Forward. One of two Hall of Fame brothers. Played 13 NHL seasons, all but last with Chi. Black Hawks. Left wing on famed Pony Line (brother Max and Bill Mosienko two others) of Hawks. Played senior hockey in home at 16, two seasons as junior, then three as senior at Moose Jaw. After one season at Drumheller, Alta., joined Black Hawks in 1939–40 season. Missed 1944–45 season during World War II, then returned to Hawks until traded to N.Y. Rangers in 1953, retiring after 1953–54 season. Three times All-Star first team, once on second. Coached amateur teams in Saskatchewan after retirement. Victim of cancer.

NHL record: 219 goals, 324 assists in 13 seasons; 9 goals, 8 assists in 23 playoff games.

BENTLEY, MAXWELL HERBERT LLOYD (Max) B. 3/1/20, Delisle, Sask. Forward. Other half of Bentley Hall of Fame team, played 12 years in NHL, teaming with Doug on Chi. Black Hawks until 1947–48 when sent to Tor. Maple Leafs. Later rejoined him for one season with N.Y. Rangers. Weighed only 145 lbs. at height of career, and was turned down by Bos. Bruins and Mont. Canadiens, the doctor of latter team telling him he had heart condition and should not play at all. Went on to become playmaking center. Joined Hawks in 1940, missed two years during war, returning in 1945, then sent to Maple Leafs in 1947–48 for five NHL players and an amateur. Rejoined brother Doug with Rangers in 1953–54, then retired. Won Hart MVP Trophy in 1946, Lady Byng in 1943 and Art Ross in 1945 and 1946. Lives in Delisle, where he coaches amateur teams.

NHL record: 245 goals, 299 assists in 646 games; 18 goals, 27 assists in 52 playoff games.

BERENSON, GORDON ARTHUR (Red) B. 12/8/39, Regina, Sask. Forward. 6′, 190. Joined Mont. Canadiens out of U. of Michigan where he earned B.A. and M.A. degrees, in 1962. Between stints with Canadiens played with Hull-Ottawa of EPHL and Quebec of AHL. Traded to N.Y. Rangers in 1966 and St. L. Blues in Nov. 1967. Went to Det. Red Wings in 1971 and insists deal was made because he was president of players' assn. Tied league record 1/7/68 with six goals against Phila. Flyers, tied another with four goals in one period. Team Canada 1972. Lives with wife and children in off-season in Bloomfield Hills, Mich. An outdoorsman, has been involved in two near fatal boating mishaps, once lost in fog and once nearly drifting over waterfall.

NHL record: 168 goals, 283 assists in 608 games; 21 goals, 12 assists in 76 playoff games.

BERGMAN, GARY GUNNAR   B. 10/7/38, Kenora, Ont. Defenseman. 5'11", 185. Played junior hockey with Winnipeg team and turned pro with Winnipeg Warriors of WHL in 1957. Also played at Buffalo, Cleveland, and Springfield of AHL before making majors when Det. Red Wings drafted him for Mont. Canadiens in 1964. Sent to Memphis of CPHL in 1965–66 before being recalled to Wings in same season. Excellent golfer and amateur pilot. Enjoys contact and has quick temper, which showed itself 3/17/71 in dispute with Wings' coach in game against Boston. Was ordered off team bench and out of Detroit Olympia. Team Canada 1972. Lives with wife and children all year in Detroit.

NHL record: 55 goals and 212 assists in 619 games; no goals, 5 assists in 21 playoff games.

BERNIER, SERGE JOSEPH   B. 4/29/47, Padoue, Que. Foward. 6', 190. Started 1971–72 season with Phila. Flyers, went to L.A. Kings 1/28/72 in eight-player deal. Played junior hockey with Sorel, turned pro with Quebec Aces in 1967–68. Spent three years in AHL before breaking in with Flyers in 1970–71 with 23 goals and 28 assists in 77 games.

NHL record: 68 goals, 97 assists in 224 games; 1 goal, 1 assist in 4 playoff games.

BERRY, ROBERT VICTOR (Bob)   B. 11/29/43, Montreal, Que. Forward. 6', 190. Played in Russia with Canadian National team before turning pro in 1968 with Mont. Canadien organization, which sent him to Cleveland. Played season with Mont. Voyageurs in AHL and went to L.A. Kings on conditional basis in 1970, finishing season with 25 goals and 38 assists, second high on team. Proficient in baseball and football, playing a year as flanker with Quebec Rifles of United League and getting baseball tryout with Houston Astros. Holds master's degree from Sir George Williams U. Runs hockey school in Ohio during off-season.

NHL record: 78 goals, 88 assists in 235 games.

BINKLEY, LESLIE JOHN   B. 6/6/36, Owen Sound, Ont. Goalie. Caught on with Cleveland Barons as trainer and spare goalie in 1958, and stayed with AHL club until 1966, winning Rookie of Year award in 1962. Spent year at San Diego before joining Pitt. Penguins in expansion. Jumped to Ottawa Nationals of WHA after 1971–72. Wears glasses off ice and contact lenses while playing. Had undergone two operations on left knee. Lives with family in Walkerton, Ont.

NHL record: allowed 575 goals in 196 games for 3.12 average, 11 shutouts; gave up 15 goals in 7 playoff games for 2.10 average, no shutouts.

BLAKE, HECTOR (Toe) B. 8/21/12, Victoria Mines, Ont. Forward, Hall of Famer. Outstanding both as player and coach for Mont. Canadiens. Started in Sudbury-Nickel Belt League in 1929, and joined Mont. Maroons in 1934, playing only three games. Sent to minors next season, he joined Canadiens in Feb. 1936 staying with team as player until 1/10/48 when broken leg forced retirement. Won NHL scoring championship in 1939 and Lady Byng Trophy in 1946, playing on line with Elmer Lach and Maurice Richard. Coached in minors, then became Canadiens coach in 1955, leading team to eight Stanley Cups before retiring in 1968. Often fiery, Blake was acquitted in 1968 on charges of attacking fan in Los Angeles in game 11/19/67. Claude Provost, Canadiens player, also was acquitted. Lives in Montreal.

NHL record: 235 goals, 292 assists in 19 seasons; 25 goals, 37 assists in 57 playoff games.

BODNAR, AUGUST (Gus) B. 8/24/25, Fort William, Ont. Forward. Made name for himself as coach after 12-year NHL playing career with three clubs. Son of Ukrainian immigrant, joined Tor. Maple Leafs in 1943 and won Calder Trophy as Rookie of Year. Stayed until 1947–48 when he went to Chi. Black Hawks in seven-player deal. Shipped to Bos. Bruins in mid-1953–54 and retired after 1954–55 season. Scored first NHL goal in 15 seconds in Oct. 1943 against N. Y. Rangers, his first game in league. Coached Toronto Marlboros to Memorial Cup in 1966, coached Salt Lake City of WHL in 1970–71. Named Coach of Year in OHA junior as coach of Oshawa Generals. Lives in Oshawa. "I don't con the players," he says of techniques.

NHL record: 142 goals, 254 assists in 667 games; 4 goals, 3 assists in 32 playoff games.

BOIVIN, LEO JOSEPH B. 8/2/32, Prescott, Ont. Defenseman. Had 18-year NHL career before retirement 11/4/70. Played for Port Arthur West End juniors before joining Tor. Maple Leafs in 1951–52. Made Leafs next season, staying until traded to Bos. Bruins 11/9/54. Remained in Boston until 1965–66, when he went to Det. Red Wings. Was taken in 1967 by expansion Pitt. Penguins. Sent to Minn. North Stars in 1969–70, then retired. Accepted position with North Stars as scout.

NHL record: 72 goals, 251 assists in 1150 games; 3 goals and 10 assists in 54 playoff games.

BOLDIREV, IVAN B. 8/15/49, Zrenjanin, Yugoslavia. Forward. 6', 190. Sent by Bos. Bruins to Calif. Seals 11/17/71 for Chris Oddleifson. Reared in Sault Ste. Marie, Ont. Played as junior with Oshawa Generals, turned pro in 1969 in Bruins' organization. Spent two seasons at Oklahoma City, scoring 67 and 71 points respectively. Played just two games with Bruins. Registered first full NHL season with Seals in 1971–72.

NHL record: 27 goals, 48 assists in 128 games.

BOLL, FRANK THURMAN (Buzz) B. 3/6/11/ Fillmore, Sask. Forward. Played as amateur with Toronto Marlboros, joined Tor. Maple Leafs in 1933, went to N.Y. Americans in 1939, and to Bos. Bruins in 1942, retiring from NHL in 1944. Had best season there in 1942–43, with 25 goals and 27 assists in 43 games. Now retired farmer in Weyburn, Sask.

NHL record: 133 goals, 130 assists in 10 seasons; no goals, 5 assists in 17 playoff games.

BONIN, MARCEL B. 9/12/32, Montreal, Que. Forward. Played with seven pro clubs before making NHL with Det. Red Wings in 1952. Played as amateur for Quebec Aces, then started long minor league climb. After making Red Wings, he went back to Aces in 1953–54, then returned to Wings in 1954–55, sent to Bos. Bruins next season, and finished career with Mont. Canadiens, retiring 7/26/62 because of back injury. Known as rough player, he piled up 25 penalty minutes in single period against Chi. Black Hawks in 1961. All-Star five times. Scored 10 goals, 5 assists in 11 games in 1959 playoffs. Among idiosyncrasies was penchant for eating glass, which he demonstrated from time to time. Once attempted to pin bear to win $1000 bet; failed after 10 minutes, said: "After 10 mee-nuts of that bear I decide mon-ee is not for me."

NHL record: 97 goals, 175 assists in 454 games; 11 goals, 14 assists in 50 playoff games.

BOON, RICHARD R. (Dickie) B. 2/14/74, Belleville, Ont. D. 5/3/61. Defenseman. Hall of Famer. Weighed only 120 lbs. Started with Montreal Monarchs in 1897, graduated to Montreal juniors and finally to Montreal AAA seniors in 1901–02. The club won Stanley Cup from Winnipeg in 1902. Finished career as player with Montreal Wanderers in 1905. Assumed managership of club in 1903 and held it until mid-1918, also serving as director and coach after 1905. Team won three Stanley Cups during his 13-year tenure.

BORDELEAU, CHRISTIAN GERALD B. 9/23/47, Noranda, Que. Forward. 5'8", 165. Captain of Junior Canadiens before turning pro at Houston in 1967. Spent two seasons there, made Mont. Canadiens in 1968–69, sold to St. L. Blues 5/23/70. Had surgery to correct shoulder infirmity before traded to Chi. Black Hawks 2/8/72 for Danny O'Shea. Jumped to Winnipeg Jets of WHA after 1971–72. Brother of J. P. Bordeleau, also in Hawks' system.

NHL record: 38 goals, 65 assists in 205 games; 4 goals, 7 assists in 19 playoff games.

BOUCHARD, EMILE JOSEPH (Butch) B. 9/11/19, Montreal, Que. Defenseman. Hall of Famer. Played 15 seasons with Canadiens, joining team in 1941, reportedly riding bicycle 50 miles to reach training camp. Made first All-Stars in 1947, 1948 and 1950, second All-Stars in 1951 and 1952. Retired 1956. Lives in Montreal, where he has served in junior hockey as coach and president of teams since retirement from NHL after 1955–56 season.

NHL record: 49 goals, 144 assists in 785 games; 11 goals, 21 assists in 113 playoff games.

BOUCHER, FRANK (Raffles) B. 10/7/01, Ottawa, Ont. Forward. Hall of Famer won Lady Byng sportsmanship trophy seven times in eight seasons after deciding against career with North West Mounted Police, which he joined at 17. Bought way out of police for $50, which took him a year to raise. Joined Ottawa in NHL in 1921, playing 24 games, then played for Vancouver of PCL until 1926, when league broke up. Was sold to Bos. Bruins, who sold him to N.Y. Rangers before he even played a game. Stayed with N.Y. until retiring in 1938. Coached Rangers to Stanley Cup in 1940, and stayed with organization until 1944, returning in last year to play 15 games. Lives in Regina, Sask., where he sells hockey sticks.

NHL record: 161 goals, 262 assists in 557 games; 18 goals, 18 assists in 67 playoff games.

BOUCHER, GEORGE (Buck) B. 1896, Ottawa, Ont. D. 10/17/60. Defenseman. Hall of Famer. Football star also, playing halfback for three years with Ottawa Rough Riders. One of four brothers who were outstanding in hockey, three in NHL. Started in Ottawa City League, then joined Ottawa Senators in 1915. Team won four Stanley Cups between 1920 and 1927. Sold to Mont. Maroons in 1928–29 season and then to Black Hawks, ending career in Chi. in 1931–32. Coached Chi., Ott., Bos., and St. L., and assisted with Ott. RCAF team that won Olympics in 1948.

NHL record: 122 goals, 62 assists in 184 games; 9 goals, 4 assists in 12 playoffs.

BOUDRIAS, ANDRE B. 9/19/43, Montreal, Que. Forward. 5'8", 165.

Played with North Bay–Hull, Hull-Ottawa, Omaha, Houston and Kansas City, before hitting majors. Originally Mont. Canadiens' property, played only briefly with Canadiens, making NHL full time with Minn. North Stars in 1967. Spent two seasons at Minn, went to Chi. Black Hawks for part of 1968–69, then on to St. L. Blues. When with Blues, was offered in draft; no one would take him, but Scotty Bowman, then Blues' coach, prevailed on Van. Canucks to give little forward chance. Vancouver writers named him "Super Pest," and radio station started playing "The Super Pest Song." Noted for defense, held Boston's Phil Esposito to three goals in 1970–71.

NHL record: 112 goals, 188 assists in 430 games; 5 goals, 10 assists in 28 playoff games.

BOWER, JOHN WILLIAM B. 11/8/24, Prince Albert, Sask. Goalie. Sometimes known as "China Wall." Broke into NHL as goalie at late age in 1953 with N.Y. Rangers, and was traded to Tor. Maple Leafs in 1958, retiring in 1970. Won Vezina Cup in 1961 and shared it with Terry Sawchuk in 1965. Now handles Eastern Canada scouting duties for Maple Leafs.

NHL record: allowed 1347 goals in 534 games for 2.53 average, 37 shutouts; gave up 184 goals in 72 playoff games for 2.58 average, 5 shutouts.

BOWIE, RUSSELL (Dubbie) B. 8/24/80, Montreal, Que. D. 4/8/59. Forward. Hall of Famer. Remained amateur throughout his career, turning down all offers of money, even grand piano, to turn pro. Spent 10 years with Montreal Victorias, scoring 234 goals in 80 games. Once scored 10 goals in single game. Broken collarbone forced end to playing in 1908. Became outstanding referee after retirement.

BOWMAN, WILLIAM SCOTT (Scotty) B. 9/18/33, Montreal, Que. Took over as coach of Mont. Canadiens for 1971–72 after club fired Al MacNeill, despite fact MacNeill won Stanley Cup previous year. Playing career ended during junior play in 1951–52 by head injury, but coached in Canadien system from 1954–66 when he joined St. L. Blues as coach and GM in 1967, leading St. L. into cup playoffs in 1968, 1969, and 1970, and to Western Division championships in 1969 and 1970.

BREWER, CARL THOMAS B. 10/21/38, Toronto, Ont. Defenseman. 5'10", 180. Turned pro in Tor. Maple Leaf organization, made club in 1958 and spent seven seasons with Leafs, retiring in 1965 after disputes with coach Punch Imlach. Totaled more than 100 penalty minutes in five of those seasons, with 177 in 1964–65. Sat out four seasons, regained amateur standing, playing year with Canadian National team and one with Finnish team. Rights secured 3/3/68 by Det. Red Wings in six-man deal. Played 70 games in 1969–70. Retired again, then was enticed back by St.L. Blues at end of 1970–71 season.

NHL record: 25 goals, 193 assists in 584 games.

BRIMSEK, FRANCIS CHARLES (Frankie) B. 9/26/15, Eveleth, Minn. Goalie. Hall of Famer. Earned nickname "Mr Zero" when he joined Bos. Bruins in 1938. Starting with second game he recorded three straight shutouts, extended string to 231 minutes and 54 seconds, then, after string was broken, ran up three more shutouts and a goalless stretch of another 220 minutes, 24 seconds. Captured two Vezina Trophies, in 1938–39 and 1941–42. As rookie, won Vezina with 69 goals in 43 games, 1.60 average, with 10 shutouts. Missed 1943–45 seasons while in U.S. Coast Guard. Returned 1945. Traded in 1949 to Chi. Black Hawks. Ended career there in spring of 1950. Now lives in Virginia, Minn.

NHL record: allowed 1402 goals in 478 games, a 2.94 average; 40 shutouts; gave up 186 goals in 68 games, a 2.74 average, 2 shutouts.

BROADBENT, HARRY L. (Punch) B. 1892, Ottawa, Ont. D. 1971 Forward. Hall of Famer played 11 NHL seasons, once leading league in both scoring and penalties. Started in Ottawa amateur hockey, then turned pro at 16, joining Ottawa of NHA in 1912. In 1916 he left to serve in World War I, winning Military Medal. Rejoined Ottawa in 1919, then was sold to Mont. Maroons in 1924. Played for Ottawa in 1927–28, and with N.Y. Americans the next year. When stock market crashed in 1929, he quit hockey and joined RCAF. Led league in 1922 with 32 goals, and also in penalties, saying he had a "hard time controlling my elbows."

NHL record: 122 goals, 45 assists in 11 seasons; 10 goals, 3 assists in 10 playoff series.

BRODA, WALTER (Turk) B. 5/15/14, Brandon, Man. D. 10/72/72, Toronto, Ont. Goalie. Hall of Famer played 14 seasons for Tor. Maple Leafs after juvenile and junior play in Brandon and Winnipeg. Played for Det. Olympics in 1934–35, then was sold to Tor. for $8000, joining team in 1936. Until his retirement in 1952, with two seasons out during World War II, he played in 630 league games. Won Vezina Trophy in 1941 and 1948, and shared it with Al Rollins in 1951. Broda, of whom Jack Adams once said, "He could play in a tornado and never blink an eye," had weight problems, and was forced onto diet in 1949 when Conn Smythe threatened him with loss of his job. He made weight of 190, losing 10 pounds while missing only one game. Lived in Toronto. Victim of heart attack.

NHL record: allowed 1611 goals in 630 games, a 2.56 average, 61 shutouts; gave up 211 goals in 101 playoff games, a 2.09 average, 12 shutouts.

BROWN, ADAM   B. 2/4/20, Johnstone, Scotland. D. Aug. 1960 in auto crash. Forward. Had nine-year career in NHL with Det. Red Wings, Chi. Black Hawks, and Bos. Bruins. Played with Guelph Junior A's, turned pro at Omaha in 1940, broke into NHL in 1941 with Det. Red Wings. After brief trip to Indianapolis returned to stay until 12/9/46, when he was sent to Black Hawks as part of deal for Pete Horeck. Went to Bruins in 1951–52, was sent to Hershey, and stepped out of NHL after that season. Exceptionally fast skater.

NHL record: 104 goals, 113 assists in 391 games; 2 goals, 4 assists in 28 playoff games.

BROWN, STEWART ARNOLD (Arnie)   B. 1/28/42, Oshawa, Ont. Defenseman, 5'11", 185. Played junior hockey with Toronto Marlboros, turning pro in Tor. Maple Leafs system with Rochester of AHL in 1961–62. Played briefly in two seasons with Leafs and with Rochester and Baltimore in 1963–64 before getting into NHL to stay with N.Y. Rangers in 1964–65 after losing 20 lbs. Traded to Det. Red Wings midway through 1970–71 in five-player deal. Had knee surgery in June 1970 for removal of cartilage in right knee injured in '70 playoffs. To N.Y. Islanders in expansion, then traded mid-1972–73 to Atlanta. Lives year-round with wife and children in Bloomfield Hills, Mich.

NHL record: 42 goals, 135 assists in 633 games; no goals, 6 assists in 18 playoff games.

BROWN, WALTER A.   B. 2/10/05. D. 9/7/64. Hall of Fame builder. Former president of Boston Bruins and GM of Boston Garden. Also leader in amateur hockey. Was member of Hockey Hall of Fame governing committee and past president of International Olympic Ice Hockey Federation. Coached Boston Olympics to five U.S. championships and world championship between 1930 and 1940. Pioneered in basketball; co-owner and president of Boston Celtics.

BUCYK, JOHN PAUL   B. 5/12/35, Edmonton, Alta. Forward. 6', 215. Played 15 seasons with Bos. Bruins through 1971–72, getting 51 goals in 1970–71 and 116 points. Started with Edmonton Oil Kings, came up in Det. Red Wings, organization with Edmonton, winning WHL Rookie of Year award in 1955. Played next 2 seasons at Detroit, then was traded to Bos. Bruins for Terry Sawchuk for 1957–58 season. Always has cigar in mouth when not playing the game. Played 1000th game 12/11/70, and

Boston management gave him $1000 bill to mark occasion. Later that year suffered 25-stitch gash in leg in boat accident near Creston, B.C., where he makes home. Won Lady Byng Trophy in 1971.

NHL record: 435 goals, 634 assists in 1207 games; 30 goals, 45 assists in 88 playoff games.

BURNS, CHARLES FREDERICK (Charlie) B. 2/14/36, Detroit, Mich. Forward. 5'11", 170. Was both coach and player in NHL. Played junior hockey at Whitby for Wren Blair, now manager of Minn. North Stars. Fractured skull in near fatal mishap in 1954, and still wears helmet. Turned pro with Det. Red Wings in 1958–59, going to Bos. Bruins next year for four seasons. Spent next four in Western League (San Francisco) before going to Calif. Seals in 1967 expansion. Played in Pittsburgh in 1968–69, then joined Minn. North Stars. Named coach 1/14/70 and held post through end of season. Lives with family in Santa Rosa, Calif.

NHL record: 106 goals and 198 assists in 749 games; 5 goals, 4 assists in 31 playoff games.

BURROWS, DAVID JAMES (Dave) B. 1/11/49, Toronto, Ont. Defenseman. 6'1", 180. Played junior hockey in Chi. Black Hawk organization at St. Catharines, turned pro in 1969 with Hawks' Dallas farm, played for Portland in 1970 WHL playoffs, then returned to Dallas for 1970–71 season, where he was voted team's most valuable member. Claimed by Pitt. Penguins in June 1971 draft. Played 77 games in rookie year. Lives in Newmarket, Ont.

NHL record: 5 goals, 34 assists in 155 games; no goals, no assists in 4 playoff games.

BYERS, MICHAEL ARTHUR (Mike) B. 9/11/46, Toronto, Ont. Forward. 5'10", 185. Played three seasons with Toronto Marlboros and turned pro in 1967 with Tor. Maple Leafs, who sent him to Tulsa. After going to Rochester and back to Tulsa, was sent to Phila. Flyers in March 1969, shipped to Quebec Aces, and then traded to L.A. Kings. Went to Buffalo Sabres 12/16/71 for Doug Barrie. Plays soccer in off-season to stay in shape, and has agent to represent him in possible theatrical career. Jumped to New England of WHA 1972–73.

NHL record: 42 goals, 34 assists in 165 games; no goals, 1 assist in 4 playoff games.

CAHAN, LAWRENCE LOUIS (Larry) B. 12/25/33, Fort William, Ont. Defenseman, 6'2", 222. Played 13 seasons in NHL before signing contract in summer of 1972 with Chicago Cougars of WHA. Played junior hockey in hometown, joined Tor. Maple Leafs in 1954, went to N.Y. Rangers in 1957, to Calif. (Oakland) Seals organization in 1967, and L.A. Kings in 1968. Left NHL at end of 1970–71 season, spending 1971–72 in Seattle before signing Cougar contract. Also had minor league experience at Pittsburgh, Springfield, and Vancouver, winning Hal Laycoe Cup in 1967 as top defenseman in WHL while at Vancouver.

NHL record: 38 goals, 92 assists in 662 games; 1 goal and 1 assist in 29 playoff games.

CAIN, HERBERT B. 12/24/13, Newmarket, Ont. Forward. Spent 13 seasons in NHL, playing for Mont. Maroons and Canadiens and Bos. Bruins. Played for Hamilton Tigers, joined Maroons in 1933, went to Canadiens in 1938 and to Bruins next season, retiring from NHL in 1946. Won NHL scoring title in 1944 with 82 points (36 goals, 46 assists). Scored 32 goals next season.

NHL record: 208 goals, 194 assists in 13 seasons; 16 goals, 13 assists in 64 playoff games.

CALDER, FRANK B. 1877, Scotland. D. 2/4/43. Hall of Fame builder. Became first president of NHL when formed in 1917 and served until death. Earlier had served as secretary of National Hockey Assn. Never a player. Calder Trophy, annually given to NHL's outstanding rookie, donated in his name.

CAMERON, HAROLD HUGH (Harry) B. 2/6/90, Pembroke, Ont. D. 10/20/53, Vancouver, B.C. Defenseman. Hall of Famer. Scored 171 goals in 312 games over 14 years, despite being defenseman. Played on three Stanley Cup winners. Played in three major leagues: Toronto and Wanderers of National Hockey Assn.; Toronto, Ottawa and Canadiens of NHL; Saskatoon of Western Canada League. Started NHL career in 1917 with Toronto, ending it in 1923 when traded from Toronto St. Pat's to Saskatoon.

NHL record: 90 goals, 27 assists in 127 games; 7 goals, no assists in 4 playoffs.

CAMPBELL, ANGUS D. B. 3/19/84, Stayner, Ont. Hall of Fame builder. Mining engineer who became first president of Northern Ontario Hockey Assn. when it was formed in 1919. Played both hockey and lacrosse at U. of Toronto, and hockey at Cobalt, Ont., where he was student mine engineer. Later became official of Ontario Hockey Assn. Retired, lives in Toronto.

CAMPBELL, BRYAN ALBERT B. 3/27/44, Sudbury, Ont. Forward. 6′, 175. Turned pro in 1963–64 at Cincinnati, played two seasons at Memphis, one at Omaha, and then with L.A. Kings, who sent him to Springfield, then recalled him in 1969–70. Kings traded unhappy Campbell to Chi. Black Hawks 2/20/70 in deal which also sent Bill White to Chicago. Missed 1971 playoffs with severe throat infection. Jumped to Phila. Blazers of WHA after 1971–72.

NHL record: 35 goals, 71 assists in 260 games; 3 goals, 4 assists in 22 playoff games.

CAMPBELL, CLARENCE S. B. 7/9/05, Fleming, Sask. Hall of Fame builder. President of NHL, position he assumed in 1946. Graduated from U. of Alberta, then attended Oxford as Rhodes scholar. A lawyer, he commanded 4th Canadian Armored Division headquarters in World War II, joined Canadian War Crimes Unit after war. Refereed hockey and lacrosse, but made mark as adminstrator, supervising expansion of NHL from six teams to present size.

CARLETON, KENNETH WAYNE B. 8/4/46, Sudbury, Ont. Forward. 6′2″, 215. Was called "best junior hockey player ever seen" by Tor. Maple Leafs' president Stafford Smythe when with Toronto Marlboros. Carleton turned pro in 1965–66 with Leafs, and began move through

Tulsa and Rochester; finally to Leafs in 1967–68. Bounced to Rochester and Phoenix next season, was traded to Bos. Bruins in 1969–70, and got 22 goals for Boston in 1970–71 as team won Stanley Cup. Acquired by Calif. Seals in 1971 summer draft. Went to Ottawa Generals of WHL after 1971–72. Lives with family on farm in Ontario, where he raises race horses.

NHL record: 55 goals, 73 assists in 278 games; 2 goals, 4 assists in 18 playoff games.

CARR, LORNE BELL   B. 7/2/10, Stoughton, Sask. Forward. Played 13 years in NHL, seven with N.Y. Americans, five with Tor. Leafs, one with N.Y. Rangers. Started with Calgary as amateur, turned pro in 1930 with Vancouver Lions, moving up to Rangers in 1933, going to Americans next season. Traded to Leafs in 1941 for four players by financially pressed Americans, and retired from NHL after 1945–46 season. Had best season in 1943–44, with 36 goals, 38 assists for 74 points, good enough only for third place in scoring race. Twice All-Star first team. Runs bowling alley in Calgary.

NHL record: 204 goals, 222 assists in 13 seasons; 10 goals, 9 assists in 51 playoff games.

CARVETH, JOSEPH GORDON   B. 3/21/18, Regina, Sask. Forward. Played for Det. Red Wings, Bos. Bruins and Mont. Canadiens during 11 years in NHL. Played at Pontiac, Mich., as amateur. Turned pro in 1939 at Indianapolis. Joined Wings in 1940–41 for 19 games, then played 29 next season, making club full time in 1942–43. Went to Bruins 6/25/46 for Roy Conacher, then to Canadiens 12/17/47 for Jimmy Peters. Returned to Det. in mid-1949–50 and finished NHL career there in 1950–51. Had three seasons of 20 or more goals.

NHL record: 150 goals, 189 assists in 504 games; 21 goals, 16 assists in 69 playoff games.

CASHMAN, WAYNE JOHN   B. 6/24/45, Kingston, Ont. Forward. 6'1", 190. Played as teammate of Bobby Orr on Oshawa Generals as junior and now is back with him as member of Bos. Bruins. Turned pro in 1966 with Oklahoma City, spent two years there, then made Bruins in 1968, with brief 21-game trip to Hershey in the process. Does manual labor on father's farm in Kingston to stay in shape during summer. Lives in Verona, Ont., and has boat there named *Boston Gardens*. Team Canada 1972.

NHL record: 90 goals, 179 assists in 351 games; 13 goals, 15 assists in 48 playoff games.

CHABOT, LORNE B. 10/5/1900, Montreal, Que. D. 10/10/46. Goalie. Had 11-season career in NHL, starting in 1926 with N.Y. Rangers and finishing in 1937 with N.Y. Americans. Stops in between with Tor. Maple Leafs, Mont. Canadiens, Chi. Black Hawks, and Mont. Maroons. Played with Port Arthur Allan Cup champions in 1924–25 and 1925–26, then moved up to Rangers in next season. Went to Leafs in 1928, and to Canadiens in 1933, then to Hawks following season, winning Vezina Trophy with 1.83 goals-against average in 1935. Sold to Maroons in 1935–36, and finished career next season with Americans, getting into just six games and allowing 25 goals.

NHL record: allowed 861 goals in 410 games for 2.10 average, 73 shutouts; gave up 64 goals in 37 games for 1.73 average, 5 shutouts.

CHADWICK, WILLIAM L. (Bill; the Big Whistle) B. 10/10/15, New York, N.Y. Hall of Fame referee. Got his chance as official in Eastern Amateur League, where he was player. Sitting out game with injuries, was asked to fill in for referee who failed to show up, thus starting career bound for Hall of Fame. Officiating career covered hundreds of NHL regular-season and playoff games, from 1940 to 1955. Credited with devising signals for types of penalties called, similar to those used in football. Manages golf course near New York. Color man first on Ranger broadcasts, then on telecasts.

CHAMBERLAIN, ERWIN GROVES (Murph) B. 2/14/15, Shawville, Que. Forward. Played 12 seasons as center in NHL, then became colorful coach in various leagues. Played as amateur with Sudbury Frood Mines team, joined Tor. Maple Leafs in 1937, went to Mont. Canadiens in 1940, N.Y. Americans in mid-1941–42, Bos. Bruins in 1942, and returned to Canadiens in 1943, where he finished career in 1948–49. Coaching duties included stints at Sudbury of EPHL, Windsor Bulldogs, Cornwall, Vancouver, and Buffalo. In one gan.e while coaching in smaller Canadian league he expressed displeasure with officials, by throwing extra puck onto the ice, which led to total confusion among players.

NHL record: 100 goals, 175 assists in 12 seasons; 14 goals, 17 assists in 75 playoff games.

CHARRON, GUY B. 1/24/49, Verdun, Que. Forward. 5'10", 175. Started in Montreal system, turning pro in 1969–70 with Canadiens after playing with Montreal's Junior Canadiens. Played most of first pro season with Montreal Voyageurs in AHL (getting 82 points on 37 goals and 45 assists), and divided time between Voyageurs and Mont. Canadiens in 1970–71 until traded to Det. Red Wings 1/13/71 in deal that sent Frank Mahovlich to Montreal. Charron spent one of toughest days at Detroit Olympia off the ice. He was accosted in stadium parking lot in Jan. 1972 and forced at knife point to drive his car about two miles away, where he was robbed of his car, watch, wallet, and visa. Lives in LaSalle, Que. in off-season.

NHL record: 37 goals, 40 assists in 183 games.

CHEEVERS, GERALD MICHAEL (Cheesy) B. 12/7/40, St. Catharines, Ont. Goalie. 5'11", 185. Came up in Tor. Maple Leafs' organization, which tried to protect him in draft by listing him as forward, but failed and Bos. Bruins got him in 1965. Stayed with Boston organization through 1971–72 season. Signed with Cleveland of WHA for 1972–73. Played as junior at St. Michael's College. Turned pro in 1961 at Sault Ste. Marie. Played at Rochester and Sudbury until drafted by Bruins. Won Harry Holmes Memorial Trophy at Rochester, 1964–65. Sent by Boston to Oklahoma City, then made Bruins two seasons later, 1967–68. Was one of many heroes of Boston's Stanley Cup team, 1972. Selected for Team Canada 1972, but did not play because of signing with Cleveland of WHA. Owns thoroughbred race horses; raced in Boston area. Has operated hockey school with former Bruin teammate Fred Stanfield in St. Catharines.

NHL record: allowed 701 goals in 252 games for 2.86 average, 16 shutouts; gave up 102 goals in 40 playoff games for 2.51 average, 5 shutouts.

CHEVREFILS, REAL   B. 5/2/32, Timmins, Ont. Forward. Played eight NHL seasons. Started with Barrie Flyers as junior in Bos. Bruins' organization, then moved up to Hershey, and joined Bruins in 1951–52. Went to Det. Red Wings in mid-1955–56, then returned to Boston next season and finished career there in 1958–59. Had best season in 1956–57, with 31 goals and 17 assists in 70 games. Participated in two All-Star games. Serves as scout for Bruins.

NHL record: 104 goals, 97 assists in 387 games; 5 goals, 4 assists in 30 playoff games.

CLANCY, FRANCIS MICHAEL (King) B. 2/25/03, Ottawa, Ont. Defenseman. Hall of Famer played amateur hockey in Ottawa before signing as pro at 18 with Ottawa Senators. Sold to Tor. Maple Leafs in 1930 for $35,000 and two players; played with club until retirement in 1937. Coached Mont. Maroons for first half of 1937–38. Then refereed until he returned to coaching with Maple Leafs (1950–53). Moved into front office, where he now is vice president. As referee, he was once challenged to fight a fan who was heckling him; learned later that heckler was Jack Sharkey, heavyweight champion.

NHL record: 137 goals, 143 assists in 16 seasons; 9 goals, 8 assists in 13 playoffs.

CLAPPER, AUBREY VICTOR (Dit) B. 2/9/07, Newmarket, Ont. Defenseman-forward. Rugged 200-pounder. Hall of Famer was first 20-year man in NHL, from 1927 to 1947, all with Bos. Bruins. Played junior hockey at 13, and was just 19 when he joined Bruins. All-Star first team once. Bruins retired No. 5 when Clapper retired 2/12/47. Coached Bruins for two years, entered family business, then returned to coach Buffalo Bisons in 1960. Now lives in Peterborough, Ont. Survived heart attack in 1964.

NHL record: 228 goals, 248 assists in 20 seasons; 13 goals, 19 assists in 89 playoff games.

CLARKE, ROBERT EARL (Bobby) B. 8/13/49, Flin Flon, Man. Forward. 5'10", 180. A diabetic who insists condition is no problem to his play, played no minor league hockey. Was Phila. Flyers' second-round choice in draft after junior play with Flin Flon Bombers. Other teams shied away because of his illness. Missed one game in four seasons—boil on elbow. Second, league scoring, 1972–73 (104 points). Team Canada 1972. Bill Masterton Memorial Trophy 1971–72. Hart Trophy for MVP 1972–73.

NHL record: 114 goals, 180 assists in 309 games; 2 goals, 6 assists in 15 playoff games.

CLEGHORN, SPRAGUE B. 1890, Montreal, Que. D. 7/11/56, Montreal, Que. Defenseman. Hall of Famer. Started out as forward but moved to defense, where he was known as one of roughest ever, often figuring in brawls. Started with N.Y. Crescents in 1909–10, then played with Renfrew in NHA. Played 17 years with either NHA or NHL clubs, including Montreal Wanderers, Ottawa, Mont. Canadiens, and Bos. Bruins. Missed 1918 season with broken leg, and ended career with Bruins in 1927–28. Played with two Stanley Cup winners.

NHL record: 84 goals, 29 assists in 10 seasons; 5 goals, 7 assists in 8 playoffs.

COLLINS, WILLIAM EARL (Bill) B. 7/13/43, Ottawa, Ont. Forward. 6', 178. Played with Whitby Juniors before turning pro in 1963 with Denver of WHL. Was with Baltimore of AHL and Minnesota of CPHL before breaking in with Minn. North Stars in 1967–68, who paid him $2000 bonus in 1969–70, then traded him to Mont. Canadiens next season. Canadiens sent him to Det. Red Wings in mid-1970–71, where he was put into service as penalty killer, specialty badly needed by Wings. Lives with wife and children in Ottawa during off-season.

NHL record: 94 goals, 94 assists in 445 games; 2 goals, 5 assists in 16 playoff games.

COLVILLE, NEIL MACNEIL B. 8/4/14, Edmonton, Alta. Forward-Defenseman. Hall of Famer. Played entire 12-year NHL career with N.Y. Rangers. Moved through Ranger organization, starting with N.Y. Crescents in Eastern Amateur League, then to Phila. Ramblers before joining Rangers in 1935 for one game. Returned to stay in next season, retiring in 1949. Served in RCAF from 1942–45, as navigator.

NHL record: 99 goals, 166 assists in 464 games, 7 goals, 19 assists in 46 playoff games.

CONACHER, CHARLES WILLIAM, SR. (Chuck) B. 12/10/09, Toronto, Ont. D. 12/30/67, Toronto, Ont. Forward. Hall of Famer played 13 years in NHL, winning scoring title in 1933–34 and 1934–35, and sharing goal-scoring championship with Bill Cook in 1932 and Bill Thoms in 1936. Joined Tor. Maple Leafs at end of 1928–29 season after amateur club, Toronto Marlboros, had won championship. Traded to Det. Red Wings for 1938–39 season, then played with N. Y. Americans, ending career in 1941. Thrice on All-Star first team. Brothers Roy and Lionel also played in NHL. Coached Chi. Black Hawks from 1947 to 1950, then entered business. Victim of cancer.

NHL record: 225 goals, 173 assists in 13 seasons; 17 goals, 18 assists in 9 playoffs.

CONACHER, LIONEL PRETORIA B. 5/24/01, Toronto, Ont. D. 5/26/64, Ottawa, Ont. Defenseman. Brother of Roy and Hall of Famer Charles. Played 12 years as NHL defenseman, and coached N. Y. Americans. Played for North Toronto AA in 1919, and for Toronto Canoe Club in 1920, which won a junior championship. Captain and manager of Pitt. Yellow Jackets, then played in NHL for Pitt. Pirates, made up mainly of players from United States amateur league. Went to N.Y. Americans in mid-1926–27, and became coach in 1929. Joined Mont. Maroons in 1930, spent three seasons there, one with Chi. Black Hawks, and then returned to Maroons for three more years, leaving NHL at end of 1936–37 season. Conacher was rough player; engaged in fight with brother Charlie in game between Maroons and Leafs in 1936. Fight started on ice and continued up ramp and into lobby. Lionel was declared winner when Charlie unable to rise. Lionel also excelled at lacrosse, boxing, wrestling, and football—playing with Toronto Argonauts, was called by U. of Illinois coach Bob Zuppke the finest punter he had seen. Was 10-second sprinter. Played baseball in International League. Served as Liberal member of parliament. Died after collapsing in ball game, after hitting triple.

NHL record: 80 goals, 105 assists in 12 seasons; 2 goals, 2 assists in 9 playoffs.

CONACHER, ROY GORDON B. 10/5/16, Toronto, Ont. Forward. Had eight seasons of 20 or more goals in his 11-year NHL career with Bos. Bruins, Det. Red Wings and Chi. Black Hawks. Brother of Lionel and Hall of Famer Charles. Joined Bruins in 1938, scoring 26 goals in rookie season. Dropped to 18 next year, then had two 24-goal years before going off to service. Returned in 1946. Sent to Red Wings 6/25/46, and came up with 30 goals in 1946-47. When Wings attempted to trade him to Rangers for Ed Slowinksi he balked, and announced retirement. Hawks bought up contract and kept him active in league until 1952, during which time he scored 22, 26, 25, and 26 goals, winning Art Ross Trophy as league's top scorer in 1949 with 68 points.

NHL record: 226 goals, 200 assists in 11 seasons; 15 goals, 15 assists in 42 playoff games.

CONNELL, ALEX B. 1901, Oshawa, Ont. D. 5/10/58. Goalie. Hall of Famer. Was persuaded to play goalie while serving in army during World War I. After discharge Connell, who had been star baseball and lacrosse player, played in small amateur league before turning pro with Ottawa Senators in 1924. Stayed with Ottawa until 1931, spent 1931-32 with Det. Falcons, returned to Ottawa in 1932-33. Sat out the 1933–34 season, then returned to hockey, this time with Mont. Maroons, playing in 1934–35, resting one year, and playing in 1936–37, after which he retired. Connell, called "Ottawa Fireman" because he was secretary of Ottawa Fire Department, was known for little black cap he wore in nets. During 1927–28 season he got six straight shutouts and was not scored on for 446 minutes, 9 seconds. After retirement, coached junior teams.

NHL record: allowed 827 goals in 415 games for 1.99 average, 82 shutouts; gave up 26 goals in 21 playoff games for 1.24 average, 4 shutouts.

COOK, FREDERICK JOSEPH (Bun) B. 9/18/03, Kingston, Ont. Forward. Played on famed N.Y. Ranger line with brother Bill and Frank Boucher. Joined Rangers in 1926 and stayed until sale to Bos. Bruins in 1936. Played just one season in Boston and retired. Runs parking lot in Kingston.

NHL record: 158 goals, 144 assists in 11 seasons; 15 goals, 3 assists in 46 playoff games.

COOK, WILLIAM OSSER (Bill) B. 10/9/96, Brantford, Ont. Forward. Hall of Famer. Played 12 years in NHL, all with N.Y. Rangers, on famed line with brother Bun and Frank Boucher. Started in hockey with Frontenac juniors in 1916 in Kingston, Ont. Served overseas in World War I, then played at Sault Ste. Marie. Turned pro with Saskatoon Sheiks in 1922, winning three scoring titles in Western Canada League. Joined Rangers after league folded in 1926. Led league in goals twice and tied for title once. Thrice on All-Star first team. Retired in 1937.

NHL record: 229 goals, 138 assists in 475 games; 13 goals, 11 assists in 45 playoff games.

COOKE, JACK KENT B. 10/25/12, Hamilton, Ont. Owner of Los Angeles Kings. Paid $3 million to put franchise in L.A. Amassed fortune through radio, television, and publishing. Also involved in pro football and basketball. Owns L.A. Lakers of NBA, who play in L.A. Forum, which Cooke built for $16 1/4 million. Lives in L.A.

CORRIGAN, MICHAEL DOUGLAS (Mike) B. 1/11/46, Ottawa, Ont. Forward. 5'10", 175. Played junior hockey in Tor. Maple Leaf organization, then turned pro with Rochester of AHL in 1965–66, moving through rosters of Tulsa, Victoria, and Springfield on way to becoming NHL regular. Played briefly in two seasons with Kings (1967–68 and 1969–70) before being claimed by Van. Canucks in 1970 draft. Although he scored 21 goals and 28 assists in 76 games in 1970–71, Canucks' GM Bud Poile labled him "lazy hockey player" and traded him back to L.A.

NHL record: 79 goals, 88 assists in 260 games.

COTTON, HAROLD (Baldy) B. 11/5/02, Toronto, Ont. Forward. Played 12 NHL seasons. Played for Aura Lee juniors and seniors, then with Pitt. Yellow Jackets, joining old NHL Pitt. Pirates in 1925. Sent to Tor. Maple Leafs in 1928–29, staying until 1935–36, finishing career with two seasons with N.Y. Americans. After retirement coached in junior hockey for four seasons, served as scout for Bos. Bruins, and did radio and television for Maple Leafs. Now serves as director of field operations for Minn. North Stars.

NHL record: 101 goals, 103 assists in 12 seasons; 4 goals, 9 assists in 9 playoffs.

COULTER, ARTHUR EDMUND B. 5/31/09, Winnipeg, Man. Defenseman. Played 11 years in NHL with just two teams, Chi Black Hawks and N.Y. Rangers. Played for St. John's Cathedral in Winnipeg, and for Pilgrim Juveniles, Manitoba champs in 1926–27. Moved to Pittsburgh, and turned pro with Phila. Arrows in 1929, joining Hawks in 1931–32 and staying until traded to Rangers in 1935–36. Entered U. S. Navy in 1942 and never returned to NHL play. Served as first president of NHL Players Assn. Lives in Florida.

NHL record: 30 goals, 82 assists in 11 seasons; 4 goals, 5 assists in 49 playoff games.

COURNOYER, YVAN SERGE B. 11/22/43, Drummondville, Que. Forward. 5'7", 165. Played only five games as minor leaguer on loan to Quebec, before making Mont. Canadiens in 1964. Had moved to Montreal at 14, and played with Lachine in Metropolitan League and for Junior Canadiens. Became high scorer starting in 1966–67 and went over 200 goals in 1971–72. Especially dangerous on power play. Was subject of rancor between Canadiens and Canadian Olympic team when NHL club refused to loan him out for 1964 games, asserting previous players it had loaned had not been used. Timid at beginning of career. Took boxing lessons one summer and no longer was intimidated. Smythe Trophy as MVP in 1973 playoffs; record 15 goals. Team Canada 1972. Also serves as head of Montreal business firm.

NHL record: 276 goals, 259 assists in 611 league games; 44 goals, 45 assists in 102 playoff games.

COWLEY, WILLIAM MAILES (Bill) B. 6/12/12, Bristol, Que. Forward. Hall of Famer. Played 12 years with Bos. Bruins, from 1935 to 1947, after breaking into NHL with old St. L. Eagles in 1934. Won Hart Trophy as MVP in 1941 and 1943, made first All-Star team four times and second once. Was leading for scoring championship in 1944 when forced out with injury. Twice member of Stanley Cup champions. Known as exceptionally sharp passer, he coached at Renfrew, Ont., and Vancouver after retiring, then went into hotel business in Ontario. Lives in Ottawa.

NHL record: 195 goals, 353 assists in 13 seasons; 12 goals, 34 assists in 62 playoff games.

CRAWFORD, JOHN SHEA (Jack) B. 10/26/16, Dublin, Ont. Defenseman. Played 12 years for Bos. Bruins, 1938–50. Turned pro with Providence in 1937. Chipped elbow during exhibition game 11/30/39, missing several weeks for second season in NHL. Wore helmet both for protection and to disguise fact he was nearly bald. Went into coaching after stepping down as active player; his teams included Baltimore Clippers.

NHL record: 38 goals, 140 assists in 12 seasons; 3 goals, 13 assists in 66 playoff games.

CREIGHTON, DAVID THEODORE B. 6/24/30, Port Arthur, Ont. Forward. Played 11 full seasons in NHL before signed 6/29/72 as general manager of Phila. Blazers in WHA. Played for Port Arthur Bruins and Hershey of AHL. Joined Bos. Bruins in 1948, went to Tor. Maple Leafs in 1954, and to Chi. Black Hawks for cash 11/17/54, then to N. Y. Rangers 8/22/55 with Bronco Horvath for Aggie Kukulowicz in three-corner deal involving Det. Red Wings. Returned to Leafs in 1958, and ended NHL playing career after 1959–60 season. Named to first All-Star team in 1952. Served as player, coach, and general manager of Providence Reds from 1967–72 before taking WHA job.

NHL record: 140 goals, 174 assists in 616 games; 11 goals, 13 assists in 51 playoff games.

CRISP, TERRANCE ARTHUR B. 5/28/43, Parry Sound, Ont. Forward. 5'8", 177. Played as junior at Niagara Falls. Turned pro in 1963 with Minneapolis of CPHL in Bos. Bruins' organization, spent two seasons there and next two at Oklahoma City. Drafted 6/6/67 by St. L. Blues in expansion, played two seasons in St. Louis, shipped to Kansas City for four games and Buffalo of AHL in 1969–70 before being recalled at end of that season. Drafted by New York Islanders after 1971–72 season.

NHL record: 43 goals, 85 assists in 354 games; 11 goals, 17 assists in 74 playoff games.

CROTEAU, GARY PAUL B. 6/20/46, Sudbury, Ont. Forward. 6', 205. Became NHL regular with Calif. Seals in 1971–72, after failing with L.A. Kings and Det. Red Wings. Credits teammate with getting him to speed up shot, giving defense less time to get set. Came out of St. Lawrence U. to turn pro with Springfield of AHL. Played briefly with Kings and Detroit before being drafted by Seals in 1970. Lives with family in Sudbury.

NHL record: 38 goals, 58 assists in 218 games; 3 goals, 2 assists in 11 playoff games.

CROZIER, JOSEPH RICHARD B. 2/19/29, Winnipeg, Man. Defenseman. Took over as coach of Buffalo Sabres in mid-1971–72 when Punch Imlach suffered heart attack. Played only five games as defenseman in NHL, with Tor. Maple Leafs, but had long minor league career at Rochester of AHL and Vancouver of WHL, then became coach and GM at Cincinnati before moving up to Buffalo job.

NHL record: No goals, 3 assists in 5 games.

CROZIER, ROGER ALLAN B. 3/16/42, Bracebridge, Ont. Goalie.

5'8", 160. Turned pro in 1960–61 with Buffalo farm of Chi. Black Hawk organization, played in minors at Sault Ste. Marie, St. L. and Pitt. before going to Det. Red Wings in 1963–64. Named best goalie in AHL in 1963–64 with 2.34 goals-against average. Played 15 games with Det. next season, and in 1964–65 won Calder Trophy as Rookie of Year, and next year was named outstanding player of Stanley Cup playoffs. NHL All-Star team 1965. Saying confidence was gone, he "retired" from Red Wings 11/6/67, then returned 1/10/68 after playing himself back into shape briefly in Fort Worth. What shook his confidence was allowing 18 goals over three-game span. Went to Buffalo Sabres before start of 1970–71 season and was voted MVP by teammates after 1971–72. Always bothered by nerves, was told by Wings to take vacation in Miami in middle of 1966–67 season, almost unprecedented move. Bothered by pancreatitis and stomach ailments, he was hospitalized during 1970–71.

NHL record: allowed 1323 goals in 469 games for 2.83 average, 26 shutouts; gave up 68 goals in 26 playoff games for 2.61 average, 1 shutout.

CUDE, WILFRED   B. 7/4/10, Barry, Wales. D. 5/5/68. Goalie. Reputed to have thrown steak at wife as result of pressures of playing his position, then abruptly retired. Reared in Winnipeg, played in 1929 with Melville Millionaires, turned pro in that year with Pirates, but saw first NHL action in 1930–31 with old Phila. Quakers. Spent next season with Bos. Bruins and in minors, then came back to split 1933–34 between Det. Red Wings and Mont. Canadiens, and stayed in Montreal until sudden retirement in 1941. Allowed just 47 goals in 30 games in 1933–34 for 1.57 average, but did not have enough minutes played to qualify for Vezina Trophy. Stayed active in hockey after retirement in Noranda, Que.

NHL record: allowed 786 goals in 280 games for 2.81 average, 24 shutouts; gave up 51 goals in 19 playoff games for 2.68 average, 1 shutout.

CURTIS, PAUL EDWIN   B. 9/29/47, Peterborough, Ont. Defenseman. 6', 185. Took boxing lessons in off-season, and has complained that his team, L.A. Kings, is not "tough" enough. Played junior hockey in hometown, turning pro in 1967 with Houston Apollos of Mont. Canadiens' organization. Spent two seasons there and next with Montreal's AHL Voyageurs before being drafted by Kings in 1970, where he picked up 62 penalty minutes in rookie season. Scored first NHL goal in Kings' 77th 1970–71 game, passing out cigars to celebrate. Called "Hound Dog" by teammates. Traded to St. Louis mid-1972–73.

NHL record: 3 goals, 34 assists in 185 games; no goals, no assists in 5 playoff games.

DAHLSTROM, CARL (Cully) B. 7/3/13, Minneapolis, Minn. Forward. Played eight seasons with Chi. Black Hawks from 1938 to 1945. One of few American-born players of time. Played as amateur for Pillsbury House. Turned pro in 1933 with Minneapolis Millers. Named top rookie 1937–38. Retired 10/8/46; told officials at Hawks' training camp in Regina that he could not continue. Offered job at Kansas City by coach Doc Romnes, but turned it down to devote time to business interests.

NHL record: 88 goals, 118 assists in 8 seasons; 6 goals and 8 assists in 5 playoff series.

DALEY, THOMAS JOSEPH (Joe) B. 2/20/43, Winnipeg, Man. Goalie. 5'10", 160. Product of Det. Red Wing system, turning pro in 1961 with Sudbury of EPHL. Played in Cincinnati, Memphis, Pittsburgh, San Francisco, and Baltimore before being drafted by Pitt. Penguins in 1967 expansion, was claimed by Buffalo Sabres on waivers 6/9/70. Sabres won only 24 games in 1970–71, and Daley was goalie in 12 of them. Also got Buffalo 8 ties. Red Wings gave up Don Luce and Mike Robitaille 5/25/71 for Daley, who plays goal from a stand-up position. Jumped to Winnipeg Jets of WHA 1972–73. Does not wear mask. Lives with wife and children in Winnipeg in off-season.

NHL record: allowed 326 goals in 105 games for 3.35 average, 3 shutouts.

DANDURAND, JOSEPH VIATEUR (Leo) B. 7/9/89, Bourbonnais, Ill. D. 6/26/64. Hall of Fame builder. Went to Canada at 16 to make name as promoter. Became associated with Joseph Cattarinich and Louis Letourneau to buy Mont. Canadiens for $11,000 in 1921, building it into property worth $165,000 when it was sold in 1937. Was director of Montreal Royals baseball team and active in horse racing.

DARRAGH, JOHN PROCTOR (Jack) B. 12/4/91, Cornwall, Ont. D. 6/25/24. Forward. Never played anywhere but Ottawa. Started in church league, played with Cliffsides, then became a pro with Ottawa, playing with four Stanley Cup winners. Noted for strong backhand.

NHL record: 68 goals, 21 assists in 120 games; 9 goals, 2 assists in 4 playoff series.

DAVIDSON, ALLAN M. (Scotty) B. 1890s, Kingston, Ont. Defenseman-forward. Hall of Famer. Outstanding junior. Became pro star briefly before being killed in Belgium during World War I. Played with Kingston Frontenac juniors from 1909 to 1911. Joined Toronto of NHA as right winger in 1912; coached team to Stanley Cup in 1914, scoring 23 goals that season after getting 19 goals in 20 games in first pro season.

DAVIDSON, ROBERT B. 2/10/12, Toronto, Ont. Forward. Played 12 seasons with Tor. Maple Leafs. Amateur hockey. Then for Leafs, 1934–46. Known primarily as defensive forward and close checker; usually assigned to shadow opponent's top scorer. Had best scoring seasons toward end of career, with 19 goals in 1943–44 and 17 next season.

NHL record: 94 goals, 160 assists in 12 seasons; 5 goals, 17 assists in 82 playoff games.

DAY, CLARENCE HENRY (Happy) B. 6/14/01, Owen Sound, Ont. Defenseman. Hall of Famer. Played 14 years with NHL teams after studying pharmacy at U. of Toronto. Turned pro with Toronto St. Pats in Dec. 1924. Joined Tor. Maple Leafs in 1926 and stayed until 1936–37. Played final season in 1937–38 with N.Y. Americans. Refereed for two seasons, then coached Leafs from 1940 to 1950, winning five Stanley Cups, three in a row; became GM of Leafs in 1950, and retired in 1957. Now lives in St. Thomas, Ont., where he is involved with manufacture of construction tools.

NHL record: 86 goals, 116 assists in 14 seasons; 4 goals, 7 assists in 9 playoff series.

DeJORDY, DENIS EMILE B. 11/12/38, St. Hyacinthe, Que. Goalie.

5'9", 185. Played amateur hockey with St. Catharines TeePees and turned pro with Buffalo of AHL in 1957–58 season. Played first NHL game with Chi. Black Hawks in 1962–63 and since has been well-traveled goalie, playing with Sault Ste. Marie, Buffalo, St. Louis and Dallas in the minors and in NHL with Hawks, L.A. Kings, Mont. Canadiens, N.Y. Islanders and Det. Red Wings, his present club. Taken by Islanders in the draft before 1972–73 season from Canadiens, then traded to Red Wings. Won EPHL Rookie of Year with Sault Ste. Marie in 1959–60 and shared Vezina Trophy with Glenn Hall while with Hawks in 1964–65.

NHL record: allowed 925 goals in 315 games for 2.96 average, 15 shutouts; gave up 55 goals in 18 playoff games for 3.49 average, no shutouts.

DELVECCHIO, ALEXANDER PETER (Alex) B. 12/4/31, Fort William, Ont. Forward. 6', 195. Played 22d full season in NHL, all with Det. Red Wings, in 1972. Has been among top 10 scorers 11 times and won Lady Byng Trophy three times. Captain of team since 1961. Went into pro hockey from Oshawa Generals junior club, playing one game with Wings in 1950–51, and playing only minor league hockey of career with Indianapolis next year before joining Detroit to stay, becoming one of only eight players to be in league 20 years. Addicted to cigars. Son of Italian immigrant, often called "Fats" by players because of round face. Lives with wife and five children in Orchard Lake, Mich.

NHL record: 455 goals, 782 assists in 1538 games; 35 goals, 69 assists in 121 playoff games.

DeMARCO, ALBERT THOMAS, JR. (Ab) B. 2/27/49, North Bay, Ont. Forward. 6', 170. Son of former Ranger player Al DeMarco, Sr. (1943–47). Played as amateur with Canadian Nationals, turned pro in 1969 with Omaha Knights, helping CHL club to league and playoff titles for two years. Made N.Y. Rangers in 1971–72, getting into 48 games. Suffered skate gash behind left knee during playoffs in 1972, necessitating surgery. Traded to St. L. Blues for Mike Murphy 3/2/73. Lives in North Bay.

NHL record: 12 goals, 30 assists in 118 games; 1 goal, 2 assists in 13 playoff games.

DENNENY, CORBETT B. 1894, Cornwall, Ont. D. 1/16/63. Forward. Played nine years during early days of NHL, also starred in other sports. Moved to Cobalt in 1913, turned pro with Toronto, playing for Arenas and St. Pat's, as well as Ottawa, Hamilton, and Chi. Black Hawks in NHL career from 1917 to 1928. Sandwiched in was time with Vancouver, Saskatoon, and Minneapolis. Brother of Hall of Famer Cy Denneny, excelled in lacrosse, and ran the 100-yd. dash in 9.6 at Canadian National Exhibition in 1916.

NHL record: 99 goals, 29 assists in 9 seasons; 6 goals, 4 assists in 3 playoff series.

DENNENY, CYRIL JOSEPH (Cy) B. 12/23/91, Farran's Point, Ont. D. 1970. Forward. Hall of Famer. Played early hockey in Cornwall, Ont. and started as pro with Tor. Shamrocks of NHA in 1914. Played with Ottawa Senators from 1916 through 1927–28, then coached and played for Bos. Bruins in 1928–29. Refereed one season in NHL after leaving Boston, then coached junior and senior teams in Ottawa. Coached Senators in 1932–33, leaving hockey when team left league.

NHL record: 246 goals, 69 assists in 12 seasons; 15 goals, no assists in 10 playoff series.

DESJARDINS, GERARD FERDINAND (Gerry) B. 7/22/44, Sudbury, Ont. Goalie. 5'11, 185. As Chi. Black Hawks' No. 3 goalie, was cause of hockey's most confused 1971–72 deal. Sent to Calif. Seals after breaking arm at end of 1970–71 season, he was returned to Chicago as unfit to play, holding up trade in which goalie Gary Smith had gone to Hawks. Compensation eventually was made to Seals in form of Paul Shmyr and Hawks were allowed to keep Smith, plus Desjardins. He was drafted 6/6/72 by N.Y. Islanders, expansion club. Son of French-Canadian miner, played two years at Houston and one at Cleveland before making L.A. Kings for two years after trade from Mont. Canadien system. Called troublemaker by L.A. owner Jack Kent Cooke and sent to Hawks in six-player deal 2/2/70. Broke arm 3/14/71 when teammate Keith Magnuson crashed into him, jamming him into goalpost.

NHL record: allowed 622 goals in 179 games for 3.51 average, 7 shutouts; gave up 33 goals in 10 playoff games for 4.03 average, no shutouts.

DILIO, FRANCIS PAUL (Frank) B. 4/12/12, Montreal, Que. Hall of Fame builder. Served in Quebec Amateur Hockey Assn. and Junior Amateur Hockey Assn. Served as secretary of JAHA and became president in 1939. Became QAHA registrar in 1943, secretary in 1952. During work with amateur league, such stars as Maurice Richard were developed. Retired from active service in 1962, and received CAHA Meritorious Award in 1963. Lives in Montreal.

DILLON, CECIL GRAHAM B. 4/26/08, Toledo, Ohio. Forward. Played 10 seasons in NHL, nine with N.Y. Rangers, and had five 20-goal seasons. Played with Owen Sound Greys as amateur. Turned pro with

Springfield Indians in 1929. Joined Rangers in 1930, staying until going to Det. Red Wings in 1939–40 for last season of NHL career. NHL All-Star 1938. Often confused with Gordon Drillon, another right wing.

NHL record: 167 goals, 131 assists in 10 seasons; 14 goals and 9 assists in 43 playoff games.

DIONNE, MARCEL ELPHEGE   B. 8/3/51, Drummondville, Que. Forward. 5'9", 170. Det. Red Wings' No. 1 choice in 1971 amateur draft. Proved self in 1971–72 by leading club in points with 77 on 28 goals and 49 assists in 78 games. Was leading scorer of OHA two seasons in row while with St. Catharines TeePees, winning in '70–71 despite missing 14 games with broken collarbone. In three years with TeePees scored 507 points in both league and playoff games, a record. Team Canada 1972. Lives in St. Catharines.

NHL record: 68 goals, 99 assists in 155 games.

DOREY, ROBERT JAMES (Jim)   B. 8/17/47, Kingston, Ont. Defensemen. 6'1", 190. Signed in the summer of 1972 to play for New England Whalers of WHA after four-year NHL career with Tor. Maple Leafs and N.Y. Rangers. Played for London Nationals as junior, spent 1967–68 with Tulsa, Rochester, and Phoenix, made Maple Leafs next year, racking up 200 penalty minutes. Broke single game penalty mark in first NHL game 10/16/68 as father watched from stands. Held penalties to 99 minutes next year, then went back to 198 in 1970–71 and was sent to Rangers following season.

NHL record: 25 goals and 74 assists in 232 games.

DORNHOEFER, GERHARDT OTTO (Gary)   B. 2/2/43, Kitchener, Ont. Forward. 6'2", 178. Played junior hockey in Niagara Falls, turned pro in Bos. Bruins' organization with Minneapolis in 1963–64. Played with Boston for three seasons and with San Francisco and Hershey before becoming a regular when drafted by Phila. Flyers as one of charter players in 1967. Won NHL players' golf tournament three years running, and plays on Canadian tour in summer. Once shot a 63.

NHL record: 126 goals, 188 assists in 461 games; 3 goals and 4 assists in 24 playoff games.

DRILLON, GORDON ARTHUR   B. 10/23/14, Moncton, N.B. Forward. Played six seasons with Tor. Maple Leafs and one with Mont. Canadiens. Skated for Pittsburgh Yellow Jackets and Indianapolis. Joined Leafs in 1936. Retired from Canadiens in 1943. Won league scoring title in 1938 with 52 points on 26 goals, 26 assists. Often confused with Cecil Dillon, another right wing playing at same time; both were selected for All-Star team at same position in 1937–38. Next season Drillon there alone.

NHL record: 155 goals, 139 assists in 7 seasons; 26 goals, 15 assists in 7 playoff series.

DRINKWATER, CHARLES GRAHAM B. ca. 1873, Montreal, Que. D. (date not recorded). Hall of Famer. Played on four Stanley Cup winners as amateur, with Montreal Victorias in 1895, 97, 98, 99. Previously attended McGill U. where he also starred in football.

DROUIN, JUDE B. 10/28/48, Mont-Louis, Que. Forward. 5'9", 160. Second of 10 children. Turned pro in 1967 with Houston of CPHL in Mont. Canadien system, and in 1969–70 moved to Mont. Voyageurs of AHL, winning Rookie of Year award. Sent to Minn. North Stars in 1970 in exchange for Bill Collins. Met wife while playing in Houston, and lives there in off-season.

NHL record: 29 goals, 96 assists in 150 games; 9 goals, 11 assists in 19 playoff games.

DRYDEN, DAVID MURRAY (Dave) B. 9/5/41, Hamilton, Ont. 6'2", 180. Goalie. Brother of Ken, Mont. Canadiens' famed goalie. Turned pro in 1961–62 with Rochester of AHL, played one game with N.Y. Rangers. Sat out three seasons, then joined Buffalo Bisons, briefly with Chi. Black Hawks, and with St. Louis of CPHL before joining Hawks for two years. Spent season in minors with Dallas, and part of 1970–71 with Salt Lake City before being called up to Buffalo Sabres near end of season. After three-season retirement, returned to hockey as result of phone call while recovering from pneumonia; although he joined Bisons on emergency basis, he decided to stay with game. Schoolteacher, he has worked with retarded boys' group in Toronto.

NHL record: allowed 354 goals in 136 games for 2.66 average, 8 shutouts; gave up 9 goals in 3 playoff games for 3.00 average.

DRYDEN, KENNETH WAYNE (Ken) B. 8/8/47, Islington, Ont. Goalie. 6'4", 210. Won Calder Trophy in 1971–72, Rookie of Year, appearing in 64 games and allowing 142 goals for 2.24 average, with eight shutouts. Heroics with Mont. Canadiens in Stanley Cup playoffs of 1970–71 had already established him as top netminder. Played at Cornell U. and with Canada in world tournament in Stockholm in 1969. Turned pro with Mont. Voyageurs of AHL in 1970, at first on part-time basis, then full time. Called up to Canadiens for six games at end of season allowing just nine goals, then put in nets in playoffs, appearing in 20 games with 3.00 goals-against average and winning Conn Smythe

Trophy as outstanding playoff performer, as well as auto from national magazine. Combines hockey with law studies at McGill U., and works with Ralph Nader's "Raiders" as expert on water pollution. Brother of Dave Dryden, also NHL goalie. Bothered by sore back during 1971–72 season. Leading goaltender 1972–73: 2.26 average. Team Canada 1972.

NHL record: allowed 270 goals in 124 games for 2.20 average, 14 shutouts; gave up 128 goals in 43 playoff games for 2.98 average, 1 shutout.

DUDLEY, GEORGE S. B. 4/19/94, Midland, Ont. D. 5/8/60. Hall of Fame builder. Was amateur hockey pioneer who gave more than 50 years to game. Played some hockey but gave it up on becoming lawyer in 1917. Elected to Canadian Amateur Hockey Assn. executive group in 1925, served as president 1940–42, became secretary in 1945 and later served as secretary manager. Was treasurer of Ontario Hockey Assn., president of International Ice Hockey Federation and head of hockey section of 1960 Olympics. Credited with arranging first visits of Russian teams to Canada.

DUFF, TERRANCE RICHARD (Dick) B. 2/18/36, Kirkland Lake, Ont. Forward. 5'9", 166. Started 1971–72 season with Buffalo Sabres, then retired 12/4/71 after eight games, capping NHL career which began with Tor. Maple Leafs in 1954. Modeled himself after star Ted Lindsay. Played as junior at St. Michael's College, moving directly into NHL. Stayed with Maple Leafs until going to N.Y. Rangers in mid-1963–64, then to Canadiens in mid-1964–65. Grabbed by L.A. Kings in mid-1969–70, and in middle of next season was sent to Buffalo Sabres. Lives in Kirkland Lake, and has expressed interest in area politics as Liberal.

NHL record: 283 goals, 289 assists in 1030 games; 30 goals, 49 assists in 114 games.

DUMART, WOODROW WILSON CLARENCE (Woody; Porky) B. 12/23/16, Kitchener, Ont. Forward. Played 15 seasons with Bos. Bruins; member of club's Kraut Line, with Milt Schmidt and Bobby Bauer. Played for Kitchener as junior and for Bos. Cubs before making Bruins in 1936, same year as his line mates, who also came from Kitchener area. Stayed until 1942, when all three entered service. Returned 1945. Retired after 1953–54 season, when he scored but four goals in 69 games. Lives in Boston.

NHL record: 211 goals, 218 assists in 15 seasons; 12 goals, 15 assists in 88 playoff games.

DUNN, JAMES A. (Jimmy) B. 3/24/98. Hall of Fame builder. Served as president of Manitoba Amateur Hockey Assn. for six years from 1945–51, in hockey career that began in 1918. Served various amateur leagues until MAHA took over in 1927, became vice president in 1942 and then president. Also was vice president and president of Canadian Amateur Hockey Assn. Active as official in other amateur sports. Won Military Medal for service in World War I. Lives in Winnipeg.

DUPERE, DENIS GILLES B. 6/21/48, Jonquiere, Que. Forward. 6'1", 195. Started as junior at Kitchener, then played a year with Canadian National team before turning pro in 1969 with Omaha. Started 1970–71 with Tulsa, of N.Y. Ranger organization, then went to Tor. Maple Leafs as part of Tim Horton deal.

    NHL record: 17 goals, 35 assists in 128 games; no goals, no assists in 11 playoff games.

DUPONT, ANDRE B. 7/27/49, Three Rivers, Que. Defenseman. 6'1", 200. Started 1971–72 season with N.Y. Rangers but traded to St. L. Blues 11/15/71. Traded to Phila. Flyers mid-1972–73. Played for Junior Canadiens as they won Memorial Cup before being first-round amateur draft choice of Rangers in 1969. Sent to Omaha's CHL championship club for two seasons. Made NHL in 1971–72 with 60 games. Lives in Three Rivers.

    NHL record: 8 goals, 38 assists in 138 games; 2 goals, 2 assists in 22 playoff games.

DURNAN, WILLIAM RONALD (Bill) B. 1/22/15, Toronto, Ont. D. 10/31/72, Toronto, Ont. Goalie. 6'2", 200. Hall of Famer. Played only seven seasons in NHL, which he did not reach until he was 28. In OHA amateur hockey from 1933 until 1940, then joined Mont. Royals and finally Mont. Canadiens in 1943–44, winning Vezina Trophy in rookie season with 2.18 goals-against average. Stayed with team through career and won trophy in six of seven seasons. Played in three All-Star games. Nerves and injuries ended Durnan's career in 1950. Was much troubled by nausea and insomnia. In middle of playoff series with N.Y. Rangers, he asked to be replaced and never returned to nets. "Nothing was worth that kind of agony," he said. Lived in Toronto, where he worked as public relations man for brewery till death.

    NHL record: allowed 901 goals in 383 games for 2.35 average, 34 shutouts; gave up 99 goals in 45 playoff games for 2.20 average, 2 shutouts.

DUTTON, MERVYN (Red) B. 7/23/98, Russell, Man. Defenseman.

Hall of Famer. Parlayed a reputation for roughness as player into presidency of NHL and place in Hall of Fame. Was injured seriously in World War I, but went on to play with Calgary from 1921 through 1925, then joined Mont. Maroons in 1926 and played until 1930, going to N.Y. Americans, ending playing career there in 1936. Coached and managed Americans until club folded in 1942. Took over as president of NHL in 1943 on death of Frank Calder, serving until 1946. Lives in Calgary, where he has business interests, and is member Hall of Fame selection committee.

NHL record: 29 goals, 67 assists in 10 seasons; 1 goal, no assists in 4 playoff series.

DYE, CECIL HENRY (Babe)   B. 5/13/98, Hamilton, Ont. D. 1/2/62, Chicago, Ill. Forward. Hall of Famer. After junior hockey in Toronto, joined Tor. St. Pats in 1919. Went to Chi. Black Hawks in 1926, broke leg in 1927 training camp. Attempted to return with N.Y. Americans in 1928, but gave up and retired after scoring just one goal in 41 games. Led league in scoring four times, getting five goals in game twice. Coached Chi. Shamrocks in old American Assn. and was NHL referee for five years. Later worked for Chicago contractor as foreman. In youth was football star and also was offered contract to play with Phila. Athletics' baseball club.

NHL record: 202 goals, 41 assists in 9 seasons; 9 goals, 2 assists in 3 playoff series.

ECCLESTONE, TIMOTHY JAMES (Tim) B. 9/24/47, Toronto, Ont. Forward. 5'10", 180. Played junior hockey with Kitchener Rangers of OHA, turned pro in 1967 with N.Y. Rangers, who traded him to St. L. Blues over the summer. Blues sent him to Kansas City of CPHL, then recalled him after only 13 minor league games. Traded to Det. Red Wings 2/6/71 with Red Berenson for Garry Unger and Wayne Connelly. Can play all three forward positions and is considered good defensive man and penalty killer. Was chosen most improved player by Blues in 1969–70. Lives with wife and son in Toronto during off-season.

NHL record: 188 goals, 151 assists in 407 games; 6 goals, 8 assists in 40 playoff games.

EDESTRAND, DARRYL B. 11/6/45, Strathroy, Ont. Defenseman. 5'11", 185. Played junior hockey in OHA with Toronto and London, turned pro with Rochester in 1965. Also played at Kansas City, Quebec, and Hershey, as well as briefly with St. L. Blues and Phila. Flyers. Went to Pitt. Penguins after 1970–71 season. Lives in London, Ont.

NHL record: 25 goals, 47 assists in 169 games; no goals, 2 assists in 4 playoff games.

EDWARDS, ALLAN ROY B. 3/12/37, Seneca Township, Ont. Goalie. 5'8", 165. Came back from fractured skull to appear in 15 games with Pitt. Penguins in 1971–72, allowing 36 goals for 2.55 average, in 14th pro season. Started as pro in 1958 at Calgary, played at Buffalo, Sault Ste.

Marie, Pittsburgh, Portland, Spokane, St. Louis, and Fort Worth in minors before making it with Det. Red Wings at age of 30 in 1967–68. "Retired" from Wings 6/4/71 after suffering fractured skull 12/6/70 when Craig Cameron of St. L. Blues crashed into him, smashing head against goal post. Had dizzy spells during rest of season. Put on waivers by Detroit, grabbed by Pittsburgh, and "unretired." Traded back to Wings in Oct. 1972 Plays wearing protective helmet. Lives with family in Caledonia, Ont.

NHL record: allowed 619 goals in 232 games for 2.69 average, 12 shutouts; gave up 11 goals in 4 playoff games for 3.43 average, no shutouts.

EGAN, MARTIN JOSEPH (Pat) B. 4/25/18, Blackie, Alta. Defenseman. Spent 11 seasons in NHL, from 1940 to 1951, with year out during war. Played for Sudbury Tigers, Seattle and Springfield before joining N.Y. Americans in 1939–40. Went to Det. Red Wings, then Bos. in 1943–44, and to N.Y. Rangers in 1949. All-Star game 1949. After leaving NHL, played for Cincinnati.

NHL record: 77 goals, 153 assists in 11 seasons; 9 goals, 4 assists in 44 playoff games.

EGERS, JOHN RICHARD (Jack) B. 1/28/49, Sudbury, Ont. Forward. 6'1", 175. Turned pro in 1968 at Omaha, and next year led CHL in scoring with 42 goals and 48 assists for 90 points. Joined N.Y. Rangers at end of 1969–70 season, and made club to stay next year. However, season was marred by concussion suffered against Minn. North Stars in Nov. 1970, and though he appeared in 60 games, he got little ice time. Traded 11/15/71 to St. L. Blues in six-player deal and scored 20 goals for team through rest of season. Lives in Kitchener, Ont., in off-season.

NHL record: 57 goals, 60 assists in 224 games; 4 goals and 6 assists in 24 playoff games.

ELLIOTT, EDWIN S. (Chaucer) B. 1879, Kingston, Ont. D. 3/13/13. Hall of Fame referee. For 10 years between 1903 and 1913 was considered Canada's best hockey referee. Played university hockey, also football and baseball. In 1906, coached Toronto Argonauts and Hamilton Tigers. Joined Montreal AAA as football coach in 1907. Victim of cancer.

ELLIS, RONALD JOHN EDWARD (Ron) B. 1/8/45, Lindsay, Ont. Forward. 5'10", 175. Scored 46 goals in 1963–64 for Toronto Marlboros as amateur, turned pro with Tor. Maple Leafs the next year without ever playing minor league hockey. Wears No. 6, originally retired after Ace

Bailey was forced out of hockey by injury. Bailey suggested that Ellis be given his old numeral. Plays guitar to relax and attends college in off-season. Team Canada 1972. Lives near Toronto.

NHL record: 221 goals, 204 assists in 655 games; 9 goals, 4 assists in 38 playoff games.

EMMS, LEIGHTON (Happy) B. 1/16/05, Barrie, Ont. Defenseman-forward. Played 10 seasons in NHL, then went on to front office career. Started in NHL with Mont. Maroons in 1926, then to N.Y. Americans in 1931 and Det. Red Wings same season. Released in 1934, signed with Bos. Bruins who returned him to Americans 12/13/34 for Red Jackson. Remained with N.Y. until leaving NHL after 1937–38 season. Following retirement, became owner and coach of Niagara Falls team, affiliate of Bruins, post he held for nearly 20 years until becoming GM of Bruins in 1965. Then became managing director of Canadian National team.

NHL record: 36 goals, 53 assists in 10 seasons; no goals, no assists in 6 playoff series.

ESPOSITO, ANTHONY JAMES (Tony) B. 4/23/44, Sault Ste. Marie, Ont. 5'11, 185. Goalie. Played at Michigan Tech after junior hockey in Sault Ste. Marie. Turned pro in Mont. Canadien organization with Vancouver in 1967. Was drafted by Chi. Black Hawks after playing 13 games for Canadiens in 1968. Won Vezina and Calder trophies in 1969–70, and lost Vezina race next season by just seven goals. Combined with net partner, Gary Smith, to win Vezina Trophy again in 1971–72 with two-man average of 2.12. Esposito's average was 1.76 for 48 games. Admits pressure gets to him, saying once about goaltending job: "I don't like it." Team Canada 1972. Wears contact lenses. Owns home in Elmhurst, Chicago suburb.

NHL record: allowed 518 goals in 237 games for 2.19 average, 36 shutouts; gave up 131 goals in 46 playoff games for 2.85 average, 3 shutouts.

ESPOSITO, PHILIP (Phil) B. 2/20/42, Sault Ste. Marie, Ont. Forward. 6'1", 210. Brother of Chi. Black Hawk goalie Tony. Smashed all league scoring records as Bos. Bruins' center in 1970–71 with 76 goals and 76 assists for 152 points, and followed through by leading league the next two years. Acquired by Bruins from Black Hawks with Fred Stanfield and Ken Hodge for Gil Marotte, Pit Martin, and Jack Norris 5/15/67 in deal which still has Chicago fans in tears. Quit high school to play junior hockey for St. Catharines TeePees in Hawks' organization, played six games with Sault Ste. Marie of EPHL in 1961–62, then spent two seasons in minors with St. Louis before moving up to Hawks in 1964. Although always 20-goal man with Hawks, came into own in Boston with 35, 49, and 43 before his big season. Scored record 23 points in 1970 playoffs, tied by Frank Mahovlich of Tor. Maple Leafs next season. Won Hart Trophy in 1969 as league's MVP. Signed four-year, $400,000 contract in Sept. 1971. Team Canada 1972. Associated in hockey equipment business with Stanfield and brother Tony. Lynnfield, Mass., permanent home.

NHL record: 398 goals, 500 assists in 691 games; 37 goals, 54 assists in 81 playoff games.

EVANS, STEWART B. 6/19/08, Ottawa, Ont. Defenseman. Spent eight years in NHL from 1930 to 1939 with three teams. Played amateur hockey in Ottawa, signed by Portland Buccaroos in 1928, went to Victoria in 1929, and was sold to Det. Falcons in 1930. Traded to Mont. Maroons in 1933–34 for Teddy Graham, and finished his career in 1938–39 with Mont. Canadiens. After retirement opened auto agency in Detroit; highly successful.

NHL record: 28 goals, 49 assists in 8 seasons; no goals, no assists in 6 playoff series.

EZINICKI, WILLIAM (Wild Bill) B. 3/11/24, Winnipeg, Man. Forward. Was known as one of roughest of NHL players. Broke into NHL with Tor. Maple Leafs in 1944, going to Bos. Bruins in 1950, leaving NHL for 1952–53 and 1953–54 seasons, then returning to finish career with N.Y. Rangers in 1954–55. All-Star 1947, 1948. After quitting hockey, became professional golfer.

NHL record: 79 goals, 105 assists in 368 games; 5 goals, 8 assists in 40 playoff games.

FAIRBAIRN, WILLIAM JOHN (Billy)   B. 1/7/47, Brandon, Man. 5'10", 190. Forward. Overcame mononucleosis which limited playing time with N.Y. Rangers in 1970–71. Bounced back with 22 goals and 37 assists in 1971–72. Part of training camp routine to get strength back was 200 pushups a day. Played as junior with Brandon Wheat Kings. Turned pro in 1967 at Omaha. Three seasons later with Rangers, scoring 23 goals rookie year on line with Walt Tkaczuk and Dave Balon that scored 203 points. Lives in Brandon.

NHL record: 82 goals, 126 assists in 289 games; 6 goals, 16 assists in 36 playoff games.

FAVELL, DOUGLAS ROBERT (Doug)   B. 4/5/45, St. Catharines, Ont. 5'10", 172. Goalie. Played junior hockey at Niagara Falls, turned pro in 1965 with Oklahoma City. Went to San Francisco in rookie season, back to Oklahoma, and joined Phila. Flyers in 1967–68. Played briefly with Quebec before making Flyers for good next season. Suffered severed Achilles tendon in that season, and worked as backup for Bernie Parent in next. However, Flyers traded Parent after 1970–71, leaving No. 1 job to Favell. Says he always wanted to be goalie. Professes to hate practice. "I'd rather face guys like Hull and Howe in a game than stand out there fielding a couple of hundred shots in practice," he explains.

NHL record: allowed 559 goals in 215 games for 2.80 average, 34 shutouts; gave up 50 goals in 16 games for 3.13 average, 1 shutout.

FERGUSON, JOHN BOWIE B. 9/5/38, Vancouver, B.C. Forward. Spent eight seasons with Mont. Canadiens after getting hockey start as stick boy in native Vancouver. Played there as bantam, midget and junior, then went to Fort Wayne Komets as junior, turned pro with Cleveland Barons, then joined Mont. Canadiens in 1963, retiring in 1971 to look after Montreal knitwear business interests. One of most belligerent players, he held records for penalty minutes, and was suspended for six games 11/28/69 as result of brawling. A onetime lacrosse goalie, was original nominee to be president of Toronto entry in Canadian Lacrosse League. Owns and drives trotting horses.

NHL record: 145 goals, 155 assists in 500 league games; 16 goals, 12 assists in 67 playoff games.

FERGUSON, NORMAN GERARD (Norm) B. 10/16/45, Sydney, N.S. Forward. 5'8", 165. As Calif. Seals' right wing, was runner-up to Minn. North Stars' Danny Grant for Rookie of Year in 1968–69; had 34 goals. Turned pro in 1966–67 with Houston after playing for Junior Canadiens. Moved to Cleveland, then grabbed by Seals in 1968. Broke shoulder in 1970–71 year. Jumped to N.Y. Raiders of WHA after 1971–72. Lives in Sydney, N.S., in off-season with son and wife, working for family cartage company.

NHL record: 73 goals, 66 assists in 279 games; 1 goal, 4 assists in 10 playoff games.

FIELDER, GUYLE ABNER B. 11/21/30, Potlatch, Idaho. 5'9", 165. Forward. Scored 76 points for Portland of WHL in 1971–72 to pass Gordie Howe as all-time point scorer in hockey. Howe's record was 1809, Fielder's near 1900 during 1972–73. Played only 11 games in NHL, but has dominated minor league play as perhaps no other player. Played as junior with Lethbridge Native Sons. Turned pro with Chi. Black Hawks in 1950, playing three NHL games. Got into six with Det. Red Wings in 1957–58. Was in two playoff games for Bos. Bruins in 1954. And, except for 1952–53 season at St. Louis of AHL, has played all rest of his hockey in West. Teams include New Westminster, Edmonton, Seattle from 1957 to 1970, then Salt Lake City. Won Rookie of Year award with New Westminster in 1952. Added eight scoring titles, six MVP awards. Set WHL scoring record in 1957 with 122 points. Has won "gentlemanly player" award thrice. Known to western fans as "Golden Guyle."

NHL record: no goals, no assists in 9 games; no goals, no assists in 2 playoff games.

FINLEY, CHARLES O. B. 2/22/18, Birmingham, Ala. Owner of Calif. Golden Seals bailed out club by buying it in 1970 when it was in default of loans. An insurance broker, he also owns Oakland Athletics of American Baseball League, garbing both teams in green and gold. Also involved in Finley's operations is mule named Charlie O., Athletics' mascot who has traveled about league on personal appearances. Finley is considered erratic in handling of sports enterprises, firing managers frequently. Lives on estate near La Porte, Ind.

FINNIGAN, FRANK B. 7/9/03, Shawville, Que. Forward. Had 14-year NHL career, playing 11 of them with Ottawa Senators. Played as amateur for Ottawa Montagnards. Signed with Senators in 1924, staying until being sent to Tor. Maple Leafs in 1931–32. Then returned to Ottawa for two more years. Went to St. Louis in 1934 when Ottawa franchise became St. L. Eagles. Finished that season with Tor. Maple Leafs. Retired end of 1936–37.

NHL record: 115 goals, 88 assists in 14 seasons; 6 goals and 9 assists in 9 playoff series.

FLAMAN, FERDINAND CHARLES (Fernie) B. 1/25/27, Dysart, Sask. Defenseman. Spent 11 full seasons with Bos. Bruins in 15-year NHL career. Played as junior with Olympics in Saskatchewan. Moved up in minors through Hershey and Pittsburgh before making Bruins in 1946 after two brief appearances in two previous years. Remained until mid-1950–51, when he went to Tor. Maple Leafs. Returned to Bruins in 1954–55 and finished career there in 1961. All-Star games 1952, 1955–59. Known for roughness, picked up four penalties in one period in 1951 Cup game. After retirement served as GM and coach of Providence Reds 1961–65. Was coach of Fort Worth Wings in 1968–69. Named hockey coach at Northeastern U. 3/11/70.

NHL record: 34 goals, 174 assists in 910 games; 4 goals, 8 assists in 63 playoff games.

FLEMING, REGINALD STEPHEN (Reggie) B. 4/21/36, Montreal, Que. Defenseman-forward. Signed contract in summer of 1972 with Chi. Cougars of WHA when it looked as if hockey career was about over. Came up in Mont. Canadien organization, played for Kingston Frontenacs, got weekend trial with Montreal at left wing in Feb. 1960, also played at Shawinigan Falls, was sent to Chi. Black Hawks next season after injuring Bob Courcey and Ed Kachur in Montreal practice. Went to Bos. Bruins in 1964 with Ab McDonald for Doug Mohns, causing Chicago fans to picket Stadium. Went to N.Y. Rangers 8/7/65 for Earl Ingarfield, to Phila. Flyers in 1969 and Buffalo Sabres in 1970–71.

Shipped to minors next season, playing at Cincinnati and Salt Lake City. One of game's roughest players, participant in some of most memorable fights, also slashed linesman Brian Sopp with stick in incident Jan. 1966.

NHL record: 108 goals, 132 assists in 749 games; 3 goals, 6 assists in 50 playoff games.

FLETT, WILLIAM MYER (Bill)   B. 7/21/43, Vermilion, Alta. Forward. 6'1", 195. Played briefly with Rochester and Denver before joining Victoria for 23 games in 1964–65. Moved through Tor. Maple Leaf organization to three seasons at Tulsa, then was grabbed in 1967 expansion draft by L.A. Kings. Got 26 goals in rookie season. Traded to Phila. Flyers in mid-1971. Once was in rodeos in Alberta, getting nickname "Cowboy." Inadvertently cost teammates $100 apiece by scoring goal 1/3/69 against St. L. Blues which referee disallowed. When no one protested, Kings' owner Jack Kent Cooke fined each member of team.

NHL record: 138 goals, 140 assists in 423 games; 7 goals, 10 assists in 28 playoff games.

FONTEYNE, VALERE RONALD (Val)   B. 12/2/33, Wetaskiwin, Alta. Forward. 5'9", 155. Played 17th season as pro and 13th full one in NHL (1971–72)—68 games for Pitt. Penguins. Turned pro in 1954 with New Westminster of WHL. Played minor league hockey at Seattle, Baltimore, Pittsburgh. Six seasons with Det. Red Wings, two with N.Y. Rangers before going to Penguins in expansion of 1967. Jumped to Alberta Oilers of WHA after 1971–72. Used as penalty killer, he went 168 league games without drawing penalty himself. Known as "Beezer." Lives with family in Wetaskiwin.

NHL record: 75 goals, 154 assists in 820 games; 3 goals, 10 assists in 59 playoff games.

FONTINATO, LOUIS   B. 1/20/32, Guelph, Ont. Defenseman. Career ended by broken neck 3/9/63 after nine NHL seasons, seven with N.Y. Rangers. Played for Guelph Biltmores as junior, joined Rangers for 27 games in 1954, went to Mont. Canadiens for Doug Harvey in 1961–62, retired in 1963 from Montreal club. One of roughest of players, with 202 penalty minutes in 1955–56. Earned nickname "Louie the Leaper." Coached Guelph juniors in Western Ontario League after retirement, and in 1964 took a Canadian hockey team to Italy. Has successful business career.

NHL record: 26 goals, 76 assists in 536 games; no goals, 2 assists in 21 playoff games.

FOYSTON, FRANK C. B. 2/2/91, Minesing, Ont. D. 1/24/66, Seattle, Wash. Forward. Hall of Famer. Played junior hockey and moved into seniors with Eatons in Toronto before turning pro with Toronto of NHA in 1912. Went to Seattle in 1915 and Victoria in 1924, scoring 186 goals in Western Canada League. When Detroit bought Cougars in 1926 he went into NHL and played two years before retiring.

NHL record: 17 goals, 7 assists in 2 seasons; 15 goals, 2 assists in 4 Stanley Cup years.

FRANCIS, EMILE PERCY (Cat) B. 9/13/26, North Battleford, Sask. Goalie. Now GM and coach of N.Y. Rangers. Played goalie for 14 years. In NHL played for Chi. Black Hawks 1946–48, and Rangers from 1948–52. Retired as player in 1960, coached Ranger farm team at Guelph, Ont., in 1961, named asst. GM in New York in 1963, GM in 1964, and coach 12/6/65. Stepped aside for Bernie Geoffrion for part of 1968–69, returning as coach 1/17/69 when Geoffrion became ill. Lives in Long Island.

NHL record: allowed 355 goals in 95 games for 3.74 average, 1 shutout; gave up 3 goals in 1 playoff game for 3.00 average, no shutouts.

FREDERICKSON, FRANK B. (date unknown) Winnipeg, Man. Forward. Hall of Famer. Played 11 years of professional hockey, then coached. Played senior hockey in Winnipeg in 1913–14 and at U. of Manitoba. After World War I led Winnipeg Falcons to Olympic title in 1920 at Antwerp. Joined Victoria club of PCL in Dec. 1920, and when league was sold went to Det. Cougars in 1926, also playing for Bos. Bruins in same season, then to Pittsburgh in mid-1928–29, and finishing playing career as forward with Detroit in 1930–31. After retiring due to leg injury, coached Winnipeg and Princeton U. Served in RCAF during World War II, then became coach of U. of British Columbia. Lives in Vancouver.

NHL record: 39 goals, 34 assists in 5 years; 2 goals, 5 assists in 2 playoff series.

GADSBY, WILLIAM ALEXANDER (Bill) B. 8/8/27, Calgary, Alta. Defenseman. Hall of Famer survived a torpedoing in the Atlantic, polio, and 600 stitches in cuts administered by opponents to play 20 years in NHL. Played junior hockey in Edmonton, then joined Chi. Black Hawks organization. Summoned to Hawks in 1946–47, traded to N.Y. Rangers in 1954, and to Det. Red Wings in 1961–62, finishing career there in 1966. Gadsby, 12, and his mother were returning from England during World War II when ship they were on was torpedoed, and he spent five hours in Atlantic before being rescued. Polio attack came in 1952, when he was captain of Hawks. All-Star 1953, 54, 56, 57, 58, 59, 60, 65. Gadsby was named coach of Red Wings for 1968–69, but was fired after one season and two games of 1969–70 when new regime took over club. Hired as scout, he was fired from that job 4/22/70. Lives in Detroit area.

NHL record: 130 goals, 437 assists in 1248 games; 4 goals, 23 assists in 67 playoff games.

GAGNON, JOHN (Black Cat) B. 6/8/05, Chicoutimi, Que. Forward. Played 10 years in NHL, mostly with Mont. Canadiens. Started as amateur with Sons of Ireland in Quebec City, turned pro with Quebec in 1926, and went to Providence in 1927. Sold to Canadiens in 1930. Went briefly to Bos. Bruins in 1934–35. Returned to Canadiens, staying until traded to N.Y. Rangers in 1939–40, where he ended NHL career in same season. Now employed as scout for Rangers; based in Rhode Island.

NHL record: 120 goals, 141 assists in 10 seasons; 12 goals, 12 assists in 9 playoff series.

GAMBLE, BRUCE GEORGE B. 5/24/38, Port Arthur, Ont. Goalie. 5'9", 200. Phila. Flyer No. 2 goalie. Suffered heart attack in Feb. 1972 in game at Oakland, putting career in doubt. Played junior hockey with Guelph Biltmores, from whom he was called up by N.Y. Rangers in 1958 to provide backup help as playoffs neared. Won WHL Rookie of Year award next season in Vancouver. Played minor league hockey in Providence, Vancouver, Portland, Kingston, Springfield, Tulsa, and Rochester, and in NHL with Bos. Bruins and Tor. Maple Leafs before joining Flyers at end of 1970–71 season. Did not begin to use goalie mask until that campaign.

NHL record: allowed 992 goals in 372 games for 3.23 average, 22 shutouts; gave up 25 goals in 5 games for 7.29 average, no shutouts.

GARDINER, CHARLES ROBERT (Chuck) B. 12/31/04, Edinburgh, Scotland. D. 6/13/34. Hall of Famer. Goalie. Was struck down by brain tumor at age 29, at height of career. Family moved to Canada in 1911. Was in intermediate hockey at 14, turned pro in 1926 with Winnipeg Maroons. Tended goal because of poor skating. Joined Chi. Black Hawks in 1927, playing for seven seasons. Won Vezina Trophy in 1932 and 1934, was first All-Star three times and second All-Star once.

NHL record: Allowed 673 goals in 316 games for 2.13 average, 43 shutouts; gave up 35 goals in 21 playoff games for 1.67 average, 5 shutouts.

GARDINER, HERBERT MARTIN (Herb) B. 5/8/91, Winnipeg, Man. Defenseman. Hall of Famer. Had many interests besides hockey, and they kept him from reaching NHL until age of 35, where he played only two seasons. Began playing in 1908, but was away from game from 1910 to 1919, first on survey for the Canadian Pacific R.R. and then in World War I with Canadian army, where he won commission and was wounded. Returned to game in 1919, and played from 1920 to 1925 for Calgary of Western Canada League. Joined Mont. Canadiens in 1926, winning Hart Trophy in first season. Loaned to Chi. Black Hawks in 1929 as manager, but recalled for playoffs. Sold to Bos. Bruins, then to Philadelphia of Canadian-American League, where he was coach and manager. Also coached Ramblers and Falcons in Philadelphia until stepping out in 1949. Now lives in Philadelphia.

NHL record: 10 goals, 9 assists in 2 seasons; 1 goal, 1 assist in 3 playoff series.

GARDNER, CALVIN PEARLY B. 10/30/24, Transcona, Man. For-

62

ward. Played 12 years in NHL for four clubs, from 1945 to 1957. Amateur with N.Y. Rovers and on 1943 Memorial Cup-winning Winnipeg Rangers. Joined N.Y. Rangers in 1945, staying until going to Tor. Maple Leafs in 1948. Spent 1952-53 with Chi. Black Hawks. Finished career with four seasons as Bos. Bruin. All-Star 1948, 1949. Lives in Toronto. Has served as broadcaster for Bruins.

NHL record: 154 goals, 238 assists in 695 games; 7 goals, 10 assists in 61 playoff games.

GARDNER, GEORGE EDWARD   B. 10/8/42, Lachine, Que. Goalie. 5'10", 160. Turned pro in 1963 with Minneapolis of CPHL, played in minors with Memphis, Pittsburgh, Vancouver and Rochester. NHL experience came with Det. Red Wings before he joined the Van. Canucks' organization. Brought up by Canucks in 1970–71. Jumped to L.A. Sharks of WHA after 1971–72.

NHL record: Allowed 207 goals in 66 games for 3.75 average, no shutouts.

GARDNER, JAMES HENRY (Jimmy)   B. 5/21/81, Montreal, Que. D. 11/7/40, Montreal, Que. Forward. Hall of Famer. Product of sidewalk hockey, he played with Montreal Hockey Club and Montreal Wanderers. Then to Calumet, Mich., for two seasons, Pittsburgh, back to Montreal with Shamrocks, back to Wanderers, New Westminster of PCL, finally Mont. Canadiens for two seasons. Retired 1917. After two years as Canadiens' coach, shifted to officiating. Tried coaching again with Hamilton Tigers in 1924–25, until team quit league.

GEE, GEORGE   B. 6/28/22, Stratford, Ont. D. 1/14/72, Wyandotte, Mich., after collapsing while playing in Det. Red Wing Old Timers game. Forward. Played nine seasons in NHL with Chi. Black Hawks and Red Wings. Served with Kansas City Pla-Mors, and served in Canadian navy before joining Hawks in 1945. Traded to Det. prior to 1948 season with Bud Poile for Jim Conacher and Doug McCaig. Returned to Hawks after 1950–51 season with five other players for $75,000. Retired from NHL in 1954. Threatened with legal action in 1946 when he jumped contract with Kingston Ponies baseball club to play hockey, but was given release by Kingston when NHL threatened to bar him.

NHL record: 135 goals, 183 assists in 551 games; 6 goals, 13 assists in 41 playoff games.

GENDRON, JEAN GUY (Smitty)   B. 8/30/34, Montreal, Que. Forward. 5'9" 165. Amateur hockey at Three Rivers. Turned pro in 1954 with Providence. Then with N.Y. Rangers, Bos. Bruins, Mont. Canadiens, and Rangers and Bruins again before going to Quebec Aces for four seasons, where he expected to finish career. Phila. Flyers bought club, and Gendron returned to big league in 1968. Jumped to Quebec Nordigues after 1971–72. Plays pro golf in off-season.

NHL record: 182 goals, 201 assists in 863 games; 7 goals, 4 assists in 42 playoff games.

GEOFFRION, BERNARD (Boom Boom) B. 2/14/31, Montreal, Que. Forward. Hall of Famer. Played 14 seasons with Mont. Canadiens, two with N.Y. Rangers—teams made playoffs every year. Joined Canadiens in 1950, played 18 games. Next season, 1951–52, his first full season, won Calder Trophy as Rookie of Year. Added Hart MVP Trophy in 1961. Retired from Canadiens 1964. Returned to play with Rangers 1966–67, 1967–68. All-Star first team 1961. Led league in scoring, 1955—75 points (38 goals); 1961—95 points (50 goals). After leaving Canadiens, coached Quebec Aces to two AHL titles. After retiring as Ranger player, became their coach, 1968, until forced to step down because of stomach ailment. Asst. GM, Rangers, Aug. 1969. Scout in Province of Quebec for Rangers, 1971–72. Coach, NHL expansion Atlanta Flames, 1972–73.

NHL record: 393 goals, 429 assists in 883 games; 58 goals, 60 assists in 132 playoff games.

GERARD, EDWARD GEORGE (Eddie) B. 2/22/90, Ottawa, Ont. Defenseman. D. 8/7/37, Ottawa, Ont. Hall of Famer. Starred as player and was successful coach. Turned pro with Ottawa Senators in 1917 and stayed with them for six years. Played on four Stanley Cup winners, including 1921–22 when he was loaned to Tor. St. Pats to help them win Cup. Retired after 1923 season. Coached Mont. Maroons to Stanley Cup in 1926, joined N.Y. Americans as manager in 1930, returned to Maroons in 1932. Was with St. L. Eagles in 1934 but quit halfway through season.

NHL record: 50 goals, 30 assists in 128 games; 7 goals, 1 assist in 5 playoffs.

GIACOMIN, EDWARD B. 6/6/39, Sudbury, Ont. Goalie 5'11", 175. Broke into pro hockey in 1960 with Providence Reds by masquerading as brother Rollo, whom Reds had summoned for emergency duty but never seen. Went on to win Vezina Trophy with N.Y. Rangers in 1971. after sharing the trophy with Gilles Villemure in 1970. Amateur with N.Y. Rovers of Eastern League, turning down football and baseball scholarships to San Fernando College. Off-season stove explosion badly burned both his legs, but he returned to five seasons with Reds before being traded by Providence to Rangers in May 1965 for four players.

Played 36 games in rookie year, plus seven at Baltimore, then did "ironman" duty for four seasons for Rangers, playing in 68, 66, 70 and 70 games, respectively, until Gilles Villemure came along to provide relief. Considered exceptionally good skater for goalie. Called by some the Rangers' third defenseman.

NHL record: allowed 1134 goals in 442 games for 2.57 average, 43 shutouts; gave up 139 goals in 50 playoff games for 2.78 average, 1 shutout.

GIBBS, BARRY PAUL   B. 9/28/48, Lloydminster, Sask. Defenseman 5'11", 195. Posted his fifth straight 100-penalty-minute year in 1971–72, with 128. His professional violence began in 1967–68, when he accumulated 154 minutes at Oklahoma City. Played as junior at Estevan, stayed at Oklahoma City in Bos. Bruins' organization until going to Minn. North Stars 5/11/69 in exchange for draft choice. Got 182 penalty minutes next season. Wears helmet while piling up penalties, which included record 194 minutes in 1968–69 season at Oklahoma City. Lives with family in Bloomington, Minn.

NHL record: 22 goals, 72 assists in 286 games; 3 goals, 2 assists in 30 games.

GILBERT, RODRIQUE GABRIEL (Rod)   B. 7/1/41, Montreal, Que. Forward. 5'9", 175. Had two spinal fusion operations and almost was written off as finished. Has worn back brace since 1965. Sneaked onto N.Y. Rangers' list when Rangers got permission to sponsor Junior B. team that included him and Jean Ratelle, although Mont. Canadiens had exclusive rights to every player within 50 miles of city. Rejected baseball offer from Milwaukee Braves, played Junior A at Guelph, injuring back for first time. Operation kept him well 3 1/2 years, then operated on again. Played briefly with Three Rivers in 1959–60, then with Kitchener in 1961–62, making Rangers in 1962–63. Team Canada 1972. First team All-Star 1972. Lives in New York City. Once engaged to Thailand girl, but broke engagement because of rigors of hockey traveling.

NHL record: 269 goals, 408 assists in 748 games; 30 goals, 25 assists in 63 playoff games.

GILBERTSON, STAN   B. 10/29/44, Duluth, Minn. Forward. 6', 175. Played amateur hockey at Jacksonville and turned pro in 1964–65 with Minneapolis at age 20. Played with San Francisco, California, and Vancouver in minors before putting in three seasons with Hershey of AHL. Drafted from Bos. Bruins' system by Calif. Seals 6/8/71 and became regular left wing in first season.

NHL record: 22 goals, 31 assists in 144 games.

GILMOUR, HAMILTON LIVINGSTONE (Billy) B. 3/21/85, Ottawa Ont. D. 3/13/59, Mount Royal, Que. Hall of Famer. Made name in early days of century. Attended McGill U., then helped Ottawa Silver Sevens to win three Stanley Cups, 1903–1905. After sitting out season, returned with Montreal Victorias of Eastern Canada Amateur League, then played for Ottawa Senators in 1908–09. After retiring for six seasons, he played two games in 1915–16 for Ottawa, then retired again permanently.

GLOVER, FREDERICK AUSTIN B. 1/5/28, Toronto, Ont. Forward. Made it in NHL as coach, though never as player, but posted one of finest minor league playing records in history of game as right wing. Had brief tryouts with Det. Red Wings and Chi. Black Hawks. Played as junior with Galt Red Wings, turned pro in 1947 with Omaha of USHL. Played 19 years in minors, last 15 with Cleveland Barons of AHL, where he also served as coach at end of career. Named coach by Calif. Seals in 1970, also serving as temporary GM, fired 10/15/71. Coached L.A. Kings for 68 games in 1971–72, let go at end of season. Rehired on interim basis by Seals 11/7/72 when Garry Young resigned. Between Seals and Kings jobs performed as personnel director for Cleveland Crusaders, resigned because of "personal reasons." During playing career scored 1413 points, with just 24 of them in 92 games in NHL. Career point totals bettered by just three players in history of game— Gordie Howe, Maurice Richard, and Guyle Fielder. Brother of Howie Glover.

NHL record: 13 goals, 11 assists in 92 games; no goals, no assists in 4 playoff games.

GODFREY, WARREN EDWARD (Rocky) B. 3/23/31, Toronto, Ont. Defenseman. Hard-checking player in NHL from 1952 to 1968, playing for Bos. Bruins and Det. Red Wings. Played as Junior for Waterloo Hurricanes, joined Bruins in 1952, went to Det. in 1955, returned to Bruins for one season in 1962–63, then was shipped back to Det. 10/9/63 for Gerry Odrowski. Wings shipped him to Pittsburgh minor league club, then recalled him in Dec. However, Godfrey never again was full-time NHL performer, tearing cartilage in Dec. 1965, and finally left league after 1967–68 season after appearing in just 55 games in five seasons.

NHL record: 32 goals, 125 assists in 787 games; 1 goal and 4 assists in 52 playoff games.

GOLDHAM, ROBERT JOHN B. 5/12/22, Georgetown, Ont. Defenseman. Rode in back of fruit truck from native Georgetown to Maple Leaf

Gardens to see first NHL game. Played at Georgetown High, went on to Toronto Marlboros after moving to Toronto at age of 16. Played at Hershey in 1941–42, getting into 19 games with Tor. Maple Leafs at end of season. Joined Leafs for good in 1945. Went to Chi. Black Hawks in 1947–48 in seven-player deal, which sent him, Gaye Stewart, Gus Bodnar, Bud Poile, and Ernie Dickens to Chi. for Max Bentley and Cy Thomas. Sent to Red Wings in 1950–51 in another big swap which peddled Al Dewsbury, Don Morrison, Pete Babando, Jack Stewart, and Harry Lumley to the Hawks for Goldham, Gaye Stewart, Metro Prystai, and Jim Henry. Finished career in Det. in 1955–56. First-team All-Star 1952. After retirement, took over microphone as one of Leafs' TV announcers, and coached at St. Michael's College in Toronto.

NHL record: 28 goals, 143 assists in 650 games; 3 goals, 14 assists in 66 playoff games.

GOLDSWORTHY, LEROY   B. 10/18/08, Two Harbors, Minn. Defense-man-forward, Played 9 NHL seasons. Started with Edmonton Eskimos as Junior, went to Springfield in 1926, to N.Y. Rangers in 1929. Sold to Det. in 1930, and played for Falcons, Olympics, and London that season, Olympics in 1931–32. Started 1933–34 with London, but was sold to Chi. Black Hawks, then went to Mont. Canadiens in 1934–35, Bos. Bruins in 1936, and finished career in 1938–39 with N.Y. Americans.

NHL record: 66 goals, 57 assists in 9 seasons. 1 goal, no assists in 26 playoff games.

GOLDSWORTHY, WILLIAM ALFRED (Billy)   B. 8/24/44, Kitchener, Ont. Forward. 6′, 200. Played junior hockey at Niagara Falls, turned pro in Bos. Bruins organization in 1964–65, playing minor league hockey at Oklahoma City and Buffalo before going to Minn. North Stars in 1967 expansion draft. Was suspended and sent to Memphis in Dec. 1968, for "poor and indifferent" play. Recalled, and next season scored 36 goals. Career also spotted by fine at Oklahoma City for "detrimental" conduct of swearing at officials, and three-game suspension 3/16/68 for slugging linesman. Began wearing helmet after being knocked unconscious three times. Team Canada 1972. Lives with family in Bloomington, Minn.

NHL record: 162 goals, 159 assists in 474 games; 18 goals, 19 assists in 40 playoff games.

GOODFELLOW, EBENEZER R. (Ebbie)   B. 4/9/07, Ottawa, Ont. Defenseman-forward. Hall of Famer. Played 14 seasons with Detroit. Amateur hockey with Ottawa Montagnards. Assigned by Detroit to Olympics of International League. Joined NHL in Detroit in 1929. (Detroit team had three names during his tenure—Cougars, Falcons,

Red Wings.) Moved from center to defense. Won Hart MVP Trophy in 1939–40. Named first All-Star twice, second once. Captain of Red Wings for five years. Retired after 1942–43 season, but remained in Detroit area.

NHL record: 134 goals, 190 assists in 14 seasons; 8 goals, 8 assists in 8 playoff series.

GORDON, JOHN (Jack)   B. 3/3/28, Winnipeg, Man. Forward. Minn. North Stars coach, played only bits of three seasons in NHL as forward, all with N.Y. Rangers, getting in 31 games in 1948–49, one in 1949–50, and four in 1950–51. In minor league career played with New Haven, Cincinnati, and finally 10 seasons with Cleveland Barons. He spent 17 years with Cleveland, also serving as coach and GM, handled scouting for Rangers for three seasons, then coached Cleveland a year before getting Minnesota job in 1970. Lives in Edina, Minn.

GORING, ROBERT THOMAS (Butch)   B. 10/22/49, St. Boniface, Man. Forward. 5′9″, 170. Resumed an NHL career in 1971–72 that was interrupted by mononucleosis in 1970–71. Played with Canadian National team, and as amateur with Winnipeg Jets before being grabbed by L.A. Kings in amateur draft 1968–69. Played at Springfield and with Kings next season, but in 1970 was stricken and sent to Springfield, leading team to Calder Cup.

NHL record: 64 goals, 88 assists in 219 games.

GORMAN, THOMAS PATRICK   B. 6/9/86, Ottawa. Ont. D. 5/15/61. Hall of Fame Builder. One of founders of National Hockey League in 1917, was owner of Ottawa franchise. Coached Chi. Black Hawks to Stanley Cup in 1934 and Mont. Maroons to Cup in 1935. Managed Ottawa Senators when they won Cup in 1920, 21, 23, and was GM of Mont. Canadiens when they won Cup in 1944, 46. Played on Canadian Olympic lacrosse team in 1908, and served as sports editor of *Ottawa Citizen* for many years.

GOTTSELIG, JOHN   B. 6/24/06, Odessa, Russia. Forward. Played 16 seasons with Chi. Black Hawks. Listed as born in 1906, but in middle of his career it became necessary to send to Russia for his birth certificate, which he says indicates he was born in 1907, and he credits this extra year of youth for extending his career. Moved to Canada in his youth. After retiring in 1945 helped run Hawks' farm system and coached team from 1945 to 1947. Served as public relations director for club until fired in 1963 for "violations of club policy." Opened hockey schools in the Chicago area. In 1949, extended scope of sports activities by managing

Kenosha Comets, a girls' softball team.

NHL record: 176 goals, 195 assists in 16 seasons; 13 goals, 14 assists in 43 playoff games.

GOYETTE, JOSEPH GEORGES PHILIPPE (Phil) B. 10/31/33, La-chine, Que. Center. 5'11", 170. Has flirted with retirement for years. Played just three regular-season games in 1971–72 after N.Y. Rangers acquired him from Buffalo Sabres for playoff insurance in his 16th NHL season. Played as amateur with Cincinnati Mohawks of IHL, turned pro in 1955 with Montreal Royals, joined Mont. Canadiens in 1956–57 and stayed until traded to Rangers 6/4/63 in multiplayer deal. Drafted by St. L. Blues in 1969, and won Lady Byng Trophy during his one year in St. Louis. Drafted by Sabres next season, retired, then returned to score 15 goals. Rangers got him back for 1972 playoffs after he sat out most of 1971–72 season. Then hired to coach expansion N.Y. Islanders, but lasted only until Jan. 1973 when fired. Suffers from tracheal bronchitis. Has business partnership with Donnie Marshall.

NHL record: 207 goals, 467 assists in 941 games; 17 goals, 29 assists in 94 playoff games.

GRANT, DANIEL FREDERICK B. 2/21/46, Fredericton, N.B. For-ward. 5'10" 192. Turned pro in Mont. Canadiens' system, playing in 1966–67 with Houston and getting into 22 games with Canadiens next season. Sent to Minn. North Stars 6/11/68 for amateur draft choices, winning 1969 Rookie of Year award with 34 goals and 31 assists. Operates hockey school in off-season. Lives in Fredericton, spending vacation time fishing.

NHL record: 150 goals, 146 assists in 408 games; 10 goals, 12 assists in 41 playoff games.

GRANT, MICHAEL (Mike) B. 1870s. D. 1961. Hall of Famer. Was outstanding speed skater as boy. Joined Montreal Victorias hockey club in 1894, eventually playing also on Shamrocks and Crystals in Montreal. Also refereed. In later years toured U.S. to demonstrate hockey and organize exhibition games.

GREEN, EDWARD JOSEPH (Ted) B. 3/23/40, Eriksdale, Man. De-fenseman. 5'10", 200. Came back from 1969 injury in which skull was smashed, to regain place on Bos. Bruins. Played with St. Boniface Canadiens as junior. Spent two seasons at Winnipeg before making Bruins in 1961. Wayne Maki of Canucks hit him with stick in exhibition game in Sept. 1969, leaving him paralyzed on left side. Three brain operations were needed to save Green's life, and he missed all of

1969–70, but returned to play all 78 games next season. Fans tendered him night in Boston 1/24/71. Says he bears Maki no ill will. Wears acrylic plastic plate in head, protected on ice by special helmet. Trace of speech impediment is only reminder of near fatal injury. Lives in Lynnfield, Mass. Jumped to New England Whalers after 1971–72.

NHL record: 48 goals, 206 assists in 620 games; 4 goals, 8 assists in 31 playoff games.

GREEN, WILFRED THOMAS (Shorty) B. 7/17/96, Sudbury, Ont. D. 4/19/60. Forward. Hall of Famer. Scored first goal in old Madison Square Garden as member of N.Y. Americans. Played intermediate hockey, then seniors, before joining army in 1916. Returning home in 1919, played amateur hockey until turning pro with Hamilton Tigers in 1923. Hamilton franchise moved to New York in 1925, and he played with Americans until retiring in 1927. Continued to coach until 1933.

NHL record: 33 goals, 8 assists in 4 seasons.

GRIFFIS, SILAS SETH (Sox) B. 1880s. D. July 1950. Hall of Famer. Starred in rowing, golf, and bowling in addition to hockey. Played for Kenora, Ont., Stanley Cup winners in 1907, then retired until 1911, joining Vancouver Millionaires of PCL until 1918, captaining Cup winner of 1915.

GUEVREMONT, JOCELYN M. (Josh) B. 3/1/51, Montreal, Que. Defenseman. 6'2", 190. Top selection by Van. Canucks in 1971 amateur draft. Team Canada 1972, but quit team in Moscow when not listed for first of four-game series. Excellent shot.

NHL record: 29 goals, 64 assists in 153 games.

GUIDOLIN, ARMAND (Bep) B. 12/9/25, Thorold, Ont. Forward. Played nine seasons as NHL forward, then went into coaching, taking charge of Bos. Bruins 2/5/73 after Tom Johnson was fired. Joined Bruins in 1942, at age 16, staying until 1947 when he went to Det. Red Wings, who sent him to Chi. Black Hawks in mid-1948–49. Retired from NHL in 1952. Coached Boston Braves in AHL 1971–72.

NHL record: 107 goals, 171 assists in 519 games; 5 goals, 7 assists in 24 playoff games.

HADFIELD, VICTOR EDWARD (Vic)   B. 10/4/40, Oakville, Ont. Forward. 6', 185. N.Y. Ranger left wing and captain. Is golf pro off-season. Played as junior in Chi. Black Hawk organization at St. Catharines. Turned pro in 1960 at Buffalo of AHL. Drafted by Rangers in June 1961. Made team same season. Amassed 151 penalty minutes in 1963–64, first season as regular. Keeps total around the 100 mark. Vic, Jean Ratelle, Rod Gilbert give Rangers explosive line. Team Canada 1972. Owns golf course in partnership with Harry Howell and Andy Bathgate.

NHL record: 235 goals, 276 assists in 761 league games; 21 goals, 19 assists in 45 playoff games.

HAINSWORTH, GEORGE   B. 6/26/95, Toronto, Ont. D. 10/9/50, auto accident. Goalie. Hall of Famer. Replaced George Vezina in goal for Mont. Canadiens after latter's death. Moved to Kitchener, Ont., as youth and played junior hockey there. Turned pro with Saskatoon in 1923. Moved to Canadiens in 1926. Won Vezina Trophy in first three seasons. Traded to Tor. Maple Leafs 1933–34, returned to Canadiens at end of 1936–37 season, then retired. In a 44-game season in 1928–29 he shut out opposition 22 times (and his team won 22 games) for 0.98 average.

NHL record: allowed 938 goals in 465 games for 2.02 average, 91 shutouts; gave up 112 goals in 52 playoff games for 2.15 average, 8 shutouts.

HALL, GLENN HENRY B. 10/3/31, Humboldt, Sask. Goalie. Started as regular in NHL as goaltender in 1955 and stayed until 1971 despite constant threats to quit because of nervous stomach. Turned pro with Indianapolis of AHL in 1951 and played with Edmonton of WHL before joining Det. Red Wings to stay, in 1955. During minor league career, also played six games with Detroit in 1952–53 and two in 1954–55. In 1955–56, officially his first season, he was named rookie of year. In 1957 he went to Chi. Black Hawks, then to St. L. Blues in 1967, retiring in 1971 after being waived out of league. Won or shared three Vezina Trophies. Nervous stomach caused him to become ill before games, and on occasion he was forced to leave ice to vomit, then return to continue game. Threatened frequently to retire, but always was lured back by offer of bigger contracts. Despite nerves, at one time played 502 straight games. Retired to farms he owns near Edmonton, Alta.

NHL record: allowed 2168 goals in 863 games for 2.50 average, 81 shutouts; gave up 312 goals in 111 playoff games for 2.84 average, 6 shutouts.

HALL, JOSEPH HENRY (Joe) B. 4/5/82, Staffordshire, England. D. 1919. Defenseman. Hall of Famer played 14 seasons as pro, starting in 1905 with Kenora, Ont., after amateur play in Brandon, Man., and Winnipeg. Played for Montreal Wanderers and Quebec Bulldogs, finished career with Mont. Canadiens. With them, he had 15 goals and an assist in 37 games. During career, Hall, known for aggressive play, was on four Stanley Cup winners.

HAMILTON, ALLAN GUY B. 8/20/46, Flin Flon, Man. Defenseman, 6'1", 195. Joined St. Paul in 1964–65, and bounced back and forth among N.Y. Rangers, Omaha, and Buffalo of AHL before being drafted by Buffalo Sabres in 1970. Played junior hockey with Edmonton Oil Kings, who won Canada championship over Bobby Orr's Oshawa team. Jumped from Sabres to Alberta Oilers of WHA after 1971–72.

NHL record: 6 goals, 63 assists in 226 games; no goals, no assists in 6 playoff games.

HAMPSON, EDWARD GEORGE (Ted) B. 12/11/36, Togo, Sask. Forward. 5'8", 173. Minn. North Stars' center known as a playmaker rather than scorer. First full season in 1957–58 at Providence. Played at Vancouver, Rochester, Baltimore, and Pittsburgh, as well as in NHL with Tor. Maple Leafs, N.Y. Rangers, and Det. Red Wings before going to Calif. Seals for three seasons. Sent to Minnesota in latter part of 1970–71 season. Won Masterton Trophy for sportsmanship and perseverance in 1969. Lives in Flin Flon, Man.

NHL record: 108 goals, 245 assists in 676 games; 7 goals, 10 assists in 35 playoff games.

HARBARUK, MIKOLAJ NICHOLAS (Nick) B. 8/16/43, Drohiczyn, Poland. Forward. 6', 195. Pitt. Penguins' right wing was born at height of World War II. Immigrated to Toronto as child. Played hockey in Tor. Maple Leafs' system, turned pro with Pittsburgh Hornets in 1961–62. Played one game, then sat out two years, returning in 1964–65 with Rochester and Tulsa. Stayed at Tulsa through 1968–69 with brief stop at Vancouver in WHL. Drafted by Penguins in 1969. Will always remember 3/4/71 for stitches it brought him—three when hit back of head with puck in morning practice; four when hit by puck in forehead in pregame practice for Montreal; and 14 when hit in head by shot by Canadiens' Guy Lapointe in second period. Lives with family in Toronto.

NHL record: 40 goals, 61 assists in 308 games; 3 goals, 1 assist in 14 playoff games.

HARKNESS, NED B. (date unknown) Ottawa, Ont. Det. Red Wings' GM stirred family quarrel when he joined club as coach in 1970 after successful college career. As result of political infighting, veteran Wings executive Sid Abel quit to go to St. L. Blues. Attended school in Glens Falls, N.Y., and Worcester, Mass. Served with RCAF for four years, last two as bombardier. Played senior hockey and won RCAF middleweight boxing title. After war spent 21 1/2 years coaching hockey and lacrosse at Rensselaer Poly and Cornell U., winning national championships in both sports, with his hockey record 351–145–13. After joining Wings as coach, he faced near rebellion over disciplinary standards. Named GM 1/8/71.

HARPER, TERRANCE VICTOR (Terry) B. 1/27/40, Regina, Sask. Defenseman. 6'1", 197. Became defenseman after childhood accident badly burned his legs, reducing skating speed. Played as junior for Regina Pats, turned pro with Montreal of EPHL in 1960, then played two seasons at Hull-Ottawa, moving up to Mont. Canadiens at end of 1962–63 and stayed. Finished third in Rookie of Year voting in 1964, and also in 1964 suffered chipped vertebrae. Took troubles with Montreal fans philosophically, explaining steady rain of boos on him: "I'm not a very stylish player." Traded to L.A. Kings before 1972–73 season.

NHL record: 15 goals, 120 assists in 631 games; 4 goals, 12 assists in 84 playoff games.

HARRIS, EDWARD ALEXANDER (Ted) B. 7/18/36, Winnipeg, Man. Defenseman. 6'2", 183. Ranked one of NHL's very best at preventing other team from scoring. Started as pro in 1956–57 at Springfield, also played in 1958–59 at Victoria before spending four more years at Springfield. Played 1963–64 at Cleveland, then joined Mont. Canadiens for seven seasons. Traded to Minn. North Stars in summer of 1970. Lives on Lake Winnipeg during summer.

NHL record: 29 goals, 146 assists in 641 games; 1 goal, 18 assists in 84 playoff games.

HARRIS, RONALD THOMAS (Ron) B. 6/30/42, Verdun, Que. Defenseman. 5'10", 180. Played junior hockey with Hamilton Red Wings, turned pro in Det. Red Wings' organization with Pittsburgh of AHL in 1962. Played briefly with Wings in 1962–63, but worked most at Pittsburgh and Cincinnati of CPHL, then with Memphis, and Pittsburgh again in 1964–65. Traded to Bos. Bruins in 1965, was sent to San Francisco of WHL, then played with California of WHL in 1966–67. Made it into NHL in 1967 when drafted by Calif. Seals. Traded to Wings 5/27/68 in five-player deal. Has played left wing, but says he prefers defense where he can "line up a forward and hit him." Lives in off-season in La Salle, Que., with wife and children.

NHL record: 12 goals, 57 assists in 306 games; no goals, no assists in 4 playoff games.

HARRIS, WILLIAM EDWARD B. 7/29/35, Toronto, Ont. Forward. Coached Swedish Olympic team to fourth-place finish in 1972 after 13-year NHL career. Played for Marlboro juniors, joined Tor. Maple Leafs in 1955, spent time at Rochester and Pittsburgh before returning to Leafs in 1957, went to Det. Red Wings in 1969 in eight-player deal, was grabbed by Oakland in 1967 and finished career in 1968–69 after being traded to Pitt. Penguins in midseason. Regained amateur standing to play with Canadian National team briefly after retirement, then coached Hamilton and Red Wings' junior club in 1970–71 before taking Swedish job. Joined Ottawa National of WHA as coach in 1972–73. Partner in hockey camp. Holds B.A. from U. of Toronto; studied 13 years for it.

NHL record: 126 goals, 219 assists in 769 games; 8 goals, 10 assists in 62 playoff games.

HARRISON, JAMES DAVID (Jim) B. 7/9/47, Bonnyville, Alta. Forward. 5'11", 185. Played as junior with Estevan Bruins and in 1966 Memorial Cup playoffs for Edmonton. Turned pro in 1968–69 with Bos. Bruins, playing 16 games for Bruins and 43 with Oklahoma City. Started next season with Bruins, then was traded 12/10/69 to Tor. Maple Leafs for Wayne Carleton. Jumped to Alberta Oilers of WHA after 1971–72. Has a temper, as evidenced by 104 penalty minutes in 1971–72, 108 the previous season, and a fight in Kamloops, B.C., bar during off-season which cost him $450 fine. Nicknamed "Max" by teammates; owns sheepdog with same name.

NHL record: 43 goals, 50 assists in 214 games; 1 goal, 1 assist in 11 playoff games.

HARVEY, DOUGLAS NORMAN B. 12/19/24, Montreal, Que. Defenseman. Hall of Fame. Winner of seven Norris Trophies for top defenseman, NHL All-Star first team 10 times (seven in a row). Played for Mont. Canadiens from 1947–61 in in 19-year NHL career, which also included play with N.Y. Rangers (1961–64), Det. Red Wings (1966–67), and St. L. Blues (1968–69). Also played season of pro baseball in Ottawa in 1949. Harvey's Montreal career ended when he became active in players' association. Traded to Rangers, he became player-coach (head coach in 1961–62), leaving club in 1964 to join Quebec Aces of AHL. Played in minors with Quebec, Pittsburgh, Baltimore, and Kansas City until 1967, when Red Wings called him for two games, then went to Blues for 1968 playoffs and stayed next full season, playing 70 games and serving as asst. coach. Went to L.A. Kings as asst. coach in 1970. Asst. coach, Houston Aeros, WHA, 1973. Intensity of sports interest was evidenced on 8/12/62 in Montreal. Demonstrating football play on blackboard for friends, Harvey pushed the chalk so hard that it broke, and he fractured a knuckle.

NHL record: 88 goals, 452 assists in 1113 games; 8 goals, 64 assists in 137 playoff games.

HAY, GEORGE W. B. Jan. 1898, Listowel, Ont. Forward. Hall of Famer. Played early hockey as junior with Winnipeg Monarchs, then in 1920–21 with Regina before turning pro with Regina Caps. Spent four years in Regina, then with Portland Rosebuds, moving to NHL when team was sold to Chicago and became Black Hawks. Shoulder injury caused him to be sent to Detroit next season (1927–28), where he stayed until 1932–33 season, in which he got into only one game. Uncle of Bill Hay, who played eight seasons with Black Hawks.

NHL record: 74 goals, 60 assists in six seasons; 2 goals, 3 assists in 3 playoff series.

HAY, WILLIAM CHARLES (Red) B. 12/8/35, Saskatoon, Sask. Forward. Played eight years for Chi. Black Hawks. Son of former goalie for Regina, mother was track and field star, uncle also played for Hawks. Started as junior for Regina Pats, studied geology at Colorado College. Originally signed by Mont. Canadiens, who loaned him to Calgary Stampeders of WHL. Hawks bought contract and brought him up in

1959, and he stayed in Chicago until retirement in 1967. Won Calder Trophy as Rookie of Year in 1959–60 with 18 goals and 37 assists. Now pursues career in geology with oil firm.

NHL record: 113 goals, 273 assists in 506 games; 15 goals, 21 assists in 67 playoff games.

HAYMES, PAUL B. 3/1/10, Montreal, Que. Forward. Known as playmaker who ranked near top of league in assists in his 11 years in NHL. Played for Montreal AAA as amateur, joined Mont. Maroons in 1930, went to Bos. Bruins in mid 1934–35, then to Mont. Canadiens next season, and left league as Canadien at end of 1940–41.

NHL record: 61 goals, 134 assists in 11 seasons; 2 goals, 8 assists in 8 playoff series.

HEBENTON, ANDREW ALEX (Andy) B. 10/3/29, Winnipeg, Man. Forward. 5'9", 182. Released by Mont. Canadiens' organization as being injury-prone, went on to play 630 consecutive NHL games for N.Y. Rangers and Bos. Bruins—a record. Played for Montreal Royals seniors, turned pro with Cincinnati in 1949, spent five years at Victoria before joining Rangers in 1955. Put together nine straight 70-game years from then until 1964. Streak began 10/7/55 in Chicago Stadium and he set record when he played 581st straight game there 12/4/63. Left league in 1964–65 after being traded to Toronto in Ron Stewart deal, and has played at Victoria and Portland of WHL since. Won Lady Byng Trophy in 1957.

NHL record: 189 goals, 202 assists in 630 games; 6 goals, 5 assists in 22 playoff games.

HELLER, EHRHARDT HENRY (Ott) B. 6/2/10, Kitchener, Ont. Defenseman. Played 15 seasons with N.Y. Rangers from 1931 to 1946. Started with Kitchener as junior, turned pro with Springfield in 1929, and then moved up to Rangers. Lives in Kitchener.

NHL record: 55 goals, 176 assists in 647 games; 6 goals, 8 assists in 61 playoff games.

HENDERSON, PAUL GARNET B. 1/28/43, Kincardine, Ont. Forward. 5'11", 180. Scored 49 goals for Hamilton Red Wings in 1963 as team won Memorial Cup, turned pro in 1963–64 in Det. Red Wings' organization with Pittsburgh of AHL, finishing that season with Red Wings and spent three more seasons there. Traded to Tor. Maple Leafs 3/3/68 in deal that sent Frank Mahovlich to Detroit. Has had share of physical problems, including broken jaw in 1970–71, which forced him to wear cumbersome "bird cage" as protection, and respiratory ailment while with Detroit, which caused him to wear surgical mask while playing. Extremely fast skater, and coach has said that his speed sometimes causes him to miss scoring chances. Team Canada 1972— hero, scoring winning goal in final game with Russia. Lives in Goderich, Ont., in off-season.

NHL record: 205 goals, 204 assists in 608 games; 11 goals, 12 assists in 48 playoff games.

HENDY, JAMES CECIL VALDAMAR (Jim) B. 5/6/05, Barbados, British West Indies. D. 1/14/61, Cleveland, Ohio. Hall of Fame builder. Known for contributions as executive and historian of hockey. Grew up in Vancouver. In youth worked as rancher, sailor, telegrapher, writer. Published *The Hockey Guide* in 1933, turning over rights to NHL in 1951. Worked on publicity for N.Y. Rangers. President of U.S. Hockey League. GM of Cleveland in AHL.

HENRY, CAMILLE (Eel) B. 1/31/33, Quebec City, Que. Forward. After spending 13 full seasons in NHL was signed 5/19/72 to coach N.Y. Raiders of WHA. Started out as stick boy for Quebec seniors, joined N.Y. Rangers in 1953, winning Calder Trophy as Rookie of Year, and picked up Lady Byng Trophy in 1958. Sent to Chi. Black Hawks in 1964–65, then returned to Rangers following season. Went to St. L. Blues in 1968, and retired during 1969–70 season after appearing in just four games for Blues. Coached at Kansas City after retirement. Always battled weight problem, trying to put on pounds, with little success. Wife is Dominique Michel, Canadian television performer.

NHL record: 279 goals, 249 assists in 817 games; 6 goals, 12 assists in 48 playoff games.

HENRY, SAMUEL JAMES (Sugar Jim) B. 10/23/20, Winnipeg, Man. Goalie. Played eight seasons in NHL. Started with Brandon Wheat Kings as junior, then played with Regina Rangers, New Haven, Kansas City, Omaha, Indianapolis in minors. Made N.Y. Rangers in 1941, spent next three years in Canadian army, went to Chi. Black Hawks in 1948–49. Then shipped to Detroit in nine-man deal in 1950–51, but spent season in Indianapolis as Terry Sawchuck made his spectacular debut. Traded to Bos. Bruins in 1951–52, and retired after 1954–55 season. All-Star game 1952.

NHL record: allowed 1165 goals in 405 games for 2.88 average, 29 shutouts; gave up 81 goals in 29 playoff games for 2.79 average, 2 shutouts.

HERN, WILLIAM MILTON (Riley) B. 12/5/80, St. Marys, Ont. D.

6/24/29, Montreal, Que. Hall of Famer. Played goalie with teams in Ontario before going to Houghton, Mich., with Portage Lake team in 1904. Signed with Montreal Wanderers in 1906. Starred with Wanderers until 1911, team winning Stanley Cup in 1906, 08, 10. Retired from hockey 1911. Business career, but continued as referee and goal judge.

HEWITSON, ROBERT W. (Bobby) B. 1/23/92, Toronto, Ont. D. 1/9/69. First curator of Hockey Hall of Fame, of which he is member (referee division), and Canada's Sports Hall of Fame. Played football and lacrosse, then turned to sports writing, retiring as sports editor of *Toronto Telegram* in 1957. Refereed 10 years in NHL, also served as secretary of Canadian Rugby Union.

HEWITT, FOSTER WILLIAM B. 11/21/02, Toronto, Ont. Hall of Fame builder. Made name as broadcaster throughout Canada and parts of U.S., starting with pioneer broadcast from Toronto in March 1923. Son of W.A. Hewitt, he was boxing champion at U. of Toronto, and has broadcast all major sports. Owns radio station in Toronto.

HEWITT, WILLIAM ARCHIBALD B. 5/15/75, Cobourg, Ont. D. 9/8/61. Hall of Fame builder. Spent 41 years as newspaperman, 31 as sports editor of *Toronto Star*. Credited with devising first set of goal nets when he strung fishing net between goalposts to end arguments about whether puck had gone between them. Was secretary of Ontario Hockey Assn. from 1903 to 1961, and registrar and treasurer of CAHA for 39 years. Managed three Canadian Olympic hockey champions.

HEXTALL, BRYAN ALDWYN B. 7/31/13, Grenfell, Sask. Forward. Hall of Famer. Played as amateur in Manitoba before turning pro with Vancouver Lions in 1934. After playing at Philadelphia, made NHL with N.Y. Rangers in 1936 and played there through 1947–48. Led NHL in points in 1941–42. Picked for first All-Stars three times and second team twice. Scored 20 or more goals in seven NHL seasons.

   NHL record: 187 goals, 175 assists in 447 games; 8 goals, 9 assists in 37 playoff games.

HEXTALL, BRYAN LEE B. 5/23/41, Winnipeg, Man. Forward. 5'11", 170. Son of Hall of Famer Bryan A. Hextall. Has brother, Dennis, also in NHL. Played with Kitchener-Waterloo, moved up to N.Y. Rangers in 1962, then returned to minors at Baltimore and Vancouver. Drafted by Oakland, sold to Tor. Maple Leafs, who sent him to Rochester and Vancouver again. Purchased by Pitt. Penguins and made NHL to stay in 1969–70. Rough player, with 259 penalty minutes over last two seasons.

Lives in Brandon, Man.

NHL record: 69 goals, 110 assists in 319 games; no goals, 3 assists in 14 playoff games.

HEXTALL, DENNIS HAROLD B. 4/17/43, Poplar Point, Man. Forward. 6′, 175. Son of Hall of Famer Bryan Hextall and brother of Pitt. Penguins' Bryan. Played college hockey at U. of North Dakota, studied biology and natural science. Turned pro in 1967–68 at Omaha, and also played at Buffalo and Springfield. Played in NHL with N.Y. Rangers, L.A. Kings, and Calif. Seals before going to Minn. North Stars after 1970–71 season. Amassed 217 penalty minutes with Seals in 1970–71. Has continued science studies in off-season, and also has instructed at hockey schools. Lives in Poplar Point.

NHL record: 63 goals, 104 assists in 230 games; 2 goals, 2 assists in 15 playoff games.

HICKE, ERNEST ALLEN (Ernie) B. 11/7/47, Regina, Sask. Forward. 5′11″, 180. Brother of Billy was acquired by Calif. Seals from Mont. Canadiens in exchange for player and Seals' first draft choice in May 1970 and scored 20 goals in rookie year. Had played amateur hockey for Pats in hometown, then turned pro in 1967–68 with Houston, spending two years there and one in Salt Lake City before moving up to Seals. Went to Atlanta Flames in expansion draft in 1972. Traded to N.Y. Islanders mid-1972–73.

NHL record: 47 goals, 60 assists in 205 games.

HICKE, WILLIAM LAWRENCE (Bill) B. 3/31/38, Regina, Sask. Forward. 5′8″, 170. Pitt. Penguins' right wing played only 12 NHL games in 1971–72 before being sent to minors after long career in NHL. Product of Mont. Canadiens' organization and originally intended as replacement for Maurice Richard when called up to big club in 1960 from Rochester, where he led AHL in scoring, won MVP and Rookie of Year. Went to N.Y. Rangers in 1964–65 and was drafted by Calif. Seals in 1967. Acquired by Penguins in summer of 1971. Overcame serious lung ailment in 1967–68, still getting 21 goals in 52 games. Jumped to Alberta Oilers after 1971–72. Brother of Ernie Hicke. Lives in Regina.

NHL record: 168 goals, 234 assists in 729 games; 3 goals, 10 assists in 42 playoff games.

HILLMAN, LARRY MORLEY B. 2/5/37, Kirkland Lake, Ont. Defenseman. 6′, 185. NHL veteran who played with Det. Red Wings, Bos. Bruins, Tor. Maple Leafs, Minn. North Stars, Mont. Canadiens, Phila. Flyers and L.A. Kings before going to Buffalo Sabres 12/16/71 in four-player deal. Turned pro with Red Wings, playing in first NHL game at 17 in 1954. Played minor league hockey in Buffalo, Edmonton, Providence, Rochester, and Springfield. Won Shore Award as top AHL defenseman in 1960, and picked up 159 penalty minutes that season. Played on four Stanley Cup teams. Brother of defenseman Wayne Hillman.

NHL record: 36 goals, 196 assists in 790 games; 2 goals, 9 assists in 74 playoff games.

HILLMAN, WAYNE JAMES B. 11/13/38, Kirkland Lake, Ont. Defenseman. 6'1", 175. Played as junior with St. Catharines, turned pro with Buffalo of AHL in 1956–57. Moved up to Chi. Black Hawks in 1960–61, and went to N.Y. Rangers in 1964–65, Minn. North Stars in 1968–69, and to Phila. Flyers next season for John Miszuk, where he played two seasons alongside brother Larry before latter left club. Conducts NHL Players Assn. Hockey School in Wilmington, Del., in association with Lew Morrison, Bernie Parent, and Barry Ashbee.

NHL record: 18 goals, 86 assists in 691 games; no goals, 3 assists in 28 playoff games.

HITCHMAN, LIONEL B. 1903, Toronto, Ont. Defenseman. NHL career stretched from 1922–23 to 1933–34, with Ottawa Senators and Bos. Bruins. Played as amateur in Ottawa before joining Senators. Went to Bruins mid-1924–25. Teamed with Eddie Shore on defense. Stayed with Boston till retirement. Lives in Ottawa.

NHL record: 28 goals, 33 assists in 12 seasons; 4 goals, 1 assist in 8 playoff series.

HODGE, CHARLES EDWARD B. 7/28/33, Lachine, Que. Goalie. Retired from Vancouver in 1971 after NHL career spanning 13 seasons. Played as midget and juvenile in Mont. Canadiens' organization and for Junior Canadiens before joining big club in 1954. Saw limited service and spent time with Quebec Aces before getting into 30 games with Canadiens in 1960–61. Stayed with team until going to Oakland Seals in 1967. During stay at Montreal won Vezina Trophy in 1964 and shared it with Gump Worsley in 1966. Went to Vancouver in 1970, and retired after one season there. Was North American canoeing champion in 1958, and has street (Hodge Ave.) named after him in Ste. Dorothee, Que., where he lived at one time before going to Vancouver.

NHL record: allowed 927 goals in 343 games for 2.70 average, 24 shutouts; 32 goals in 16 playoff games for 2.00 average, 2 shutouts.

HODGE, KENNETH RAYMOND (Ken) B. 6/25/44, Birmingham, England. Forward. 6'2", 216. Was one of players involved in trade that sent Phil Esposito and Fred Stanfield to Bos. Bruins from Chi. Black Hawks in 1967. Moved to Canada and played hockey in Hawks' organization, moving to big club after being picked hockey's top junior at St. Catharines in 1964–65. Played 1965–66 and 1966–67 seasons with Hawks. Coach Billy Reay considered him "slow starter" and used electric bull horn to "push him" in practice. Became All-Star after going to Bruins, making *Hockey News* lst team in 1972 despite suffering broken ankle during season, which kept him out of 18 games. Lives in Lynnfield, Mass., where he has swimming pool in backyard in shape of No. 8, his Bruins' number.

NHL record: 207 goals, 293 assists in 565 games; 23 goals, 30 assists in 66 playoff games.

HOLLETT, WILLIAM (Flash) B. 4/13/12, North Sydney, N.S. Defenseman-forward. Played with four teams in NHL career that spanned 13 years. Son of fisherman who died of influenza in 1916. Moved to Toronto that year. Played with Acadian Juveniles and West Toronto juniors. Survived pneumonia. Played for Toronto Marlboro seniors, then turned pro with Syracuse of AHL. Also played for Buffalo at time when club had just seven players. Joined Tor. Maple Leafs in 1933, and also played for Ottawa during that season, returning to Leafs in 1934. Went to Bos. Bruins in mid-1935–36; stayed until sent to Det. Red Wings in mid-1943–44. Retired in 1946. Former professional lacrosse player. Lives in Port Credit, Ont.

NHL record: 132 goals, 181 assists in 13 seasons; 8 goals, 26 assists in 82 playoff games.

HOLMES, HAROLD (Hap) B. 4/15/89, Ontario. D. 6/27/41, Florida. Goalie. Hall of Famer. Played his amateur hockey in Ontario, turned pro in 1913 with Toronto of NHA on team which included Scotty Davidson, Harry Cameron, Frank Foyston, Jack Walker, and Frank Nighbor, all in Hall of Fame. Jumped to Seattle in Pacific Coast League in 1915, returned to Toronto Arenas of NHL in 1918, went back to Seattle for seven seasons, then one at Victoria. Returned to NHL with Detroit (1926–28) after coast league folded. Sixteen-year career included play on four Stanley Cup winners. Led NHA goalies in 1914 and coast league goalies seven times. After retirement moved to Florida, where had papaya farm. Campaigned to take hockey teams on Australian tour, and made trip to Australia to promote idea. Holmes Memorial Trophy, awarded to leading goalie in American League, is named for him.

NHL record: allowed 269 goals in 106 games for 2.54 average, 17 shutouts; gave up 28 goals in 7 playoff games for 4.00 average, no shutouts.

HOOPER, CHARLES THOMAS (Tom) B. 11/24/83, Rat Portage (now Kenora), Ont. Hall of Famer. Played organized hockey only eight years, helped lead Kenora Thistles to Stanley Cup victory over Montreal Wanderers, 1/07. Played first organized hockey in high school, 1900. Then joined Thistles for series of Cup challenges. Switched to Wanderers, and retired 1908.

HORNER, GEORGE REGINALD (Red) B. 5/28/09, Lynden, Ont. Defenseman. Hall of Fame. One of roughest and most penalized players in NHL history. Joined Tor. Maple Leafs from juniors in 1928 and never played anywhere else until retiring 12 years later in 1940. Weighed 200 lbs., and led league in penalties eight straight years, 1933 through 1940, with 167 minutes in 43 games in 1935–36, a record which stood for 20 years. Retired from business, he has home in Portugal, summer home in Toronto, and farm near Owen Sound, Ont.

NHL record: 42 goals, 110 assists in 12 seasons; 7 goals, 10 assists in 11 playoff series.

HORTON, MILES GILBERT (Tim) B. 1/12/30, Cochrane, Ont. Defenseman. 5'10", 180. Played 17 seasons with Tor. Maple Leafs before going to N.Y. Rangers 3/30/70. Pitt. Penguins drafted him at age 42 from Rangers in 1971 and Buffalo Sabres drafted him in 1972. Started pro career with Pittsburgh of Tor. Maple Leafs' organization in 1949. Played only minor league hockey there before making Leafs in 1952. "Retired" in 1969 in successful effort to get salary increase, which paid off when he was raised from $42,500 to $85,000. Now is estimated to be $100,000-a-year man. Lives in Toronto. Owns chain of 30 doughnut shops in Ontario.

NHL record: 115 goals, 397 assists in 1391 games; 11 goals, 39 assists in 126 playoff games.

HORVATH, BRONCO JOSEPH B. 3/12/30, Port Colborne, Ont. Forward. Had hockey career which included coaching, long minor league experience, and nine seasons in NHL. Tied for league lead in goals scored one year. Played as junior with Galt Black Hawks. Came to N.Y. Rangers in 1955. Sent to Mont. Canadiens next season, then to Bos. Bruins in 1957. Stayed four seasons, tied Bobby Hull with 39 goals 1959–1960. Hull got one more assist to win scoring crown by point. Went to Chi. Black Hawks in 1961, then split 1962–63 between Rangers and Tor. Maple Leafs. Dropped into minors afterwards, ending career by playing eight years for Rochester Americans, although was recalled briefly for 14 games by Minn. North Stars in 1967–68. Once had tryout with Dodgers in baseball.

NHL record: 141 goals, 185 assists in 434 games; 12 goals, 9 assists in 36 playoff games.

HOULE, REJEAN B. 10/25/49, Rouyn, Que. Forward, 5'11", 165. Mont. Canadiens' right wing has been known as a "shadow" of opposing stars, notably Bobby Hull in 1972 playoffs. Hull was angered enough to complain that the strategy was "not hockey." Played with Junior Canadiens, turned pro in 1969 with Montreal's AHL club, and made Canadiens in 1970.

NHL record: 34 goals, 62 assists in 224 league games; 5 goals, 11 assists in 43 playoff games.

HOWE, GORDON (Gordie) B. 3/31/28, Floral, Sask. Forward. Hall of Famer. Announced retirement 9/9/71 after longest career in history of NHL—25 seasons. Considered by many greatest player in history of game. A big youngster who was to turn into one of bigger men (6', 210) to play in NHL, he excelled at junior hockey and spent only one season (1945–46) with Omaha of now disbanded United States Hockey League before joining Det. Red Wings, with whom he played entire major league career. Although often troubled by injuries and in later years by arthritic wrist, Howe set and holds these major league records: most games, 1687; most goals, 786; most assists, 1023; most points, 1809; most points which won games, 122. Selected for All-Star team 21 times, including 12 on first team. Played in 22 All-Star games, getting 18 points on 10 goals and 8 assists. Named Canada's outstanding male athlete in 1963 and 6/25/71 selected among 25 persons to receive medal of service of Order of Canada. On 7/17/67, named to Madison Square Garden Hockey Hall of Fame. Once turned down by N.Y. Rangers. Lives in Detroit area. Vice president of Red Wings. Also has business interests in Detroit. Signed in summer 1973 to play with Houston of WHA, joining two sons on roster.

NHL record: 786 goals, 1023 assists in 1687 games; 67 goals, 91 assists in 154 playoff games.

HOWE, SYDNEY HARRIS (Syd) B. 9/28/11, Ottawa, Ont. Forward. Hall of Famer. Shares with Red Berenson record for most goals in single game, six against N.Y. Rangers in Detroit 2/3/44. Started skating at age three on double runners, played junior and senior hockey in Ottawa, turned pro in the NHL with Ottawa Senators in 1929–30. Played with Philadelphia Quakers, on loan basis in 1930–31, returned to Ottawa in 1932. Team transferred to St. Louis in 1934–35, and was sold to Det. Red

Wings during that season, staying in Detroit until retiring from NHL in 1945–46.

NHL record: 237 goals, 291 assists in 16 seasons; 17 goals, 27 assists in 9 playoff series.

HOWELL, HENRY VERNON (Harry) B. 12/28/32, Hamilton, Ont. Defenseman. NHL veteran who has played 21 seasons. Joined N.Y. Rangers after only one minor league game (Cincinnati 1951–52) and spent 17 seasons there. Back injury forced him to undergo spinal fusion in summer of 1969, and was sold to Calif. Seals. Sold to L.A. Kings in Feb. 1971. Brother of Ron Howell, former Canadian pro football star, Harry was honored at "night" in Madison Square Garden in 1966–67 by normally blasé N.Y. hockey fans. Won Norris Trophy as NHL's top defenseman in same season. Served as color man on nationally televised Stanley Cup playoff of 1971–72.

NHL record: 94 goals, 324 assists in 1411 games; 3 goals, 3 assists in 38 playoff games.

HUGHES, BRENTON ALEXANDER (Brent) B. 6/17/43, Bowman-ville, Ont. Defenseman. Turned pro in 1964 with Minneapolis after playing in Eastern League with New Haven Blades. Played minor league hockey with Memphis, Pittsburgh and Springfield. Then three years with L.A. Kings before going to Phila. Flyers in May 1970 for Mike Byers. Philadelphia sent him to Quebec next season, but recalled him after 25 games. Traded to St. Louis mid-1972–73.

NHL record: 13 goals, 78 assists in 298 games; 1 goal, 3 assists in 22 playoff games.

HULL, DENNIS WILLIAM B. 11/19/44, Point Anne, Ont. Forward. 5'11", 194. Played junior hockey at St. Catharines, joined Chi. Black Hawks in 1964, sent to St. Louis of CPHL for seasoning next year, then recalled to stay at end of season. Overcame handicap of being Bobby's "kid brother," still is partner with him in three ranches in Canada, has home in Elmhurst, Chicago suburb. Joined Bobby in flap over curved blades in 1972 playoffs in which brothers threatened to lead strike if they were denied use of curved blades. Team Canada 1972.

NHL record: 210 goals, 226 assists in 606 games; 26 goals, 29 assists in 96 playoff games.

HULL, ROBERT MARVIN (Bobby; Golden Jet) B. 1/3/39, Point Anne, Ont. Forward. 5'10", 193. One of hockey's big stars. Storm center in recent years. Has more than 600 goals in league play, more than any other man in history of league except Gordie Howe. One of strongest men ever to play game. Also has strong opinions, battling league over use of curved blade, which he loves, and club over salary, which he has always considered too low. Came up to Chi. Black Hawks in 1957 after junior play at St. Catharines, Ont. (where, he said, he "wasn't very good"), for Rudy Pilous, later to coach Hawks and Hull to Stanley Cup. Led NHL in scoring in 1960, 1962 and 1966. Led in goals scored six times, going over 50 mark on five occasions. Won Hart MVP Trophy in 1965 and Lady Byng in 1965. Fought Hawks' management before start of 1968–69 season, holding out for $100,000. Settled for about $60,000 after sitting out 11 games, and was forced into public apology, which always irritated him. Had battle in 1971 with NHL over curtailment of curved sticks, threatening to lead players in strike, which never came off, and saying restriction would drive players into other leagues. Stunned NHL when he jumped June 1972 to new World Hockey Assn. Winnipeg club in a $2,750,000 deal ($1,000,000 initially). Has cattle ranches in Saskatchewan. WHA's MVP 1972–73.

NHL record: 604 goals, 549 assists in 1036 games; 62 goals, 66 assists in 116 playoff games.

HUME, FRED JOHN B. 5/2/92, New Westminster, B. C. D. 2/17/67. Hall of Fame builder. Entered politics at 29, starting as alderman in New Westminster and eventually serving as mayor, and later as mayor of Vancouver. Helped form Western Hockey League, and was owner of Vancouver Hockey Club. Was also active in lacrosse and soccer, and helped put professional baseball into Vancouver in 1955.

HUTTON, JOHN BOWER (Bouse) B. ca. 1880. Goalie. Hall of Famer. Played on championship teams around turn of century. Was member of Ottawa amateur champions in 1898–99, then played six seasons with Silver Sevens, allowing 28 goals in 12 Stanley Cup games. Retired as player in 1904, continuing to coach for several years in Ottawa area.

HYLAND, HARRY B. 1/2/89, Montreal, Que. Forward. D. 8/8/69, Montreal, Que. Hall of Famer. Played early hockey in Montreal and turned pro with Shamrocks in 1908. Played with Wanderers, then joined New Westminster in PCL in 1911, returned to Montreal, and split last year of career in 1917–18 between Montreal and Ottawa. Scored eight goals 1/27/13 for Wanderers in game with Quebec. In his one NHL season in 1917–18 he scored 14 goals in 16 games.

IMLACH, GEORGE (Punch) B. 3/15/18, Toronto, Ont. Buffalo Sabres' coach and GM. Coached 10 years with Tor. Maple Leafs (1958–1969), also serving as GM to bring tenure with team to 11 years, won four Stanley Cups, and holds to prediction Sabres will be first expansion club to win Cup. Before getting Toronto job, spent time with Quebec Aces, eventually becoming part owner. Took over as manager-coach of Springfield Indians in 1957. Went to Buffalo in 1970 when club joined NHL. Suffered severe heart attack in Jan. 1972 and had to give up coaching reins for three months while recovering.

ION, FRED J. (Mickey) B. 2/25/86, Paris, Ont. D. 10/26/44, Seattle, Wash. Made Hall of Fame for work as referee in career which started in 1913 and lasted until 1943. Played baseball and lacrosse, became hockey referee in New Westminster, B.C., in amateur games, and worked first pro game there in 1913. Joined NHL staff when PCL folded in 1926, and finished career by working the Howie Morenz Memorial Game in Montreal Forum in 1943. Hailed by King Clancy, later to be great referee himself, for controlled manner of handling games.

IRVIN, JAMES DICKENSON (Dick) B. 7/19/92, Limestone Ridge, Ont. D. 5/16/57, Montreal, Que. Forward. Hall of Famer who excelled as player and coach. Played amateur hockey in Winnipeg, turning pro in 1915 with Portland Rosebuds. After service in army during World War I, returned to Regina Caps in 1921, then went back to Portland. Played for Chi. Black Hawks in NHL from 1926 to 1929, collecting a fractured skull. Coached Hawks. Then coached Tor. Maple Leafs to Stanley Cup in 1931–32; coached Mont. Canadiens from 1940 to 1955, winning three more Cups.

NHL record: 29 goals, 23 assists in 3 seasons; 2 goals, no assists in 1 playoff series.

IRVINE, EDWARD AMOS (Ted) B. 12/8/44, Winnipeg, Man. Forward. 6'2", 195. N.Y. Rangers' left wing blamed warm weather in Los Angeles for inability to concentrate on hockey when he played for Kings. Traded to Rangers in Feb 1970 for Juha Widing and Real Lemieux, and performance improved. Played as junior with St. Boniface, turned pro in Minneapolis of CHL in 1964. Played two seasons there and two more at Oklahoma City, joined NHL with Kings in 1967, although originally a product of Bos. Bruins' organization. Borrowed one of Bobby Hull's sticks in 1966–67 season, and adopted curved blade.

NHL record: 87 goals, 213 assists in 432 games; 13 goals, 16 assists in 61 playoff games.

IVAN, THOMAS N. (Tommy) B. 1/31/11, Toronto, Ont. Chi. Black Hawks' GM, was outstanding amateur in CAHA before injury ended career. Started as scout with Det. Red Wings, and in 1945–46 coached Omaha of USHL. Coached Indianapolis of AHL next season, then joined Det. Red Wings as coach in 1947, leading team to six straight league titles and three Stanley Cups in seven years. Joined Hawks as GM in 1954, serving as coach for 1 1/2 years when Dick Irvin became fatally ill. Under Ivan, Hawks won first cup in 23 years in 1961, first NHL title in 1967, another in 1970, and West crown in '71. Lives in Chicago suburb.

JACKSON, ARTHUR B. 12/15/15, Toronto, Ont. Forward. Brother of Hall of Famer, Harvey. Played in NHL as center from 1934 to 1945. Played for St. Michael's College, turned pro with Syracuse, started with Tor. Maple Leafs in 1934–35, went to Bos. Bruins in 1937 and N.Y. Americans next season, returning to Bruins in 1939 to play until 12/23/44, when he was sent back to Toronto to finish out career at end of season.

NHL record: 123 goals, 178 assists in 11 seasons; 8 goals, 12 assists in 9 playoff series.

JACKSON, HARVEY (Busher) B. 1/19/11, Toronto, Ont. D. 6/25/66, Toronto, Ont. Forward. Hall of Famer. Starred for Tor. Maple Leafs, N.Y. Americans and Bos. Bruins in 15 seasons from 1929 to 1944. Joined Bruins after extended holdout forced his sale for $7500. Led league in scoring in 1933 and was first All-Star four times, and second team once.

NHL record: 241 goals, 234 assists in 15 seasons; 18 goals, 12 assists in 12 playoff series.

JARRETT, DOUGLAS WILLIAM (Doug) B. 4/22/44, London, Ont. Defenseman. 6'1", 205. Played junior hockey at St. Catharines and moved up to St. Louis of CPHL before joining Chi. Black Hawks in 1964. Suffered severely dislocated shoulder in fall of 1970 in collision with teammate Jim Pappin.

NHL record: 28 goals, 146 assists in 575 games; 7 goals, 15 assists in 82 playoff games.

JARRETT, GARY WALTER B. 9/3/42, Toronto, Ont. Forward. 5'8", 170. Was Calif. Seals' wing, right and left, before jumping to Cleveland Crusaders of WHA after 1971–72. Considered one of the fastest skaters. Played amateur hockey with Marlboros before turning pro in 1960–61 at Sudbury in Tor. Maple Leaf organization. With Rochester, Denver, Tulsa, and Pittsburgh in minors before making it as regular with Det. Red Wings, to whom he was traded in 1965. Went to Seals in May 1968 as part of six-player deal. Lives in Scarborough, Ont., in off-season with wife and children.

NHL record: 72 goals, 92 assists in 341 league games; 3 goals, 1 assist in 11 playoff games.

JOHNSON, DANIEL DOUGLAS (Danny) B. 10/1/44, Winnipegosis, Man. Forward. 5'11", 170. Det. Red Wing left wing joined team from Van. Canucks in mid-1971–72, then jumped to Winnipeg Jets of WHA after season. Turned pro in 1965 with Tulsa in CPHL in Tor. Maple Leaf organization. Played one game for Toronto in 1969–70, and was drafted by Canucks, then divided 1970–71 between Rochester and Vancouver, scoring 15 goals for Canucks in rookie season while playing on line with Orland Kurtenbach and Bob Schmautz.

NHL record: 18 goals, 19 assists in 121 games.

JOHNSON, ERNEST (Moose) B. 1886, Montreal, Que. D. 3/25/63, White Rock, B.C. Played way into Hall of Fame with 99-inch reach, achieved with longest stick ever used. "The year I quit they buried my stick," he said. "In those days there were no size regulations and they couldn't take it away from me." Started as junior and as intermediate once played three games in two days. Turned pro with Montreal Wanderers and played with Stanley Cup winners in 1906, 07, 08, 10. In 1912 joined New Westminster in PCL and played with such teams as Victoria, Los Angeles, and Portland before retiring in 1931.

JOHNSON, IVAN WILFRED (Ching) B. 12/7/97, Winnipeg, Man. Defenseman. Hall of Famer. Was noted not only for rough play, but for injuries, including broken leg, broken collarbone, broken jaw. In 1935 he even burned himself with sun lamp while treating his other afflictions, causing an infection. All this in addition to shrapnel wounds he picked up while serving overseas in World War I. Played with Winnipeg Monarchs after returning from war in 1919, then with Eveleth (Minn.) Miners and three years with Minneapolis before joining N.Y. Rangers in 1926, where he stayed until 1937–38, when he ended NHL career with one season with N.Y. Americans. Left NHL at 41, but continued to play until 46 in Minneapolis, Marquette, Mich., Washington, D.C. Finished career as player-coach of Hollywood Wolves, winning Helms Award.

NHL record: 38 goals, 48 assists in 12 seasons; 5 goals, 2 assists in 60 playoff games.

JOHNSON, NORMAN JAMES (Jimmy) B. 11/7/42, Winnipeg, Man. Forward. 5'9", 190. Played junior hockey with Winnipeg Rangers. Turned pro in 1962 with Sudbury, then played four years in Minnesota and Omaha of CPHL while getting brief tryouts with N.Y. Rangers. Sent to Phila. Flyers in 1967–68, who sent him to Quebec, then recalled him next year. Traded to L.A. Kings 1/28/72. Worked during summer of 1971 as member of staff of Andre Lacroix hockey school in New Jersey. Minnesota, WHA, 1972–73.

NHL record: 75 goals, 111 assists in 302 games; no goals, 2 assists in 7 playoff games.

JOHNSON, THOMAS CHRISTIAN (Tom) B. 2/18/28, Baldur, Man. Defenseman. Hall of Famer. Coached Bos. Bruins until fired 2/5/73. Played junior hockey in Winnipeg, senior hockey with Montreal Royals, then was sent to Buffalo in 1947. Joined Mont. Canadiens for game 1947–48, then made team in 1950, playing 13 seasons before joining Bos. Bruins for last two seasons. Injury to nerve in leg ended career in 1965. Played on six Stanley Cup winners.

NHL record: 51 goals, 213 assists in 978 games; 8 goals, 15 assists in 111 playoff games.

JOHNSTON, EDWARD JOSEPH (Eddie) B. 11/24/35, Montreal, Que. Goalie. 6', 190. Bos. Bruins veteran is sensitive about age, claiming that years ago most goalies were in their 30s before they made it into NHL. Played with Junior Canadiens, turned pro in 1956 with Winnipeg, then played at Shawinigan and Edmonton before getting amateur standing back in 1959 to play season with Johnstown Jets of Eastern League. Returned to pros with Hull-Ottawa in 1960–61, leading EPHL goalkeepers and setting record for regular-season shutouts, with 11. Played next season at Spokane, then made Bruins to stay in 1962–63. Outstanding golfer, and teamed with Bruin Derek Sanderson to win team title in players' tourney in 1971. Lives with family in Reading, Mass., and owns night club.

NHL record: allowed 1384 goals in 444 games for 3.13 average, 27 shutouts; gave up 37 goals in 13 playoff games for 2.85 average. 1 shutout.

JOHNSTON, JOSEPH JOHN (Joey) B. 3/3/49, Peterborough, Ont. Forward. 5'9", 175. Calif. Seal center made NHL as regular in 1971–72 after four-year minor league service. Went to Seals in trade with Minn. North Stars, after stint with Cleveland of AHL in 1970–71. Turned pro in 1967 with Omaha after playing junior hockey with Peterboro Petes.

NHL record: 44 goals, 38 assists in 160 games.

JOHNSTON, LARRY MARSHALL B. 6/6/41, Birch Hills, Sask. Defenseman. 5'11", 175. Became regular for first time in NHL in 1971–72 with Calif. Seals, playing 74 games and getting two goals and 11 assists, after being purchased from Mont. Canadiens' organization. Won Eddie Shore Trophy in 1970–71 with Cleveland as outstanding defenseman of AHL. Turned pro in 1967–68 after playing with Canadian National team, joining Minn. North Stars and playing 49 games with them over four seasons as well as 50 games with Iowa team of CHL.

NHL record: 12 goals, 36 assists in 201 games; no goals, no assists in 6 playoff games.

JOLIAT, AUREL B. 8/29/01, Ottawa, Ont. Forward. Hall of Famer became hockey player after broken leg ended football playing with Ottawa Rough Riders. Started in Ottawa and Iroquois Falls. Took harvest excursion west, played with Saskatoon Sheiks, and ended up with Mont. Canadiens in 1922, staying with club until retirement in 1938. Canadiens traded Hall of Famer Newsy Lalonde to get Joliat, who seldom weighed more than 135 lbs. Won Hart Trophy in 1934. Joined Canadian National Railway after quitting hockey. Now retired, lives in Ottawa.

NHL record: 270 goals, 190 assists in 16 seasons; 13 goals, 17 assists in 14 playoff seasons.

JOYAL, EDWARD ABEL (Eddie) B. 5/8/40, Edmonton, Alta. Forward. 6', 180. Played as junior with Edmonton Oil Kings. Turned pro in 1960 with Edmonton of WHL. Played minor league hockey with Pittsburgh, Rochester, and Tulsa as well in NHL with Det. Red Wings and Tor. Maple Leafs before going to L.A. Kings in 1967. Went to Phila. Flyers 1/28/72 in eight-man deal. Jumped to Minn. Fighting Saints after 1971–72. Started 20-minute brawl in Jan. 1971, when he skated into Tor. Maple Leaf goalie Jacques Plante, knocking him down. Owns part interest in grocery chain in St. Albert, Alta.

NHL record: 128 goals, 134 assists in 466 games; 11 goals, 8 assists in 11 playoff games.

KANNEGIESSER, SHELDON BRUCE   B. 8/15/47, North Bay, Ont. Defenseman. 6′, 185. Started in N.Y. Rangers' system in 1967 at Omaha, also played in minors at Buffalo, Kansas City, and Amarillo. Called up by Pitt. Penguins in 1971. Traded to N.Y. Rangers mid-1972–73. Lives in North Bay.

NHL record: 2 goals, 7 assists in 78 games.

KARLANDER, ALLAN DAVID (Al)   B. 11/5/46, Lac la Hache, B.C. Forward. 5′8″, 170. Det. Red Wing center is college product, playing at Michigan Tech, where in one season he scored 31 in 32 games. Was grabbed by Wings in 1967 amateur draft, turned pro with Fort Worth in CHL in 1969–70, and played 41 games with Wings in that season, being voted team's Rookie of Year by broadcasters. Returned to Texas for further seasoning in 1970–71 after starting season with Detroit; made club for full season in 1971–72. Bachelor, lives in Lac la Hache in off-season.

NHL record: 36 goals, 56 assists in 212 games; no goals, 1 assist in 4 playoff games.

KEARNS, DENNIS McALEER   B. 9/27/45, Kingston, Ont. Defenseman. 5′10″, 180. Made it as regular in NHL with Van. Canucks in 1971–72. Drafted in 1971 from the Chi. Black Hawks by Vancouver Coach Hal Laycoe, who had coached the blocky Kearns at Portland in WHL. Turned pro with Portland in 1967 and spent three seasons there, then went to Halifax and Dallas before breaking in as NHL regular. Was Canucks' No. 1 selection in draft.

NHL record: 7 goals, 59 assists in 145 games.

KEATS, GORDON BLANCHARD (Duke) B. 3/1/95, Montreal, Que. Forward. Hall of Famer. Played hockey in many places, but only three years in NHL. Was paid $75 a month to play in Cobalt area of Ontario at age 14, and was with Toronto of NHA at 17. Returned to amateurs, then went overseas with army in World War I, returned to amateurs in Edmonton. Turned pro in 1919 in Western Canada League. Joined Bos. Bruins on sale of league in 1926. Also played for Detroit Cougars that season. With Detroit and Chi. Black Hawks in 1927–28. Started in 1929 with Hawks, then had quarrel with Major Frederic McLaughlin, owner of Hawks, who sent him to American Assn. where he played with Tulsa. Lives in Edmonton, Alta.

NHL record: 30 goals, 19 assists in 3 seasons.

KEELING, MELVILLE SIDNEY (Butch) B. 8/10/05, Owen Sound, Ont. Forward. Played 12 years in NHL, 10 of them with N.Y. Rangers. Started with London senior team, signed with London Panthers in 1926, and went to Tor. Maple Leafs in 1927. Sent to Rangers in spring of 1928, and remained with team until retiring from NHL in 1938.

NHL record: 157 goals, 63 assists in 12 seasons; 11 goals, 11 assists in 47 playoff games.

KELLY, LEONARD PATRICK (Red) B. 7/9/27, Simcoe, Ont. Defenseman-forward. Hall of Famer. Reversed usual order, starting as defenseman and finishing playing career as center. Joined Det. Red Wings in 1947 at 19 to begin 20-year career in which his team made playoffs 19 times. Spent 12 1/2 years with Red Wings, then joined Tor. Maple Leafs in mid-1959–60, and became forward. Maple Leaf trade was consummated after Kelly refused to report to Rangers in previously arranged deal. Ended playing career in 1967 in Toronto and joined L.A. Kings as coach in next season in move punctuated by lawsuits, charges and countercharges, and near fistfight between L.A. owner Jack Kent Cooke and Toronto sports writer over deal. Got Kings into playoffs twice, then was fired 6/3/69 and became coach of Pitt. Penguins. Named Coach of Year for bringing Penguins home second in 1970. Fired by Penguins Jan. 1973. Won Lady Byng Trophy four times, James Norris Memorial Trophy for defensemen once. First All-Star six times, second team once. On eight Stanley Cup winners. Served in parliament from 1962 to 1965; married to former figure skating champion Andra McLaughlin.

NHL record: 281 goals, 542 assists in 1316 games; 33 goals, 59 assists in 164 playoff games.

KELLY, ROBERT JAMES (Bob)   B. 11/25/50, Oakville, Ont. Forward. 5'10", 190. Phila. Flyer left wing moved directly into NHL from junior hockey in 1970, and played every game of Flyers' schedule in 1971–72. Started with Oshawa Generals of OHA, picked 32nd in 1970 amateur draft. One of roughest players in league, piled up 227 penalty minutes in first 154 games. Former Flyer coach Vic Stasiuk called him "Reggie Fleming with polish."
NHL record: 38 goals, 44 assists in 231 games.

KENNEDY, FORBES TAYLOR   B. 8/18/35, Dorchester, N.B. Forward. Battled way up through long minor league career to play 11 years in NHL for five clubs. Played as amateur with Junior Canadiens, made Chi. Black Hawks in 1956, went to Det. Red Wings next season, then to Bos. Bruins in 1962. Taken by Phila. Flyers in 1967, and sent to Tor. Maple Leafs in mid-1968–69. Fined $1000 and suspended four games for April 1969 brawl. Learned in May of 1969 while listening to radio that he had been traded to Pitt. Penguins, and called it quits. Minor league teams included Montreal Royals, Shawinigan Falls, Edmonton, Hershey, Spokane, San Francisco, and California of WHL. After retirement accepted job as coach of Halifax Atlantics in Maritime Junior A league.
NHL record: 70 goals, 107 assists in 580 games; 2 goals, 4 assists in 12 playoff games.

KENNEDY, THEODORE S. (Teeder)   B. 12/12/25, Humberstone, Ont. Forward. Hall of Famer. Played 14 full seasons and part of 15th with Tor. Maple Leafs. Barely missed being a Mont. Canadien. Reported to Canadiens' camp at age of 16, but became homesick and left. Leafs traded for him next year, and in 1942–43 season he joined NHL with Toronto at age of 18. Won Hart MVP Trophy in 1955, his last full season in NHL. Ended retirement briefly in Jan. 1957 when injured Leafs prevailed on him, but quit for good at end of season. Twice on first All-Stars, once on second. Lives in Ontario.
NHL record: 231 goals, 329 assists in 696 games; 29 goals, 31 assists in 78 playoff games.

KEON, DAVID MICHAEL (Dave)   B. 3/22/40, Noranda, Que. Forward. 5'9", 163. Tor. Maple Leafs center finished 14th season with Toronto. Played at St. Michael's College and moved directly to Leafs in 1960 after participating in EPHL play offs with Sudbury the previous year. First season in NHL produced 20 goals. Rookie of Year in 1961, won Lady Byng in 1962 and 1963, and Conn Smythe Trophy in 1967 as most valuable player in playoffs. Serves as Leafs' captain. Owns hockey schools with ex-Toronto player Billy Harris, and sells insurance.

NHL record: 324 goals, 422 assists in 910 games; 31 goals, 28 assists in 78 games.

KERR, DAVID ALXANDER B. 1/11/10, Toronto, Ont. Goalie. Played 10 seasons in NHL, last seven with N.Y. Rangers. Played as junior in Toronto and as senior in Iron Falls, came up to Mont. Maroons in 1930, then bounced to Windsor, Philadelphia, and Montreal in the Canadian-American League before returning to Maroons in 1932–33. Went to Rangers in 1934, and retired at end of 1940–41 season. During 1937 playoffs registered four shutouts in nine games as New York won Stanley Cup. Lives in Toronto.

NHL record: allowed 955 goals in 428 games for 2.23 average, 51 shutouts; gave up 76 goals in 40 playoff games for 1.90 average, 8 shutouts.

KILPATRICK, GEN. JOHN REED B. 6/15/89. D. 5/7/60. Hall of Fame builder. Served in both world wars. Starred in football and track at Yale, twice making All-America. Member of Football Hall of Fame. Served as president of Madison Square Garden and N.Y. Rangers for 22 years, and as NHL governor starting in 1936. An original director of NHL Players Pension Society.

KILREA, HECTOR J. (Hurricane Hec) B. 6/11/07 in Novar, Ont. Forward. Won Distinguished Service Cross as sergeant serving in Europe with U. S. Army in World War II. Excelled as a speed skater in youth, winning $400 first prize in *Montreal Star* stakes, beating Howie Morenz, among others. Played amateur hockey with Ottawa Rideaus. Signed into NHL in 1925 with the old Ottawa Senators. Stayed there until 1932, when he played one year for Det. Falcons. Then returned to Ottawa. Played with Tor. Maple Leafs for two years (1933–35), and finished career with four years with Det. Red Wings in 1939.

NHL record: 167 goals, 129 assists in 14 seasons; 8 goals, 7 assists in 10 playoff series.

KLUKAY, JOSEPH FRANCIS B. 11/6/22, Sault Ste. Marie, Ont. Forward. Spent 11 years in NHL. Played for Cornwallis Navy Club. Military service 1943–45. Returned to play for Pittsburgh in 1945–46. Joined Tor. Maple Leafs in 1946. Went to Bos. Bruins in 1952. Returned to Leafs 11/9/54 for Leo Boivin, and stepped out of NHL after 1955–56 season.

NHL record: 109 goals, 127 assists in 566 league games; 13 goals, 10 assists in 71 playoff games.

KORAB, GERALD JOSEPH (Jerry) B. 9/15/48, Sault Ste. Marie, Ont. Defenseman. 6'3", 215. Played junior hockey at Sault Ste. Marie and at St. Catharines, went to Port Huron in 1968–69, then to Portland Buckaroos for one season and part of next. Called up by Chi. Black Hawks for 46 games in 1970–71—totaled 152 penalty minutes. Traded to Vancouver 5/17/73 with Gary Smith for Dale Tallon.

NHL record: 25 goals, 34 assists in 196 games; 1 goal, 1 assist in 30 playoff games.

KOROLL, CLIFFORD EUGENE (Cliff) B. 10/1/46, Canora, Sask. Forward. 6', 195. Chi. Black Hawk right wing had first 20-goal season in NHL in 1971–72, getting 22. Played at Denver U., turned pro in 1968 with Dallas, Hawks' CHL farm, made big club next season as replacement for Ken Wharram after latter was felled by heart attack. Had brilliant playoff in 1971, with 16 points in 18 games.

NHL record: 89 goals, 100 assists in 298 games; 12 goals, 19 assists in 24 playoff games.

KURTENBACH, ORLAND JOHN B. 9/7/36, Cudworth, Sask. Forward. 6'2", 195. Van. Canucks' center and captain had finest NHL season in 1971–72 at age of 35, getting 24 goals and 37 assists in 78 games. Considered league's prime fighter, but never has been penalized 100 minutes in a season. Turned pro in 1954–55 with Saskatoon of WHL, playing minor league hockey with Vancouver, Buffalo, Springfield, Providence, San Francisco, and Omaha. Was regular at various times with N.Y. Rangers, Tor. Maple Leafs, and Bos. Bruins, spending four years in N.Y. (1966–70) before being picked up by Canucks. Attimes has been hobbled by injuries, including one with Rangers, which required him to undergo spinal fusion 12/10/68.

NHL record: 111 goals, 200 assists in 587 games; 2 goals, 4 assists in 19 playoff games.

LACH, ELMER JAMES   B. 1/22/18, Nokomis, Sask. Forward. Made Hall of Fame through centering famed Punch Line with Maurice Richard and Toe Blake, playing 14 years with Mont. Canadiens from 1940 to 1954. Played as amateur with Regina, Weyburn, and Moose Jaw. Led NHL in scoring in 1945, winning Art Ross Trophy and also Hart MVP Trophy in same season. First All-Stars 1952. Lives in Montreal, public relations director for transport firm.

   NHL record: 215 goals, 408 assists in 14 seasons; 19 goals, 45 assists in 76 playoff games.

LACROIX, ANDRE JOSEPH   B. 6/5/45, Lauzon, Que. Forward. 5'8", 170. Played junior hockey in OHA, twice edging Bobby Orr for MVP. Spent first full pro season with Quebec in 1966–67, and joined Phila. Flyers at end of next season. Worked way into doghouse by 1971, prompting trade to Chi. Black Hawks 10/15/71 for Rick Foley. Jumped to Phila. Blazers of WHA after 1971–72. Lives in Philadelphia in off-season, and owns hockey school in New Jersey.

   NHL record: 76 goals, 105 assists in 296 games; 2 goals, 5 assists in 16 playoff games.

LAFLEUR, GUY DAMIEN   B. 9/20/51, Thurso, Que. Forward. 6', 175. Mont. Canadiens' right wing was tabbed "Player of Future" when drafted from Quebec Ramparts juniors in 1971, responded in rookie season with 29 goals and 35 assists in 73 games. Was one of wealthy "amateurs" with Ramparts, getting reported $20,000 a year. Scored 130 goals in 1970–71 for Ramparts, and had 147 year before, 44 in playoffs.

NHL record: 57 goals, 62 assists in 143 games; 4 goals, 9 assists in 23 playoff games.

LALONDE, EDOUARD (Newsy) B. 10/31/87, Cornwall, Ont. D. 11/21/70, Montreal, Que. Defenseman-forward. Hall of Famer. Also was fine lacrosse player, voted Canada's outstanding player of half century in that sport. Lalonde worked as Linotype operator in printing plant in his youth, acquiring his nickname. Began hockey career in 1905 in Cornwall, and played in several cities in Ontario and Vancouver and Saskatoon. Was charter member of Mont. Canadiens. Played from 1917 to 1922, once scoring 38 goals in 11-game schedule, and came back to coach team 1932–34. As old-timer, he refused to insist that the old players were better, often saying that the modern players were much better stick handlers.

NHL record: 124 goals, 27 assists in 98 games; 16 goals, 1 assist in 2 playoff series.

LAPERRIERE, JOSEPH JACQUES HUGUES B. 11/22/41, Rouyn, Que. Defenseman. 6'2", 190. Won Rookie of Year award in 1963–64 with Mont. Canadiens, his only team in NHL. Played with Junior Canadiens, made token appearances with Hull-Ottawa of EPHL from 1959–62, then turned pro for good in 1962–63, playing 40 games at Hull-Ottawa and six with Canadiens. Came up to stay next season, and in 1965–66 won James Norris Trophy as league's top defenseman. Often hobbled by injuries, including cracked bone in arm which he ignored in 1972 cup playoffs, and shoulder separation 1/15/72. Assigned Doug Harvey's old No. 2 when he joined club. Not known as belligerent player, but was suspended for three games in 1969 for "cross checking" official Bill Friday in on-ice dispute. Team Canada 1972.

NHL record: 38 goals, 232 assists in 649 games; 9 goals, 22 assists in 88 playoff games.

LAPOINTE, GUY GERARD B. 3/18/48, Montreal, Que. Defenseman. 6', 185. Became regular with Mont. Canadiens 1970 when Serge Savard broke leg. Played as junior with Junior Canadiens, turned pro in 1968 with Houston, then moved to Montreal entry in AHL before going to big team in 1970. Scored 15 goals in rookie season.

NHL record: 45 goals, 102 assists in 229 league games; 10 goals, 13 assists in 43 playoff games.

LAROSE, CLAUDE DAVID B. 3/2/42, Hearst, Ont. Forward. 6', 170.

Mont. Canadiens' right wing returned to team after having two best NHL seasons with Minn. North Stars. Played as junior at Peterborough, turned pro at Hull-Ottawa in 1962, played next season at Omaha, with some games with Canadiens, then made Montreal club in 1964. Sent to Houston 1/29/68, but was recalled less than month later. Traded to North Stars along with Danny Grant 6/11/68 for future draft choices. Stayed two seasons, getting 25 goals and 24 goals, respectively, and in 1968–69 won both Masterton Trophy and North Star MVP award. Traded back to Canadiens 6/10/70 for Bobby Rousseau.

NHL record: 148 goals, 174 assists in 624 league games; 12 goals, 15 assists in 83 playoff games.

LAVIOLETTE, JEAN BAPTISTE (Jack) B. 7/27/79, Belleville, Ont. D. 1/10/60, Montreal. Defenseman-forward. Member of both Hockey Hall of Fame and Canada's Sports Hall of Fame (as lacrosse player). Formed Mont. Canadiens out of battle between Canadian Hockey Assn. and National Hockey Assn. for supremacy. Moved to Valleyville, Que., at young age and played amateur hockey in that province. Then played for Sault Ste. Marie, Mich., before forming Canadiens. Started as defenseman but moved to forward and stayed with Canadiens through 1918–19. Stanley Cup was canceled that season by flu epidemic. Although he lost foot in accident in 1919, ending his playing career, he was able to return as referee.

LAWSON, DANIEL MICHAEL (Danny) B. 10/30/47, Toronto, Ont. Forward. 5'11", 180. Played junior hockey at Hamilton in Det. Red Wings' organization, playing briefly with Wings and with Fort Worth before being sent to Minn. North Stars, who farmed him to Iowa club, then recalled him for two seasons and allowed Buffalo Sabres to draft him in 1970. Jumped to Phila. Blazers of WHA after 1971–72. His slap shot is one of hardest in league.

NHL record: 28 goals, 29 assists in 219 games; no goals, 1 assist in 16 playoff games.

LAYCOE, HAROLD RICHARDSON (Hal) B. 6/23/22, Sutherland, Sask. Defenseman. Now coach of Van. Canucks after surviving incident in which he was kicked upstairs after coaching L.A. Kings for just 24 games. Played 11 years with N.Y. Rangers, Mont. Canadiens, and Bos. Bruins from 1945 to 1956. Moved to WHL as New Westminster coach, followed franchise to Victoria, then led Portland to seven championships in nine years. Joined Kings for abortive NHL coaching debut, then became coach of Canucks in 1970. Fired by Canucks after 1971–72 season.

NHL record: 25 goals, 77 assists in 531 games; 2 goals, 5 assists in 40 playoff games.

LEACH, REGINALD JOSEPH (Reg) B. 4/23/50, Riverton, Man. Forward. 6', 185. Calif. Seals' right wing was obtained from Bruins 2/23/72 with Rick Smith for Carol Vadnais. Played as junior at Flin Flon, Man., where 65 goals made him Bos. Bruins' No. 1 amateur pick of 1970. Sent to Oklahoma City in first pro year, scored 24 goals and 18 assists in 41 games until Bruins called him up in mid-Jan. 1971. Known to friends as "Little Beaver" because he is part Indian.

NHL record: 38 goals, 36 assists in 172 games; no goals, no assists in 3 playoff games.

LEADER, GEORGE ALFRED (Al) B. 12/4/03, Barnsley, Man. Hall of Fame builder. Started as secretary of Seattle City League in 1933, also playing, coaching, managing, and officiating. Elected secretary-manager of PCL in 1944, and became first president of pro Western Hockey League in 1948, a position he held until resignation in May 1969. A U.S. citizen, naturalized in 1933, he lives in Seattle.

LEBEL, ROBERT (Bob) B. 9/21/05, Quebec City, Que. Hall of Fame builder. Former mayor of Chambly, Que., where he lives, LeBel played junior and senior hockey there and in upstate New York. Founded Interprovincial Senior League in 1944. Then headed Quebec Amateur Hockey League, Canadian Amateur Hockey Assn., and International Ice Hockey Federation.

LEDUC, ALBERT (Battleship) B. 7/31/01, Valleyfield, Que. Defenseman. Played 10 years in NHL, all but one with Mont. Canadiens. Skated with such uncontrolled speed that he earned nickname "Battleship." Joined Canadiens in 1925, spent season of 1933–34 with N.Y. Rangers and Ottawa, then returned to finish NHL career next season with Canadiens. Coached Quebec for two seasons, then at Providence, where one of his pupils was Toe Blake. Built rink in Valleyfield, financing team there, and started hockey-stick factory in town. Lives most of year in Florida, where he owns motel.

NHL record: 57 goals, 35 assists in 10 seasons; 5 goals, 6 assists in 31 playoff games.

LEHMAN, FREDERICK HUGH (Hughie) B. 10/27/85, Pembroke, Ont. D. 4/8/61, Toronto, Ont. Goalie. Hall of Famer was also called "Old Eagle Eyes." Played for 23 years. Career started in Pembroke, and took him to Sault Ste. Marie, Berlin, New Westminster and Vancouver in the PCL and finally into NHL with Chi. Black Hawks in 1926–27. Retired after 1927–28 season, during which he shared Hawks' coaching reins with Barney Stanley.

NHL record: allowed 136 goals in 48 games for 2.83 average, 6 shutouts. Gave up 10 goals in 2 playoff games for 5.00 average, no shutouts.

LEITER, ROBERT EDWARD (Bob) B. 3/22/41, Winnipeg, Man. Forward. 5'9", 175. Pitt. Penguins' center made it back to NHL in 1971–72 after bouncing between Bos. Bruins and Hershey for several years. Started with Winnipeg WHL, played at Kingston, moved up to Bruins in 1962 for two years, then started career which also took him to California in WHL, expansion Atlanta Flames (1972–73). Led Hershey in scoring in 1971 with 33 goals and made All-Star team. Lives in Winnipeg with family.

NHL record: 60 goals, 79 assists in 291 games; 3 goals, no assists in 4 playoff games.

LEMAIRE, JACQUES GERALD B. 9/7/45, La Salle, Que. Forward. 5', 10", 170. Mont. Canadiens' center practices in summer with steel puck to develop shot which has enabled him to average more than 28 goals a season. Played for Junior Canadiens, spent just one season in minors (1966–67) at Houston before making Canadiens, and scored at least 20 goals in every big league season. Shot considered one of hardest in league. Also can play left wing.

NHL record: 187 goals, 210 assists in 445 games; 29 goals, 32 assists in 70 playoff games.

LEMIEUX, REAL GASTON B. 1/3/45, Victoriaville, Que. Forward. 5'11", 180. L.A. Kings' left wing had to learn to curb aggressiveness before becoming NHL regular. Played junior hockey with Hamilton Red Wings and turned pro in Det. Red Wings' organization, which assigned him to Memphis in 1964–65. In third season there, racked up 150 penalty minutes in first 35 games, prompting league president to caution him that if he did not calm down he would be suspended. Finished year with 211 minutes. Taken by L.A. in expansion draft of 1967, sent to N.Y. Rangers after two seasons, returned to Kings a year later. Divided 1970–71 between L.A. and Springfield. Played junior baseball for five years, hitting .394 in last year as catcher despite fact he wears contact lenses. Lives in Sorel, Que., with family.

NHL record: 50 goals, 103 assists in 418 games; 2 goals, 4 assists in 18 games.

LEPINE, ALFRED B. 7/31/01, Ste. Anne de Bellevue, Que. D. 1948. Forward. Played for Mont. Canadiens for 13 seasons, from 1925 to 1938, and coached squad for year. Started with Montreal Nationals as amateur, joined Canadiens in 1925. Had best season in 1929–30 when he scored 24 goals. Coached Canadiens in 1939–40 after retirement as player.

NHL record: 143 goals, 98 assists in 13 seasons; 7 goals, 5 assists in 10 playoff series.

LESUEUR, PERCY B. 11/18/81, Quebec City, Que. D. 1/27/62, Hamilton, Ont. Forward-goalie. Hall of Famer. Played both right wing and goal in addition to serving as coach, manager, referee, writer and in radio. Played amateur hockey in Quebec and Smith Falls, Ont. Joined Ottawa in 1906, playing, coaching, and managing until traded to Toronto in 1914. After army service, he quit as player but refereed and coached. Was first manager of Detroit Olympia. Credited with inventing goaler gauntlet glove. Worked in radio as member of Hot Stove League.

LESUK, WILLIAM ANTON (Bill) B. 11/1/46, Moose Jaw, Sask. Forward. 5'8", 180. Joined L.A. Kings as right wing after being obtained from Phila. Flyers 1/28/72 in eight-player deal. Played as junior with Weyburn Red Wings. Turned pro with Oklahoma City in 1967. Got brief tryout with Bos. Bruins before going to Hershey Bears of AHL in 1969–70, who recommended that Flyers draft him. Considers defense important part of forward's role.

NHL record: 34 goals, 50 assists in 225 games; 1 goal, no assists in 7 playoff games.

LESWICK, ANTHONY JOSEPH B. 3/17/23, Humboldt, Sask. Forward. 5'6", 155. Though a little guy, "could bring out the worst in a saint," according to former referee Bill Chadwick. Played on six championship teams while playing midget, juvenile, and church hockey in Saskatoon. Played senior hockey with Saskatoon Quakers. Joined Regina Pats as junior. Turned pro with Cleveland Barons. Royal Navy 1943. Made N.Y. Rangers in 1945. Spent 12 NHL seasons, going to Red Wings in 1951, to Chi. Black Hawks in 1955, then back to Wings in 1957, retiring that season after getting into only 11 games. Six All-Star games, five as All-Star.

NHL record: 165 goals, 159 assists in 729 games; 13 goals, 10 assists in 59 playoff games.

LEWICKI, DANIEL (Danny) B. 3/12/31, Fort William, Ont. Forward. Played eight full NHL seasons, hitting stride after slipping back to minors following big buildup his first time around. Played with Stratford juniors in OHA and with Port Arthur Bruins, 1948 Memorial Cup winners, after boyhood hockey in Fort William. Joined Tor. Maple Leafs in 1950. Spent 1952–54 in minors. Shipped to N.Y. Rangers in 1954–55, he scored 29 goals and 24 assists, and stayed with club until 1958–59, when he played 58 games for Chi. Black Hawks and retired. Did radio work. Lives in Toronto.

NHL record: 105 goals, 135 assists in 461 league games; no goals, 4 assists in 28 playoff games.

LEWIS, HERBERT A. B. 4/17/06, Calgary, Alta. Forward. Spent 11 seasons with Detroit teams, going through all name changes from Cougars to Falcons to Red Wings. Joined Cougars in 1928 as wing, and stayed in Detroit until 1939, playing on line with Hall of Famer Marty Barry and Larry Aurie. Had 20-goal seasons in 1930 and 1933.

NHL record: 148 goals, 161 assists in 11 seasons; 13 goals, 10 assists in 7 playoff series.

LEY, RICHARD NORMAN (Ricky) B. 11/2/48, Orillia, Ont. Defenseman. 5′9″, 190. Was grabbed by Tor. Maple Leafs in 16-year-old midget draft. Remained in organization until jumping to New England Whalers of WHA after 1971–72. Played as junior with Niagara Falls as team won Memorial Cup in 1968, then turned pro with Tulsa in 1968–69, playing 20 games before moving up to Leafs. Has piled up 416 penalty minutes in 229 games. Works for Dave Keon in off-season as hockey instructor.

NHL record: 8 goals, 54 assists in 229 games; no goals, 2 assists in 14 playoff games.

LIBETT, LYNN NICHOLAS (Nick) B. 12/9/45, Stratford, Ont. Forward. 6′1″, 175. Det. Red Wings' left wing played in Stratford Minor Hockey Assn. as a boy and Red Wings agreed to sponsor entire operation in order to get rights to Libett. Moved up to Hamilton Red Wings juniors before turning pro in 1963–64 with Cincinnati of CPHL, played with Memphis for two seasons, then with San Diego of WHL and Fort Worth of CPHL before joining major club late in 1967–68. Played first full season with Detroit in 1968–69, scoring team's first goal of season and its last. Lives with wife and family in Hamilton, Ont. in off-season.

NHL record: 98 goals, 104 assists in 400 games; 2 goals, no assists in 4 playoff games.

LIGHTFOOT, CHARLES B. 2/4/80, West Flambora, Ont. D. (date unknown). Forward. Was a black active in hockey around turn of century in game in which few blacks have participated. Played right wing with Stratford juniors, also played at Barrie, Ont., and Portage la Prairie, Man. Coached and refereed in Ontario leagues after playing career ended.

LINDSAY, ROBERT BLAKE THEODORE (Ted) B. 7/29/25, Renfrew, Ont. Forward. Hall of Famer. Played 17 seasons in NHL, earning nickname "Terrible Tempered Ted"; also earned faceful of scars, with stitches running into hundreds. Started in junior hockey in Kirkland Lake, Ont., where father operated ice rink. Joined Det. Red Wings out of junior ranks in 1944 and played 13 seasons before being traded to Chi. Black Hawks in 1957. Retired in 1960. Comeback in 1964–65, helped Wings to league championship; played in 69 games. Then retired for good. Lives in Detroit, where he is manufacturer's agent. Boycotted Hall of Fame dinner at which he was inducted in 1966, because wife not invited. Color man on NBC hockey telecasts, 1972–73.

NHL record: 379 goals, 427 assists in 1068 games; 47 goals, 49 assists in 133 playoff games.

LISCOMBE, HARRY CARLYLE (Carl) B. 5/17/15, Perth, Ont. Forward. Played in NHL for nine seasons, all with Det. Red Wings. Joined Wings in 1937, left NHL in 1946. Later starred in minor league hockey. Voted American Hockey League MVP in both 1948 and 1949 with Providence Reds, scoring 118 points in 1948, at that time a record.

NHL record: 137 goals, 140 assists in 9 seasons; 22 goals, 19 assists in 59 playoff games.

LITZENBERGER, EDWARD C. J. B. 7/15/32, Neudorf, Sask. Forward. Was victim of tragedy 1/18/60 when his wife was killed in auto crash in Chicago as Litzenbergers were driving home after Chi. Black Hawks game, and it was blamed for stunting his career. Came up with junior Canadiens, accepting $100 hockey bonus to give up football and basketball. Played in only five games with Canadiens from 1952–54 before going to Hawks 12/11/54 for $15,000, and went on to win Calder Trophy as rookie of Year in 1955 with 23 goals and 28 assists. Had 30-goal seasons in 1957, 58, 59, but never scored as many as 20 after the accident. Remarried. Sent to Det. Red Wings 6/14/61, then bought by Tor. Maple Leafs 12/30/61 for $20,000 waiver price. Finished NHL career there in 1964. All-Star game four times.

NHL record: 178 goals, 238 assists in 618 games; 5 goals, 13 assists in 40 playoff games.

LOCKHART, THOMAS F. (Tommy) B. (date not known). Hall of

Fame builder. Has been interested mainly in amateur hockey, although he served for six years as business manager of N.Y. Rangers. Early cycling and track and field promoter, organized amateur hockey in Madison Square Garden in 1932, organized Eastern Amateur Hockey League and served as president, also organized Amateur Hockey Assn. of the United States and was president. Supervised Metropolitan Amateur League, and coached and managed New York Rovers between 1932–52. Worked for Rangers from 1946–52. Active as official of AAU, lives in New York.

LOICQ, PAUL   B. 1890, Brussels, Belgium. D. (date unknown). Was elected posthumously as Hall of Fame builder in 1960. Played on Belgian national team from 1909 until retirement after 1924 Olympics. Was president of International Ice Hockey Federation in 1927 and served federation in various capacities, including referee, for 20 years. Decorated for bravery while serving as Belgian army colonel in World War I.

LONSBERRY, DAVID ROSS   B. 2/7/47, Humboldt, Sask. Forward. 5'10", 195. Phila. Flyers' left wing was traded to Philadelphia by L.A. Kings 1/28/72 in eight-man deal. Played junior hockey at Estevan, scoring 67 goals and 77 assists in 60 games in last year. Turned pro with Bos. Bruins organization in 1966–67, playing with Minneapolis, Oklahoma City, and Buffalo of AHL before making Bruins in 1967. Almost lost tip of right little finger in final preseason game, and after 19 games was shipped down to Oklahoma City, and stayed there another season before going to Kings in 1969.
   NHL record: 84 goals, 103 assists in 344 games.

LUCE, DONALD HAROLD   B. 10/2/48, London, Ont. Forward. 6'2", 190. Buffalo Sabres' center broke into pro hockey in 1968–69 with Omaha of CHL, staying there two seasons and getting 44 goals. Played 12 games with N.Y. Rangers in 1969–70 season, then moved to Det. Red Wings and after 1970–71 went to Sabres. Played junior hockey in Kitchener, Ont.
   NHL record: 33 goals, 47 assists in 235 games; 1 goal, 2 assists in 11 playoff games.

LUMLEY, HARRY (Apple Cheeks)   B. 11/11/26, Owen Sound, Ont. Goalie. Served 16 years in NHL with Det. Red Wings, N.Y. Rangers, Chi. Black Hawks, Tor. Maple Leafs and Bos. Bruins from 1943 to 1960. Won Vezina Trophy in 1954 with Leafs. Joined Winnipeg in 1960 after leaving Bruins, and rejoined team briefly in 1968 before retiring for good.

NHL record: allowed 2210 goals in 804 games for 2.75 average, 71 shutouts; gave up 199 goals in 76 playoff games for a 2.62 average, 7 shutouts.

McDONALD, ALVIN BRIAN (Ab) B. 2/18/36, Winnipeg, Man. Forward. 6'2", 194. Played for six NHL clubs in pro career which began in 1956, before jumping to Winnipeg Jets of WHA for 1972–73. Played amateur hockey with St. Catharines juniors before turning pro in 1956 with Rochester of AHL, making NHL with Mont. Canadiens in 1958. Sold to Chi. Black Hawks in June 1960. Played with Chicago's 1962 Stanley Cup winners, then was traded to Bos. Bruins in 1964. Boston sent him to Providence for part of that season, then traded him to Det. Red Wings, which shipped him to Memphis, then used him mainly with Pittsburgh's entry in AHL in 1966–67. Drafted by Pitt. Penguins in 1967 expansion, played in Pittsburgh until traded to St. L. Blues 6/11/68. Blues traded him back to Detroit 2/19/71 in deal in which Blues got permission to negotiate with Carl Brewer, who had told Wings he was going to retire. Had surgery for ailing back at end of that season. Lives with wife and children in Winnipeg in off-season.

NHL record: 182 goals, 248 assists in 762 games; 21 goals, 29 assists in 84 playoff games.

MacDONALD, CALVIN PARKER B. 6/14/33, Sydney, N.S. Forward. Spent 15 years in NHL, also played in AHL and CPHL in pro career that ran from 1952 to 1969. Played 675 games with Tor. Maple Leafs, N.Y. Rangers, Det. Red Wings, Bos. Bruins and Minn. North Stars. After retiring as player, coached Waterloo and Cleveland to second-place finishes in their leagues, then was named GM-coach of New

Haven Nighthawks of North Star Organization. Lives in Edina, Minn.

NHL record: 144 goals, 179 assists in 675 games; 14 games, 14 assists in 75 playoff games.

McDONALD, WILFRED KENNEDY (Bucko) B. 10/31/11, Fergus, Ont. Defenseman. 5'11", 220. Played 11 years in NHL, turning to hockey after lacrosse league in which he was a professional folded. Member of five championship lacrosse teams in eastern Canada at Brampton. When league folded played bush league hockey, then signed contract with Tor. Maple Leafs in 1933. Leafs farmed him to Buffalo, then sent him to Red Wings in 1934, where he stayed until sold to Leafs in 1939. Went to N.Y. Rangers in mid-1943–44, and retired from NHL in 1945. Served in parliament from Parry Sound, and lives in Sundridge, Ont.

NHL record: 35 goals, 88 assists in 11 seasons; 6 goals, 1 assist in 63 playoff games.

McDONOUGH, JAMES ALLISON (Al) B. 6/6/50, St. Catharines, Ont. Forward. 6'1", 175. Pitt. Penguins' right wing played first full NHL season in 1971–72 after being traded in mid-season from L.A. Kings. Started as amateur in St. Catharines, Ont., drafted by Kings in 1969–70. Played 65 games next year at Springfield, getting 33 goals and 16 assists, as well as six games with L.A. club. Spends summers instructing at hockey schools.

NHL record: 47 goals, 55 assists in 152 games; no goals, 1 assist in 4 playoff games.

McGEE, FRANCIS (Frank) B. 1880s. D. 9/16/16, France, in action during World War I, serving as lieutenant in Canadian army. Hall of Famer's big date was 1/16/05 when he scored 14 goals for Ottawa in Stanley Cup game against Dawson City, Yukon. Scored eight straight in 8 min., 20 sec., four in 140-sec. span. Played center for Ottawa Silver Seven from 1903 to 1906, although blind in one eye. Scored 71 goals in 23 games and 63 goals in 22 playoff games during career.

McGIMSIE, WILLIAM GEORGE (Billy) B. 6/7/80, Woodsville, Ont. D. 10/28/68, Calgary, Alta. Hall of Famer. Led Kenora (Ont.) Thistles to Stanley Cup in 1907, making it the smallest town ever to win the cup. Played entire career with Kenora, where he moved at age of one when town was called Rat Portage. During his career, Thistles challenged for cup in 1903, 1905 and twice in 1907. Dislocated shoulder ended career after 10 years in which he was star center.

MacGREGOR, BRUCE CAMERON B. 4/26/41, Edmonton, Alta.

Forward. 5'10", 180. N.Y. Ranger right wing spent only one season in minors and 10 full seasns and part of another with Det. Red Wings before being sent to Rangers in 1971. Played as junior with Edmonton Oil Kings and broke into pro hockey in 1960 with Edmonton of WHL. Played 12 games with Red Wings at end of season, then made club for good in 1961–62. Traded to Rangers 2/2/71 with Larry Brown for Arnie Brown, Mike Robitaille, and Tom Miller. Considered outstanding defensive forward. Wears helmet which he says gives him confidence.

NHL record: 196 goals, 230 assists in 827 games; 13 goals, 26 assists in 94 playoff games.

MacKAY, DUNCAN McMILLAN (Mickey) B. 5/21/94, Chesley, Ont. D. 5/21/40, British Columbia, in auto accident. Hall of Famer. Played junior hockey in Edmonton and Grand Forks, B.C., then joined pro Pacific Coast League with Vancouver Millionaires, where he stayed until joining Chi. Black Hawks of NHL in 1926. After two seasons went to Pittsburgh Pirates for half a season in 1928, then up to Bos. Bruins to help win Stanley Cup. After next season began, he retired as active player. Involved in six playoffs, including three with Vancouver before joining NHL.

NHL record: 44 goals, 19 assists in 4 seasons; no goals, no assists in 3 playoff series.

McKECHNIE, WALTER THOMAS JOHN (Walt) B. 6/19/47, London, Ont. Forward. 6'2", 195. Calif. Seal center turned pro with Minn. North Stars after playing as amateur with London Nationals. Played at Phoenix, Iowa, and Cleveland before being sent to Seals in trade which sent Dennis Hextall of Minnesota. Hard-hitting player. Fined $250 during 1970–71 season for "accosting" referee during argument over penalty.

NHL record: 36 goals, 71 assists in 246 games; 3 goals, 2 assists in 9 playoff games.

McKENNEY, DONALD HAMILTON (Don) B. 4/30/34, Smiths Falls, Ont. Forward. 6', 175. Amateur with Barrie Flyers juniors. Turned pro 1953–54 with Hershey of AHL. Bos. Bruins in 1954. Center was traded to N.Y. Rangers in Feb. 1963 for Dean Prentice; to Maple Leafs 2/22/64 in seven-player deal. Sent to minors, Pittsburgh and Kansas City. Returned to NHL briefly with Red Wings in 1965–66 and St. L. Blues in 1967–68. Ended career at Providence of AHL, 1969. Lady Byng Trophy 1960.

NHL record: 237 goals, 345 assists in 798 games; 18 goals, 29 assists in 58 playoff games.

McKENNY, JAMES CLAUDE (Jim) B. 12/1/46, Ottawa, Ont. Defenseman, 6', 185. Tor. Maple Leafs' defenseman is sometimes called "Howie" due to physical similarity to former "bad actor" Howie Young, but isn't troublemaker himself. Played as junior with Toronto Marlboros Memorial Cup champs, turned pro in 1966 with Tulsa after playing two games in 1965–66 with Leafs. Worked at Rochester and Vancouver, with token appearances in Toronto, until making big club in 1969. Has studied acting, and appeared in movie *Face-Off*. Worked at hockey school in Finland over summer of 1971.

NHL record: 33 goals, 131 assists in 314 games; 5 goals, 1 assist in 11 playoff games.

McKENZIE, JOHN ALBERT B. 12/12/37, High River, Alta. Forward. 5'9", 175. Right wing for Bos. Bruins in 1971–72, but signed three-year contract 6/14/72 to play for and coach Phila. Blazers of WHA at reported $100,000 a year. Indicated he signed contract partly as result of unhappiness that Bruins did not protect him in draft. Stepped down as Blazers' coach in Nov. 1972, Phil Watson replacing him. Played as junior in Chi. Black Hawks' organization at St. Catharines, turned pro in 1958 at Calgary, moved up to Hawks in same season, then was shipped to Det. Red Wings. Spent 1960–62 at Hershey, then moved to Buffalo, sharing AHL playoff scoring record with eight goals and 12 assists. Returned to Hawks from 1963 to 1965, then 6/5/65 was shipped to N.Y. Rangers, who kept him until 1/10/66 and shipped him to Bruins for Reggie Fleming. Round face which led teammates to call him "Pie." Injuries include ruptured spleen, which was removed in Nov. 1963 and shoulder surgery in Jan. 1971.

NHL record: 206 goals, 268 assists in 691 games; 15 goals, 32 assists in 69 playoff games.

McLAUGHLIN, MAJ. FREDERIC B. 6/27/77, Chicago, Ill. D. 12/17/44, Chicago, Ill. Hall of Fame builder. Formed Chicago franchise in NHL out of breakup of Western Canada League 1926. Named team Black Hawks after regiment he served with in World War I. Hawks did poorly in attendance at first, playing in old Coliseum, so McLaughlin, the president, purchased controlling interest and moved team to Chicago Stadium in 1929, where it perked up. During ownership, Hawks won Stanley Cup in 1934 and 1938.

McLELLAN, DANIEL JOHN B. 8/6/28, South Porcupine, Ont. Forward. Resigned as coach of Tor. Maple Leafs end of 1972–73 season. Played only two games with Leafs in 1951–52, but in minors for nine years, helping win Calder Cups for Pittsburgh and Cleveland. As amateur played on St. Michael's team that won Memorial Cup in 1947, was with Toronto Marlboros when they won Allan Cup in 1950, and played on 1958 Belleville McFarland world championship team. Coached Nashville to two Eastern League titles, and led Tulsa of CPHL to a first-place finish and championship in two seasons. Took over Toronto post from Punch Imlach in 1969.

McLEOD, ROBERT JOHN (Jackie) B. 4/30/30, Regina, Sask. Forward Canada's Olympic coach had five-year NHL career cut short by collision with Bill Barilko in 1955 in which he suffered broken jaw and shoulder. Played as amateur for Moose Jaw Canucks, joined N.Y. Rangers in 1949, staying until 1955 although he never was full-time player. Also played at Cincinnati, Saskatoon, Vancouver, and Calgary in minors, buying his way out of Calgary contract for $1000. Represented Canada in three world tournaments, and took over reins of Olympic team in 1967.

NHL record: 14 goals, 23 assists in 106 games; no goals, no assists in 7 playoff games.

MacMILLAN, WILLIAM STEWART (Billy) B. 3/7/43, Charlottetown, P.E.I. Forward. 5'10'', 180. Atlanta Flames' right wing did not move into NHL until 1970 at age of 27 after playing many years with Canadian National team. Started out by getting 22 goals as rookie. Played as junior with Metro A League, then joined Canadian Nationals while finishing education. Played three games at Tulsa of CHL, then joined Tor. Maple Leafs. To Flames before 1972–73 season. Worked for several summers as director of camp for crippled children, and has managed one of Dave Keon's hockey schools. Named Prince Edward Island Citizen of Year in 1971. Owns farm near Charlottetown.

NHL record: 42 goals, 41 assists in 215 games; no goals, 3 assists in 11 playoff games.

McNAMARA, GEORGE B. 8/26/86, Sault Ste. Marie, Ont. D. 3/10/52. Hall of Famer. Started out with Sault Ste. Marie, Mich., team, then joining Montreal Shamrocks in 1908. Played with Halifax Crescents for three years, then for Toronto Tecumsehs in in 1912. In 1914 played for Toronto Ontarios after starting season with Ottawa. Joined army and went overseas in 1917 after playing briefly with army team in NHL. Returned to Sault Ste. Marie to coach after war, led Greyhounds to Allan Cup in 1924.

MacNEIL, ALLISTER WENCES (Al) B. 9/27/35, Sydney, N.S. Defenseman. Coached Canadiens to Stanley Cup championship in 1971 and was fired for his pains. Broke into NHL in 1955 with Tor. Maple Leafs, staying with club until 1959–60. In 1960–61 he played for Hull-Ottawa of EHL, winning top defenseman award, and returned to NHL next season with Mont. Canadiens, going to Chi. Black Hawks in 1962, N.Y. Rangers in 1966, and finishing NHL playing career with Pitt. Penguins in 1967–68. Coached Montreal team in AHL. Then named Canadiens' ass't. coach 9/9/70 and head coach, replacing Claude Ruel, 12/3/70. Constant changing of lines during 1971 playoff series with Hawks prompted Canadiens' Henri Richard to call MacNeil "the worst coach I ever saw," and MacNeil was fired. Now coaches Nova Scotia Voyageurs, Canadiens' farm team.

NHL record: 17 goals, 75 assists in 525 games; no goals, 4 assists in 37 playoff games.

McVEIGH, CHARLES (Rabbit)   B. 3/29/98, Kenora, Ont. Forward. Played nine seasons in NHL, two with Chi. Black Hawks and seven with N.Y. Americans. Started as amateur in Moose Jaw, Sask. Joined Regina Caps in 1921, Hawks in 1926, went to N.Y. Americans in 1928, left NHL in 1935. Served as official after retirement as player, assignments including Stanley Cup games.

NHL record: 84 goals, 88 assists in 9 seasons; no goals, no assists in 2 playoff series.

MAGNUSON, KEITH ARLEN   B. 4/27/47, Saskatoon, Sask. Defense-man. 6′, 185. Chi. Black Hawk defenseman, one of league's premier brawlers, has taken boxing lessons. Played junior hockey in home town and for Denver U. Made Hawks direct from college in 1969, picking up 213 penalty minutes, and next season set league record with 291. Had knee surgery in summer of 1971. Works in off-season in public relations for soft drink firm. Old schoolmate from Saskatoon once recalled that Magnuson was considered meek as a junior.

NHL record: 5 goals, 82 assists in 303 games; 1 goal, 7 assists in 41 playoff games.

MAHOVLICH, FRANCIS WILLIAM (Frank)   B. 1/10/38, Timmins, Ont. Forward. 6′, 205. Mont. Canadien left wing has had one of most checkered of all hockey careers, from record-breaking scoring to fits of depression severe enough to put him in hospital. Played at St. Michael's College. Turned pro with Tor. Maple Leafs in 1957, winning Calder Trophy as Rookie of Year by four votes over Bobby Hull. Never played in minors. Suffered two nervous breakdowns in Toronto, fighting frequently with coach Punch Imlach. On 3/4/68, was traded to Detroit in seven-man deal involving Garry Unger and Pete Stemkowski. In 1962, Leafs had turned down Jim Norris' million-dollar certified check for "Big M" in deal that would have made him Chi. Black Hawk. Detroit shuffled front office in 1970, and 1/13/71 sent Mahovlich, who had scored 400th goal 12/3/70 against L.A. Kings, to Montreal. Pushed Canadiens to Stanley Cup, setting playoff record of 14 goals; had 27 points, tying record set previous year by Phil Esposito. Team Canada 1972.

NHL record: 502 goals, 521 assists in 1110 games; 55 goals, 74 assists in 123 playoff games.

MAHOVLICH, PETER JOSEPH (Pete) B. 10/10/46, Timmins, Ont. Forward. 6'5", 205. Mont. Canadien left wing is brother of Frank and is known as "Little M" despite fact that he is considerably bigger than older brother. Played at St. Michael's High School. Drafted by Det. Red Wings and played as junior with Hamilton Red Wings before becoming pro with Wings in 1966. Played at Pittsburgh of AHL and at Fort Worth for two seasons before getting into 30 games for Wings in 1968–69. Traded to Mont. Canadiens 6/6/69 for Garry Monahan and Doug Piper, sent to Montreal AHL entry, brought up to Canadiens for end of season. Made team as regular in 1970–71, and put together two 35-goal seasons in row. Wears braces on weak knees, but still aggressive—181 penalty minutes in 1970–71. Team Canada 1972.

NHL record: 109 goals, 113 assists in 332 games; 14 goals, 17 assists in 43 playoff games.

MAKI, RONALD PATRICK (Chico) B. 8/17/39, Sault Ste. Marie, Ont. Forward. 5'10", 170. Chi. Black Hawk right wing. Played junior at St. Catharines. Won Rookie of Year honors at Buffalo in 1961 with 30 goals and 42 assists in 69 games. Played briefly with Hawks next season, but mostly at Buffalo. Made Hawks to stay in 1962–63. Brother of Wayne Maki of Canucks.

NHL record: 134 goals, 261 assists in 750 games; 17 goals, 35 assists in 98 playoff games.

MAKI, WAYNE B. 11/10/44, Sault Ste. Marie, Ont. Forward. 5'11", 185. Van. Canucks' left wing suffered through season of torment in 1969 after stick-swinging brawl with Boston's Ted Green. Latter nearly killed, requiring three operations and plastic plate in head before he was able to return to action. Charges brought against Maki, then with St. L. Blues, as result of exhibition game fight 9/21/69 in Ottawa, but later dropped. Suspended for month. Brother of Chi. Black Hawks' Ronald (Chico) Maki, turned pro with St. Louis of CPHL in 1964–65, moved through

Dallas, Chicago, Blues, and Buffalo in CPHL before coming to roost at Vancouver. Stricken with brain tumor and operated on 12/11/72.

NHL record: 57 goals, 79 assists in 246 games; 1 goal, no assists in 2 playoff games.

MALONE, MAURICE JOSEPH (Joe)   B. 2/28/90, Quebec City, Que. D. 5/15/69. Forward. Hall of Famer was prodigious scorer in 15 years of professional play. Started with junior Crescents in 1907, turned pro with Waterloo, Ont., in 1909. Played seven years with Quebec Bulldogs, four with Mont. Canadiens, and two with Hamilton, Ont. Credited with 379 goals during career, including 146 goals in 125 NHL games between 1917 and retirement in 1924. Led NHA in scoring in 1912 and 1913, and in 1918 scored 44 goals in 20 games with Canadiens in NHL. Scored 9 goals in 1913 playoff game, 8 goals in game in 1917, and scored 7 goals 1/31/20 against Toronto for NHL single game record.

NHL record: 146 goals, 18 assists in 125 games; 6 goals, 1 assist in 5 playoff games.

MANIAGO, CESARE   B. 1/13/39, Trail, B.C. Goalie. 6'3", 185. Minn. North Star veteran turned pro in 1960–61 at Sudbury of EPHL, went on to play in 12 places before ending up at Minnesota. Other stops included Tor. Maple Leafs, Vancouver, Spokane, Hull-Ottawa, Mont. Canadiens, Quebec, Buffalo, Omaha, Minneapolis, and Baltimore. Played for N.Y. Rangers in 1965–66, 1966–67 before going to North Stars in 1967. Played 52 games that season, getting three consecutive shutouts. Expressed belief that goalie does best work when rested occasionally. Attacked by fan in Madison Square Garden 3/26/72 and pressed charges, later dismissed in court. Lives in North Burnaby, B.C.

NHL record: allowed 881 goals in 304 games for 3.05 average, 16 shutouts; gave up 85 goals in 29 playoff games for 2.81 average, 1 shutout.

MANTHA, GEORGES   B. 11/29/08, Lachine, Ont. Forward. Played 13 seasons as left wing for Mont. Canadiens. Started with Bell Telephone in Montreal, joined Canadiens in 1928 and stepped out of NHL in 1941.

NHL record: 89 goals, 102 assists in 13 seasons; 6 goals, 1 assist in 10 playoff series.

MANTHA, SYLVIO   B. 4/14/02, Montreal, Que. Defenseman. Hall of Famer played 14 seasons in NHL, 13 with Mont. Canadiens. Junior and senior hockey player in Montreal. Joined Canadiens in 1923 as forward, but moved to defense in first year and helped them win first Stanley Cup. In final year with Canadiens, 1935–36, he was player-coach. Finished playing career next season with Bos. Bruins. After retiring as player, served as official in NHL and AHL, then coached amateur teams in Montreal, where he lives as retired city employee.

NHL record: 63 goals, 72 assists in 14 seasons; 5 goals, 4 assists in 10 playoff series.

MARCH, HAROLD C. (Mush) B. 10/18/08, Silton, Sask. Forward. 5'5", 140. Despite small stature, played 17 seasons with Chi. Black Hawks, joining them 12/6/28 after amateur hockey with Regina Monarchs. Feisty player; once chased off ice by own coach after fight in amateurs. Scored winning goal after 30 minutes and 5 seconds of overtime to win Stanley Cup for Hawks over Red Wings 4/10/34 in 1–0 game. Turned to officiating in NHL after retirement as player. Also became golfer, serving as teaching pro. Lives in Chicago suburb.

NHL record: 153 goals, 230 assists in 17 seasons; 12 goals and 15 assists in 11 playoff series.

MARCOTTE, DONALD MICHEL (Don) B. 4/15/47, Asbestos, Que. Forward. 5'11", 185. Bos. Bruins' left wing, has been considered "seventh man," coming off bench to fill whatever hole needs filling. Played as junior for Niagara Falls Flyers, made a couple of falses starts in pro hockey, then turned pro for good in 1967–68 at Hershey, spending two years there, and divided time between Hershey and Boston in 1969–70, then made Bruins in next season, getting into 75 games. Lives in Niagara Falls, Ont.

NHL record: 55 goals, 51 assists in 243 games; 6 goals, 1 assist in 37 playoff games.

MARIUCCI, JOHN B. 5/8/16, Eveleth, Minn. Defenseman. Played five seasons in NHL with Chi. Black Hawks, then went on to career as coach and executive. Played football and hockey for U. of Minnesota, then turned pro in hockey with Providence of AHL in 1940, joining Hawks in same season. Left Hawks in 1948; missed three seasons while serving in Coast Guard during World War II (1942–45). Played with St. Louis of AHL in 1948–49, and Minneapolis and St. Paul of USHL in 1949–50 and 1950–51. Then coached U. of Minnesota hockey team for 14 seasons before joining Minnesota North Stars in 1967, where he scouted, acted as traveling secretary, and coached twice in emergencies. Now is special assistant to GM, living in Bloomington, Minn.

NHL record: 11 goals, 34 assists in 223 games; no goals, 3 assists in 8 playoff games.

MAROTTE, JEAN GILLES B. 6/7/45, Montreal, Que. Defenseman.

5'9", 195. L.A. Kings' defenseman admitted to bitterness when he was traded to L.A. by Chi. Black Hawks in latter part of 1969–70, going from first-place team to also-ran, but now plays regularly. Played junior hockey with Niagara Falls Flyers, going directly to Bos. Bruins in 1965. Traded to Hawks 5/15/67 in deal which got Boston line of Phil Esposito, Ken Hodge, and Fred Stanfield. Offered baseball contract as catcher after three years of semipro ball, also is nine-handicap golfer.

NHL record: 42 goals, 184 assists in 559 games; 3 goals, 1 assist in 11 playoff games.

MARSHALL, ALBERT LEROY (Bert) B. 11/22/43, Kamloops, B.C. Defenseman. 6'2", 195. Calif. Seals' ace has been hampered by injuries in pro career that began in 1963–64, including collapsed lung suffered 12/28/68 while with Det. Red Wings, and undetected hairline fracture of wrist, with which he played throughout 1969–70 season. Played with Edmonton Oil Kings before turning pro with Cincinnati, moved in minors to Memphis and Pittsburgh before making Red Wings in 1965–66. Traded to Seals 1/9/68 in four-man deal. Traded to N.Y. Rangers mid-1972–73. Lives in Kamloops in off-season with wife and children, running hockey school there.

NHL record: 9 goals, 94 assists in 476 games; 1 goal, 12 assists in 29 playoff games.

MARSHALL, DONALD ROBERT (Donnie) B. 3/23/32, Verdun, Que. Forward. 5'10", 166. Tor. Maple Leafs' left wing retired in 1972. Played as amateur with Cincinnati Mohawks and was Rookie of Year in AHL with Buffalo in 1953–54 on 39-goal season. Split next season between Mont. Canadiens and Royals, then made Canadiens to stay next year. Traded to N.Y. Rangers in 1963 in seven-man deal, which included Jacques Plante and Phil Goyette. In 1970, was left unprotected and was grabbed by Buffalo Sabres in expansion draft. Toronto drafted him back for 1971–72 in what management called a hedge against retirement of George Armstrong. Was used often as penalty killer.

NHL record: 265 goals, 324 assists in 1176 games; 8 goals, 15 assists in 95 playoff games.

MARSHALL, JOHN C. (Jack) B. 3/14/77, St. Vallier, Que. D. 8/7/65, Montreal, Que. Hall of Famer starred in soccer and football in addition to being associated with five Stanley Cup winners during 17 years in hockey. Started with Winnipeg Victorias who won cup in 1900–01. Played with Montreal AAA, Montreal Wandererers and Ottawa Montagnards and Montreal Shamrocks. Joined Toronto as playing manager in 1914, then finished career with Wanderers. Career scoring record was

99 goals in 132 regular games and 13 goals in 18 playoff games.

MARTIN, HUBERT JACQUES (Pit) B. 12/9/43, Noranda, Que. Forward. 5'8", 165. Chi. Black Hawk center turned pro in Det. Red Wings' organization in 1962–63. Played at Pittsburgh in AHL and failed to make Red Wings on steady basis. Traded to Bos. Bruins 12/30/65 for Parker McDonald and spent two seasons in Boston. Sent to Hawks 5/16/67 in deal which brought Phil Esposito, Ken Hodge, and Fred Stanfield to Boston. Chicago papers said at time that Martin was not expected to make team. Assailed club in fall of 1969 for giving preferential treatment to stars, many of whom he accused of lack of ambition where the team was concerned. Won Masterton Trophy in 1970. Graduate of Windsor U., is avid golfer in off-season.

NHL record: 198 goals, 291 assists in 660 games; 23 goals, 29 assists in 67 playoff games.

MARTIN, RICHARD LIONEL (Rick) B. 7/26/51, Montreal, Que. Forward. 5'11", 165. Buffalo Sabres' left wing won *Sporting News* Rookie of Year in 1971–72. Led club in goals with 44, tied Gil Perrault for point leadership with 74. Scoring was best ever for NHL rookie. Set Ontario Hockey Assn. record for goals in 1970–71 with Junior Canadiens with 71. Attended Sir George Williams U. in Montreal and is excellent golfer. Uses slap shot and has strong wrist shot. Team Canada 1972.

NHL record: 81 goals, 66 assists in 148 games; 3 goals, 2 assists in 6 playoff games.

MASTERTON, WILLIAM (Bat) B. 8/16/38, Winnipeg, Man. D. 1/15/68. Forward. First fatality in 51 years of NHL play when he died of injuries suffered in game 1/13/68 against California. Was in his first season with Minn. North Stars, coming out of retirement to join club. Played college hockey at Denver U.; named NCAA most valuable player. Then with Hull-Ottawa of EHL in 1961–62 and Cleveland of AHL in 1962–63 before retiring. Named for him is Masterton Trophy, yearly given to player best embodying "perseverance, sportsmanship and dedication to hockey."

NHL record: 4 goals, 8 assists in 38 games.

MAXWELL, FRED G. (Steamer) B. 5/19/90, Winnipeg, Man. Hall of Famer played amateur hockey in Winnipeg all his career, finishing up playing with Monarchs from 1914–1916, then went to on to become outstanding coach. Coached Monarchs for two seasons, then coached Winnipeg Falcons until 1925, leading team to Allan Cup in 1919 and World and Olympic titles in 1920. Coached Winnipeg Rangers, then

Winnipeg Maroons of American Professional League in 1927–28. When league folded, coached amateur teams, taking Monarchs to world title in 1935. Also served as official until 1940.

MEEHAN, GERALD MARCUS (Gerry) B. 9/3/46, Toronto, Ont. Forward. 6'2", 200. Buffalo Sabres' center got chance to play as regular in NHL when Buffalo's rookie center Randy Wyrozub was injured at start of 1970–71 season. Meehan was shifted to wing and scored 24 goals and 31 assists, third on team elected captain of team in Oct. 1971. Played junior hockey with Toronto Marlboros, joined Rochester in 1965–66. Sat out 1966–67 season, then returned to score 31 goals for Tulsa in 1967–68. Had brief trials with Tor. Maple Leafs and Phila. Flyers and also played for Phoenix and Seattle before going to Sabres in 1970. Considered extremely strong puck carrier.
    NHL record: 74 goals, 92 assists in 268 games; no goals, 1 assist in 10 playoff games.

MEEKER, HOWARD WILLIAM B. 11/4/24, Kitchener, Ont. Forward. Played eight seasons with Tor. Maple Leafs from 1946 to 1954, then moved into management. Performed with Stratford, Ont., before joining Leafs in 1946 after wartime service to score 27 goals, his best season ever and good enough for Calder Trophy as Rookie of Year. Overall, however, was not high scorer. Named coach of Leafs in 1956, then was replaced by Billy Reay and moved into front office as GM. Has appeared on CBC hockey broadcasts, and is hockey instructor in Newfoundland. In 1952 won election to parliament from Waterloo District as Progressive Conservative.
    NHL record: 83 goals, 102 assists in 346 games; 6 goals, 9 assists in 42 playoff games.

MELOCHE, GILLES B. 7/12/50, Montreal, Que. Goalie. 5'10", 170. Calif. Seals' goalkeeper was part of deal that sent Gary Smith to Chi. Black Hawks in transaction which was in doubt until after season had started. Played junior hockey at Verdun, Que., and was playing with Flint (Mich.) Generals when Hawks' Gerry Desjardins was injured in March 1971. Appeared in two games for Chicago, beating Canucks 7–4 in Vancouver in maiden effort.
    NHL record: allowed 414 goals in 117 games for 3.57 average, 5 shutouts.

MICKOSKI, NICHOLAS B. 12/7/27, Winnipeg, Man. Forward. Played 12 NHL seasons with four clubs. Started with N.Y. Rovers and played as pro at New Haven. Joined Rangers in 1948, stayed until going to Chi.

Black Hawks in mid–1954–55. Hawks sent him to Det. Red Wings 12/18/57 in eight-man deal, and he was peddled to Bos. Bruins 8/25/59 for Jim Morrison. Left NHL in 1959–60 after playing 18 games for Bruins, but continued on in WHL with San Francisco, where he scored 42 goals and 53 assists in 1962. Went into coaching after retirement. Also outstanding golfer.

NHL record: 158 goals, 185 assists in 703 games; 1 goal, 6 assists in 18 playoff games.

MIKITA, STANLEY B. 5/20/40, Sokolce, Czechoslovakia. Forward. 5′9″, 165. Chi. Black Hawk center played in shadow of Bobby Hull until 1972–73, even in junior days at St. Catharines, although he has won four NHL scoring titles in own right. Real name Stanley Gvoth. Took name of uncle after moving to St. Catharines as boy. Moved to Hawks directly from amateur play in 1959–60, and went on to win—in addition to four scoring crowns in 1964, 1965, 1967, 1968—the Hart and Lady Byng trophies in both 1967 and 1968. Team Canada 1972. Has been bothered by bad back. Wears helmet which he had designed for him by engineer after head injury. Eventually went into helmet manufacturing business; believes that some day NHL will make helmets mandatory. Broke heel 2/9/73 and sidelined for six weeks. Outstanding golfer. Has helped in Chicago area with field hockey competition in Special Olympics for mentally retarded youngsters. Subject of book *I Play to Win.*

NHL record: 401 goals, 673 assists in 976 games; 48 goals, 80 assists in 126 playoff games.

MOHNS, DOUGLAS ALLEN (Doug) B. 12/13/33, Capreol, Ont. Defenseman. 6′, 184. Minn. North Stars' defenseman has also played left wing. Turned pro in 1953–54 with Bos. Bruins and spent 11 seasons at Boston, going to Chi. Black Hawks 6/8/64 for Ab McDonald and Reg Fleming. Minnesota acquired him 2/23/71 for Danny O'Shea in effort to improve power play. Has been hampered by injuries, including broken hand 12/22/68 and broken wrist in fall of 1970. Scored 200th goal 3/20/68. Bald since early days in NHL, now wears toupee. Lives in Braintree, Mass.

NHL record: 246 goals, 440 assists in 1287 games; 15 goals, 38 assists in 103 playoff games.

MOLSON, SEN. HARTLAND de MONTARVILLE, OBE B. 5/29/07, Montreal, Que. Hall of Fame builder. Retired as president of Mont. Canadiens 5/15/64. President of Molson Breweries Ltd., Montreal. Served with 1st Fighter Squadron of RCAF overseas in World War II. Lives in Montreal.

MONAHAN, GARRY MICHAEL   B. 10/20/46, Barrie, Ont. Forward. 6',
185. Tor. Maple Leaf center and wing played with Peterborough Petes
as junior, turned pro in 1967 with Mont. Canadiens' organization, which
sent him to Houston, then to Cleveland. Went to Det. Red Wings 6/7/69
in deal which delivered Peter Mahovlich to Canadiens, then was traded
in midseason to L.A. Kings for Dale Rolfe. Went to Leafs 9/4/70 in Bob
Pulford deal. Considered aggressive and used as penalty killer.

   NHL record: 45 goals, 64 assists in 320 games; 2 goals, no assists in
11 playoff games.

MOORE, RICHARD WINSTON (Dickie)   B. 1/6/31, Montreal, Que.
Forward. Played 14 years in NHL despite two bad legs sustained in
childhood accident and from which cartilage was removed during
hockey career. One of 10 children, played with Montreal Junior Royals
and Junior Canadiens, both Memorial Cup winners. Turned pro with
Royals in 1951–52, and was called up to Mont. Canadiens same year.
Remained through 1962–63, winning league scoring title in 1958 despite
playing last five weeks with cast on wrist, and repeating in 1959 with 96
points, then a record. Sent to Tor. Maple Leafs in 1964–65, then went to
St. L. Blues, where he played 27 games in 1967–68 and retired. Appeared
in eight All-Star games, seven with Canadiens. Operates several successful businesses in Montreal.

   NHL record: 261 goals, 347 assists in 719 games; 46 goals, 64 assists
in 135 playoff games.

MORAN, PATRICK JOSEPH (Paddy)   B. 3/11/87, Quebec City, Que.
D. 1/14/66, Quebec City, Que. Goalie. Made Hall of Fame as standup
goalie in days before goalers were allowed to drop to ice to stop puck.
Played juvenile hockey in home town, moved through juniors and
intermediates and turned pro with Quebec Bulldogs in 1901. Stayed with
team for 16 seasons except for 1909–10 when he played with Haileybury,
Ont. Played 201 games with just over five goals-against average. Helped
Bulldogs to Stanley Cup in 1912 and 1913.

MORENZ, HOWARTH WILLIAM (Howie)   B. 9/21/02, Mitchell, Ont.
D. 3/8/37 of complications after breaking leg in game 1/28/37. Hall of
Famer. Started hockey career in Stratford, Ont. Joined Mont. Canadiens
in 1923. Speed and daring earned him nickname "Babe Ruth of
Hockey." Played in NHL 14 years and won Hart MVP Trophy three
times. Joined Chi. Black Hawks in 1934, N.Y. Rangers 1935–36, and
returned to Canadiens for 1936–37 season.

   NHL record: 270 goals, 197 assists in 14 seasons; 14 goals, 9 assists
in 47 playoff series.

MORRISON, LEWIS (Lew) B. 2/11/48, Gainsborough, Sask. Forward. 6′, 185. Atlanta Flames' right wing. Played as junior with Flin Flon (Man.) Bombers. Turned pro in Flyers' system with Quebec Aces in 1968, and joined big team in 1969–70. Sent down to Richmond, but recalled 11/16/71. Drafted by Atlanta 6/6/72. Involved in NHL Players Association hockey school in Wilmington, Del.

NHL record: 25 goals, 31 assists in 279 games; no goals, no assists in 4 playoff games.

MORTSON, JAMES ANGUS GERALD (Gus) B. 1/24/25, New Liskeard, Ont. Defenseman. Spent 13 years in NHL, six with Tor. Maple Leafs, six with Chi. Black Hawks, one with Det. Red Wings. Played with Memorial Cup winners at Oshawa and St. Michael's, joined Leafs in 1946. Went to Hawks in 1952 after feud with Conn Smythe, and to Red Wings in 1958. Wings sent him to N.Y. Rangers 1/17/58 for waiver price of $15,000; never played for New York and stepped out of NHL. Participated in eight All-Star games, six as member of All-Star team. Took job as coach of Chatham club after retirement.

NHL record: 46 goals, 152 assists in 797 games; 5 goals, 8 assists in 54 playoff games.

MOSDELL, KENNETH B. 7/13/22, Montreal, Que. Forward. Played 15 NHL seasons, 1941–58, with time out for military service. Started with Montreal Royals junior. Came into NHL with Brooklyn in 1941. Went into service next season. Returned in 1944 with Mont. Canadiens. Played at Buffalo in 1945–46, then recalled by Canadiens, staying with them until 5/18/56 when purchased by Chi. Black Hawks. Returned to Canadiens in 1957–58; played two games, then retired from league. Had best years in 1954 and 1955 when he scored 22 goals each season. Runs gas station in Montreal. All-Star four times.

NHL record: 141 goals and 168 assists in 693 games; 16 goals, 13 assists in 79 playoff games.

MOSIENKO, WILLIAM (Bill) B. 11/2/21, Winnipeg, Man. Forward. Hall of Famer played 14 years in NHL, teaming with two other Hall of Fame members, Max and Doug Bentley, on Pony Line for Chi. Black Hawks. Turned pro with Providence in 1940, played with Kansas City, then joined Hawks in 1941 and stayed with them until retiring in 1955. Won Lady Byng Trophy in 1945 and was named first All-Star once and second once. Scored three goals in 21 seconds against N.Y. Rangers 3/23/52—a record. Was penalized only 129 minutes in entire hockey career. Helped start Winnipeg Warriors in 1955, playing with team until 1959, then coaching in 1959–60. Lives in Winnipeg.

NHL record: 258 goals, 282 assists in 711 games; 10 goals, 4 assists in 22 playoff games.

MURDOCH, JOHN MURRAY B. 5/19/04, Lucknow, Ont. Forward. Played 11 seasons with N.Y. Rangers, then served as hockey coach at Yale for 27 years, retiring 5/17/65. Started with Rangers in 1926, leaving league in 1937.

NHL record: 84 goals, 108 assists in 508 games; 9 goals, 12 assists in 55 playoff games.

MURPHY, ROBERT RONALD (Ron) B. 4/10/33, Hamilton, Ont. Forward. Played 18 seasons in NHL, from 1952 to 1970. Started as junior with London Nationals, moved up to N.Y. Rangers in 1952, went to Chi. Black Hawks in 1957, to Det. Red Wings in 1964, and to Bos. Bruins in mid-1965–66, retiring from Bruins' organization in 1970 after playing most of last two years with Springfield. Accepted job as coach of Kitchener Rangers on retirement, but resigned post 4/11/72.

NHL record: 205 goals, 274 assists in 890 games; 7 goals, 9 assists in 53 playoff games.

NANNE, LOUIS VINCENT (Lou) B. 6/2/41, Sault Ste. Marie, Ont. Forward. 6', 180. Minn. North Stars' right wing, a naturalized U.S. citizen. Captained U.S. Olympic team in Grenoble in 1968 after playing at U. of Minnesota. Played briefly with North Stars in 1967–68, then at Memphis and Cleveland before rejoining North Stars in 1968–69. Lives in Edina, Minn., in off-season, and has worked at Minneapolis printing plant.

NHL record: 46 goals, 92 assists in 337 games; 4 goals, 14 assists in 30 playoff games.

NEILSON, JAMES ANTHONY (Jim; Chief) B. 11/28/40, Big River, Sask. Defenseman. 6'2", 205. Spent one year in minors before joining N.Y. Rangers in 1962, only NHL club with which he ever has played. Started as junior with Prince Albert Mintos, spent 1961–62 with Kitchener of EPHL. Had elbow surgery in spring of 1968. Suffered burns on hands 1/7/70 saving daughter, who was five at time, from fire in home of him and his wife Donna on Long Island, N.Y.

NHL record: 56 goals, 231 assists in 738 league games; 1 goal, 16 assists in 53 playoff games.

NELSON, FRANCIS B. (date unknown). D. April 1932. Hall of Fame builder. Former sports editor of *Toronto Globe*. Served as vice president of Ontario Hockey Assn. from 1903–05, and later was life member of Canada AAU. Also known for work in horse racing.

NESTERENKO, ERIC PAUL B. 10/31/33, Flin Flon, Man. Forward. 6'2", 197. Played 20 years in NHL, 16 with Chi. Black Hawks, retiring after 1971–72 Known as outstanding defensive forward and penalty killer, and for his "intellectual" approach to game. Studied engineering at U. of Toronto, played as amateur for Toronto Marlboros. Started with Tor. Maple Leafs in 1952–53, but in 1955–56 was farmed out to Winnipeg. Sold to Hawks 5/21/56 with goalie Harry Lumley, and considered quitting hockey to concentrate on studies. Hawks' official Tommy Ivan talked him into playing for Chicago on weekends, commuting from classes in Toronto. Played full schedule next season, having only 20-goal season of career. Sometimes bothered by nervous rash. Coached squad in practice 3/14/72 when Coach Billy Reay was absent, prompting one Hawk to remark: "I'd rather have Reay. Eric worked our butts off." Tried unsuccessfully to make it as pro football player with Toronto Argonauts. Lives in Evanston, Ill. and spends time as after-dinner speaker in off-season.

NHL record: 250 goals, 324 assists in 1219 games; 13 goals, 24 assists in 124 playoff games.

NEVIN, ROBERT FRANK (Bob) B. 3/18/38, South Porcupine, Ont. Forward. 6', 190. Minn. North Stars' right wing turned pro in Tor. Maple Leaf organization, and played at Rochester and Chicoutimi before making big club in 1960. Sent to N.Y. Rangers in 1963. Became captain of N.Y. team, but earned enmity of fans, who are credited with forcing trade 5/27/71 to Stars for Bobby Rousseau. Scored 200th goal on birthday in 1970. Wears contact lenses, saying his vision without them is "very poor." Lives in Toronto.

NHL record: 243 goals, 306 assists in 893 games; 13 goals, 17 assists in 67 playoff games.

NIGHBOR, FRANK B. 1893, Pembroke, Ont. D. 4/13/66, Pembroke, Ont. Forward. Hall of Famer was ironman with Ottawa Senators from 1917 to 1929, ending playing career with Tor. Maple Leafs in last half of 1929. Turned pro with Toronto in 1913, then played season at Vancouver, helping to win Stanley Cup, then joined Ottawa. Won Hart MVP Trophy in 1924 and Lady Byng Trophy in 1925 and 1926.

NHL record: 136 goals, 60 assists in 13 seasons; 10 goals, 8 assists in 9 playoff series.

NOBLE, EDWARD REGINALD (Reg) B. 6/23/95, Collingwood, Ont. D. 1/19/62, Alliston, Ont. Defenseman-forward. Hall of Famer played his way from Collingwood Business College team to 16 seasons in NHL as left wing and defenseman. Played junior and senior hockey, then joined Toronto pro team in 1916. When club folded part way through season, he was sent to Mont. Canadiens, but ruled ineligible for playoffs. Joined Toronto Arenas in first year of NHL, 1917, scoring 28 goals in 20 games as Arenas won 1918 Stanley Cup. stayed with Toronto through name change to St. Pat's, traded to Mont. Maroons in 1924, traded to Det. in 1927, and finished NHL career with Maroons in 1932–33. Retired as player after two years in International League with Cleveland. Refereed in NHL for two years.

NHL record: 167 goals, 79 assists in 16 seasons; 2 goals, 3 assists in 8 playoff series.

NOLET, SIMON LAURENT   B. 11/23/41, St. Odilon, Que. Forward. 5'9", 185. Phila. Flyer right wing played senior amateur hockey in Sherbrooke, played briefly at Quebec Aces in 1961–62 and 1964–65, joined them as pro for good in 1965. Stayed four years, getting brief appearances with Flyers, and winning AHL scoring title in 1967–68 with 96 points. Made Flyers in 1969–70 by scoring 22 goals and 22 assists in 56 games, slumped to 9 goals and 19 assists next year, but rebounded with 23 goals in 1951–72.

NHL record: 74 goals, 91 assists in 306 games; 5 goals, 2 assists in 16 playoff games.

NORRIS, BRUCE A.   B. 2/19/24, Chicago, Ill. Hall of Fame builder. With father and brother helped hockey succeed in Detroit. President of Norris Grain Co., Norris also assumed presidency of Red Wings and Olympia Stadium in 1945, succeeding sister. Lives in Libertyville, Ill., where raises Herefords on 500-acre ranch.

NORRIS, JAMES   B. 12/10/79, St. Catharines, Ont. D. 12/4/52. Hall of Fame builder spent youth in Montreal. Played for Montreal Victorias as well as excelling at squash and tennis. Made fortune as grainbroker and bought Chicago Shamrocks of AHL in 1930. Bought Detroit Olympia in 1933 and changed name of team from Falcons to Red Wings. Struggling team went on to win Stanley Cup in 1936, 1937, and 1943. Family raised eyebrows by at one time owning interest in Chi. Black Hawks, Det. Red Wings and N.Y. Rangers when league had only six teams.

NORRIS, JAMES D.   B. 11/6/06, Chicago, Ill. D. 2/25/66, Chicago, Ill. Hall of Fame builder was co-owner of Chi. Black Hawks from 1946 until death. Inherited grain fortune from father, James Norris. Started in NHL in partnership with dad in 1933 in ownership of Red

Wings and Detroit Olympia. In 1946 joined with Arthur Wirtz to buy Hawks, bringing them from cellar to Stanley Cup in 1961. Had holdings in horse racing and operated International Boxing Club from 1949–58, latter enterprise running him afoul of Congress on charges of monopoly and hoodlum infiltration of boxing. Of sports holdings, Norris once said: "I'd rather win the Stanley Cup than the Kentucky Derby."

NORTHEY, WILLIAM M.   B. 4/29/72, Leeds, Que. D. 4/9/63. Hall of Fame builder. In 1908, at his urging, Sir Montagu Allan presented Allan Cup as symbol of senior amateur championship. Served as president of Montreal AAA and with Canada Amateur Hockey Assn. Helped to supervise building of Montreal Forum.

O'BRIEN, DENNIS FRANCIS B. 6/10/49, Port Hope, Ont. Defenseman. 6', 195. Minn. North Star defenseman kept up his average in his rookie NHL year (1971–72) by registering 106 penalty minutes in 70 games. Played in Ontario Hockey Assn. turned pro with Waterloo, Iowa, in 1969, getting 331 penalty minutes in 72 games. Added 100 in 27 games next season at Cleveland before moving up to Stars at end of 1970–71 season. One of nine children, lives in Port Hope.

NHL record: 9 goals, 19 assists in 171 games; 1 goal, 1 assist in 23 playoff games.

O'BRIEN, JOHN AMBROSE B. 5/27/85, Renfrew, Ont. D. 4/25/68, Ottawa, Ont. Hall of Fame builder. Helped develop hockey in early years. Played amateur hockey. When hometown of Renfrew was rejected for membership in Eastern Canada Assn. O'Brien, angered, organized NHA, financing four clubs, among them Jack Laviolette's Mont. Canadiens.

O'CONNOR, HERBERT WILLIAM (Buddy) B. 6/21/16, Montreal, Que. Forward. Played for Mont. Canadiens and N.Y. Rangers, spending 10 seasons in NHL and becoming first man in history to win Hart and Lady Byng trophies in same season. Started with Montreal Royals seniors, joined Canadiens in 1941, traded to Rangers before start of 1947–48 season, going on to win the Hart and Lady Byng that year on 24 goals and 36 assists. Remained with Rangers until leaving NHL at end of 1950–51 season. Weighing just 143, center was one of lightest players in NHL. After quitting as player, coached for awhile at Cincinnati Mohawks of IHL, resigning 8/12/53.

NHL record: 140 goals, 257 assists in 509 games; 15 goals, 21 assists in 53 playoff games.

OLIVER, HAROLD (Harry) B. 10/26/98, Selkirk, Man. Forward. Hall of Famer played through junior and senior hockey in Selkirk, then in WHL with Calgary as forward in 1920. Stayed there until league was sold in 1926, scoring 91 goals and 49 assists. Joined Bos. Bruins of NHL in 1926, going to N.Y. Americans in 1934, and retiring from NHL in 1937. Weighing only 155, never spent more than 24 minutes in penalty box in any one season.

NHL record: 127 goals, 85 assists in 11 seasons; 10 goals, 6 assists in 7 playoff series.

OLIVER, MURRAY CLIFFORD B. 11/14/37, Hamilton, Ont. Forward. 5'9", 170. Minn. North Stars' veteran has been in NHL since 1959. Voted MVP in Ontario Hockey Association in 1958. Turned pro with Edmonton in WHL in 1958–59, going to Det. Red Wings in 1959–60. Sent to Bos. Bruins in 1960, and to Tor. Maple Leafs in 1967. Leafs traded him to North Stars 5/31/70 for "future considerations." Played Class D baseball in Cleveland system with Batavia, N.Y., but gave up game at request of Red Wings. Signed three-year pact with North Stars in 1972. Lives in Port Credit, Ont., and sells mutual funds in off-season.

NHL record: 227 goals, 388 assists in 894 games; 9 goals, 12 assists in 29 playoff games.

OLMSTEAD, MURRAY BERT B. 9/4/26, Sceptre, Sask. Forward. Played 13 full seasons in NHL, serving briefly as playing coach of Tor. Maple Leafs, then began full-time coaching career. Played as junior with Moose Jaw Canucks. Played at Kansas City, nine games with Chi. Black Hawks in 1948–49. Returned to Chicago in 1949–50. Sent to Milwaukee next season, to Montreal in mid-1950–51, to Leafs in 1958–59. Member of Leafs' coaching staff while still a player in 1959. Retired as player in 1962. Named personnel director by N.Y. Rangers in 1964, and coached Vancouver of WHL for two seasons before being named coach by Calif. Seals in 1967. Held job for a season. Also coached senior hockey near two farms he worked near Calgary. Named coach of Mount Royal Junior College 5/13/70, but quit in 1971, expressing disgust at attitude of youngsters. In 1958 was involved in altercation in Vancouver in which he was sentenced to six months in prison for assault, but penalty was reduced on appeal to $1000 fine.

NHL record: 181 goals, 421 assists in 848 games; 16 goals, 42 assists in 115 playoff games.

O'REE, WILLIAM ELDON (Willie) B. 10/15/35, Fredericton, N.B. Forward. 5'10", 175. First black to play in NHL, appeared in two seasons for Bos. Bruins. Played as junior for Kitchener-Waterloo Canucks, turned pro with Quebec of QHL in 1956, scoring 22 goals in 68 games. Appeared in two games with Bruins in 1957–58, and in 43 in 1960–61 before drifting back to minors. Went to West Coast after leaving NHL, with six seasons at Los Angeles of WHL, then to San Diego Gulls. Reported that he had no racial troubles in NHL, but has been called names from time to time during his minor league career.

NHL record: 4 goals, 10 assists in 45 games.

ORR, ROBERT GORDON (Bobby) B. 3/20/48, Parry Sound, Ont. Defenseman. 5'11", 185. Joined Bos. Bruins in 1966–67. Referred to as "Our Moses" by teammate in becoming highest scoring defenseman in history of game. Played as junior with Oshawa Generals. Won Calder Trophy as Rookie of Year and has won trophies every year since, picking up Norris Trophy as top defenseman each year since 1968, Hart MVP Trophy in 1970, 1971, and 1972. Scored record-breaking 102 assists in 1970–71 as he finished second in league scoring, finishing second again in 1971–72. Named Canada's outstanding athlete in 1970. Team Canada 1972. Had assistance of lawyer Alan Eagleson in negotiating first NHL contract at age of 18, for two years at $75,000, and in summer of 1968 signed three-year pact for reputed $400,000. Affects observers in different ways; by some described as shy and accommodating, by others as having moments of temper and arrogance. Knee surgury before 1972–73 season; apparently successful. Operates summer sports camp outside Toronto with teammate Mike Walton.

NHL record: 181 goals, 432 assists in 467 games; 21 goals, 47 assists in 55 playoff games.

O'SHEA, DANIEL PATRICK (Danny) B. 6/15/45, Toronto, Ont. Forward. 6'1", 190. Played junior hockey at Oshawa, Ont., and then joined Canadian National team in 1968 Olympics. Signed by Minn. North Stars 6/25/68, although Mont. Canadiens originally had rights to him. Traded to Chi. Black Hawks 2/24/71 in Doug Mohns deal. Went to St. L. Blues 2/8/72 for Chris Bordeleau. Brother Kevin also on Blues.

NHL record: 64 goals, 105 assists in 370 games; 3 goals, 7 assists in 39 playoff games.

O'SHEA, KEVIN WILLIAM B. 5/28/47, Toronto, Ont. Forward. 6'2", 205. Blues' right wing, was sent to St. L. on waivers 3/4/72 by Buffalo

Sabres. Played at St. Lawrence U. and with Canadian Nationals with brother Danny, also a St. L. Blue. Turned pro in 1969–70 with San Diego in WHL, then moved up to Buffalo next season.

NHL record: 13 goals, 18 assists in 135 games; 2 goals, 1 assist in 12 playoff games.

PAIEMENT, JOSEPH WILFRID ROSAIRE   B. 8/12/45, Haileybury, Ont. Forward. 5'11", 170. Ex-Van. Canucks' right wing is a 100-minute man in the penalty box. Totaled 152 in 1970–71 with Canucks, but career high was at Quebec in 1969–70, where he spent 242 minutes in penalty box. Says he has had run-ins with all the tough ones and come out all right. Played briefly in first pro season with Phila. Flyers, and had two more brief trials with Phila. from 1967–70 while playing mostly for Quebec. Drafted 6/10/70 by Canucks in expansion. In first regular NHL season, led Canucks in goals with 34 in 78 games. Jumped to Chi. Cougars of WHA 1972–73. Spends summers working for father's construction company.

NHL record: 48 goals, 52 assists in 190 games; 3 goals, no assists in 3 playoff games.

PAPPIN, JAMES JOSEPH   B. 9/10/39, Sudbury, Ont. Forward. 6'1", 190. Went to Chi. Black Hawks 5/23/68 from Tor. Maple leafs in wake of battle with then coach Punch Imlach. Played at Sudbury and at Rochester before being called up to Maple Leafs in 1963. Bounced between Rochester and Leafs until 1967–68, when he defied Imlach and refused to report to minors, calling it "disciplinary action." Traded to Hawks for Pierre Pilote. Suffered severe facial paralysis in summer of 1970. Outstanding golfer in off-season.

NHL record: 202 goals, 206 assists in 562 games; 30 goals, 26 assists in 75 playoff games.

PARENT, BERNARD MARCEL (Bernie) B. 4/3/45, Montreal, Que. Goalie. 5'11", 180. While with Tor. Maple Leafs shared time with veteran Jacques Plante. Signed five-year contract with Phila. Blazers of World Hockey Association 6/3/72, for reported $700,000. Played as junior with Niagara Falls and turned pro with Bos. Bruins in 1965. Played 51 2/3 games at Boston over two years, but was on Oklahoma City roster when drafted by Phila. Flyers in 1967 expansion. Went to Leafs 2/1/71 in three-team deal involving Boston, which sent Bruce Gamble to Flyers. Idolized Plante as youngster in Montreal. Sometimes feisty, as evidenced by fistfight he had with Flyer trainer 4/13/68, during playoffs.

NHL record: allowed 840 goals in 310 games for 2.84 average, 15 shutouts; gave up 42 goals in 16 playoff games for 2.49 average, no shutouts.

PARISE, JEAN-PAUL B. 12/11/41, Smooth Rock Falls, Ont. Forward. 5'9", 175. Minn. North Star left wing turned pro at Kingston in 1962, played at Minneapolis, Oklahoma City, and Rochester in minors as well as with Bos. Bruins and Tor. Maple Leafs (1 game) in NHL. Went to Stars 12/26/67 in seven-man deal. Team Canada 1972. With Bill Goldsworthy, was one of players fined in 1966 at Oklahoma City for cursing officals. Teaches in North Stars' hockey school in off-season, and lives in Bloomington, Minn.

NHL record: 116 goals, 183 assists in 437 games; 11 goals, 13 assists in 45 playoff games.

PARK, DOUGLAS BRADFORD (Brad) B. 7/6/48, Toronto, Ont. Defenseman. 6', 190. Put in part of one season in minors, then joined N.Y. Rangers in 1968 and has been All-Star selection since. Played for Toronto Marlboros. Drafted by Rangers June 1966; had believed he was bound for Tor. Maple Leafs. Sent to Buffalo of AHL in 1968, played 17 games there before moving up to N.Y. Participated in bitter contract fight in Sept. 1970, along with several teammates, and was suspended until resolved. First All-Star team in 1969–70, 1971–72. Team Canada 1972.

NHL record: 55 goals, 178 assists in 309 games; 7 goals, 20 assists in 48 playoff games.

PATRICK, FRANK A. B. 12/21/85, Ottawa, Ont. D. 6/29/60. Hall of Fame builder never played in NHL, but joined with brother Lester in pioneering hockey in western Canada. Refereed in Montreal at early age, then went west to join Lester as defenseman with Renfrew Millionaires.

Brothers built first artificial ice arenas in Canada, and Frank became president of PCL when it was formed in 1911. Sold league in 1926. Became coach of Bos. Bruins in 1934–35 and 1935–36, was GM of Mont. Canadiens, and served as managing director of NHL. Credited with 22 rules now in use in NHL, including the blue line rule. Succumbed to heart attack.

PATRICK, LESTER B. 12/30/83, Drummondville, Que. D. 6/1/60, Victoria, B.C. Hall of Famer for whom Lester Patrick Trophy for outstanding service to hockey was named. Started as defenseman at Brandon, Man., in 1903, played at Westmount, Que., then joined Montreal Wanderers 1905–06. Played on two Stanley Cup winners. Moving to West Coast, Patrick and brother Frank played for Renfrew Millionaires, formed Pacific Coast Hockey League, and Lester operated the Victoria club, which won world championship in 1912–13. Patrick became manager of N.Y. Rangers in 1926 after selling Pacific Coast League. Won three Stanley Cups, 1927–28, 1932–33, 1939–40. Developed first major farm systerm as executive, also is credited with Frank with originating playoff system. Only NHL playing experience was one game at goal in 1927–28 playoffs.

PELYK, MICHAEL JOSEPH (Mike) B. 9/29/47, Toronto, Ont. Defenseman. 6'1", 188. Turned pro with year of junior eligibility remaining, and spent just part of year in minors before making Tor. Maple Leafs. Helped Toronto Marlboros to Memorial Cup in 1967, turned pro next season, playing 47 games at Tulsa before being called up to Leafs. Picked up 146 minutes in penalties next season, but managed to cut down after that. Fined $400 for helping to start major brawl 4/8/71 in N.Y. Studied for bachelor's degree at U. of Toronto, and always has lived in Toronto.

NHL record: 13 goals, 56 assists in 316 games; no goals, no assists in 15 playoff games.

PERREAULT, GILBERT B. 11/13/50, Victoriaville, Que. Forward. 6', 195. Buffalo Sabres' center dreamed from boyhood of replacing Jean Beliveau with Mont. Canadiens. When time came he went to expansion Buffalo. There he won Calder Trophy as Rookie of Year in 1970–71 by scoring 38 goals and 34 assists in 78 games, then league record for rookie. Team Canada 1972. Before turning pro, twice led Junior Canadiens to Memorial Cup. After first season, town of Victoriaville held day for him—attended by Beliveau.

NHL record: 92 goals, 142 assists in 232 games; 3 goals, 7 assists in 6 playoff games.

PHILLIPS, THOMAS (Neil) B. 5/22/80, Kenora, Ont. D. 1923. Toronto Hall of Famer played for McGill U. and Montreal AAA, as well as for Toronto Marlboros, then returned to Kenora in 1905 to captain Thistles, including team that won 1907 Stanley Cup. Literature-quoting observers of time when he played describe him as greatest player they ever saw.

PICKARD, ALLAN W. B. (date unknown) Exeter, Ont. Hall of Fame builder was pioneer in amateur hockey in western Canada. Moved west to organize Regina YMCA League in 1920s, served as president of Regina Aces senior team, and was named president of Saskatchewan Amateur Hockey Assn. in 1941. Also served as president of Western Canada Senior League, governor of Saskatchewan Junior League and Western Canada Junior League. Was president of Canadian Amateur Hockey Assn. from 1947 through 1950. Lives in Exeter.

PIKE, ALFRED B. 9/15/17, Winnipeg, Man. Forward. Played six seasons in NHL as center, then went on to checkered career in coaching, including most of two seasons with N.Y. Rangers. Played with Winnipeg Monarchs as they won Memorial Cup, then New York Rovers, and turned pro with Phila. before joining Rangers in 1939, staying until 1947 with two seasons out during World War II. Took over coaching duties of Guelph juniors, and once pulled players off ice in dispute with officials. Also coached Calgary Stampeders, and 11/12/59 was hired to coach Rangers, lasting until 3/24/61. Took over as coach of L.A. Blades in WHL, then moved to Phoenix.

NHL record: 42 goals, 77 assists in 234 games; 4 goals, 2 assists in 21 playoff games.

PILOTE, PIERRE PAUL B. 12/11/31, Kenogami, Que. Defenseman. Played 14 NHL seasons, 13 with Chi. Black Hawks and last with Tor. Maple Leafs, from 1955 to 1969. Won the Norris Trophy three times and consistently ranked as one of league's top men on defense. Moved through amateur ranks to St. Catharines TeePees. Was playing with Buffalo when discovered by Hawks, who bought franchise, although not exclusively to get Pilote, as sometimes is asserted. Now lives in Toronto and coaches amateurs.

NHL record: 80 goals, 418 assists in 890 games, 8 goals, 53 assists in 86 playoff games.

PINDER, ALLEN GERALD (Gerry) B. 9/15/48, Saskatoon, Sask. Forward. 5'8", 165. Has had stormy career, both as amateur and pro. Played with Canadian National team that faced Russians 14 times.

Walked out on team after dispute with general manager. Joined Chi. Black Hawks in 1969–70, playing two seasons and getting 32 goals and 38 assists in 149 games. Left team in fury during 1971 playoffs, claiming coach Billy Reay "shafted me" and "lied to me." Later apologized and returned, but was traded to Calif. Seals 9/9/71 for goalie Gary Smith. Jumped to Cleve. Crusaders of WHA for 1972–73. Played boyhood hockey in Saskatoon, where he recalls "playing in four leagues at the same time."

NHL record: 55 goals, 69 assists in 223 games; no goals, 4 assists in 17 playoff games.

PITRE, DIDIER (Pit) B. 1884, Sault Ste. Marie, Ont. D. 7/29/34. Forward. Hall of Famer joined with Jack Laviolette to earn for Canadiens the nickname "Flying Frenchmen," which has stuck to present day. Played in Federal Amateur Hockey League and International Pro League, then with Shamrocks in 1908, going to Pacific Coast next year with Edmonton. Joined Canadiens when they were formed in 1909, and except for 1913 season in Vancouver, remained in Montreal until retiring in 1923. Credited with 240 goals in 282 games.

NHL record: 64 goals, 17 assists in 127 games; 2 goals, 2 assists in 2 playoff series.

PLAGER, BARCLAY GRAHAM B. 3/26/41, Kirkland Lake, Ont. Defenseman. 5'11", 175. Eldest of three brothers once on St. L. Blues. Played as junior at Peterborough, Ont., turned pro in 1961–62 at Hull-Ottawa, played at Pittsburgh, Edmonton, Omaha, three years at Springfield, at Omaha again and at Buffalo before making Blues in 1967. Arrived in St. Louis as result of three-way deal, which sent him first to N.Y. Rangers in summer of 1967, then on to Blues 11/29/67 with Red Berenson in exchange for Ron Stewart and Ron Attwell. Named outstanding defenseman in CPHL in 1964 at Omaha, coming up with 208 penalty minutes. In five NHL seasons never has had less than 100 penalty minutes. Wears mask to protect nose, which has been broken more than 10 times.

NHL record: 34 goals, 134 assists in 400 games; 3 goals, 19 assists in 65 playoff games.

PLAGER, ROBERT BRYAN (Bob) B. 3/11/43, Kirkland Lake, Ont. Defenseman. 5'11", 195. One of three brothers once on St. L. Blues. Played as junior with Guelph Royals, in minors at Kitchener-Waterloo, Baltimore, St. Paul, Vancouver, Minnesota, and Kansas City, as well as part of three seasons with N.Y. Rangers before making Blues in 1967–68, coming over in four-man deal for Rod Seiling 6/6/67. Ranked by NHL coaches as one of two hardest-checking defensemen in league. Bobby Baun is other. Team cutup, once snipped ties of mates.

NHL record: 12 goals, 85 assists in 375 games; 2 goals, 17 assists in 65 playoff games.

PLAGER, WILLIAM RONALD (Bill) B. 7/6/45, Kirkland Lake, Ont. Defenseman. 5'9", 175. Youngest of three Plager brothers. Turned pro in 1966 with Houston in Mont. Canadiens' organization, played next year at Memphis and Minn. North Stars after trade 6/6/67, then returned to minors at Kansas City in Blues' organization, after bouncing to N.Y. Rangers and then to Blues in three-way deal. Split time among Blues, K.C., and Buffalo of AHL over next two seasons. Finally made it with Blues in 1971–72. Atlanta 1972–73.

NHL record: 4 goals, 31 assists in 235 games; no goals, 2 assists in 31 playoff games.

PLANTE, JOSEPH JACQUES (Omer) B. 1/17/29, Shawinigan Falls, Que. Goalie. 6', 175. Began NHL career in 1952–53 with Mont. Canadiens, and still was winning All-Star berths in 1970s with Tor. Maple Leafs, although in his 40s. Credits longevity to use of face mask, which he introduced into widespread use in NHL. Played with Montreal Royals' senior team in Quebec League in early 50s, then turned pro and played most of first two seasons at Buffalo of AHL. Made Canadiens in 1954, staying nine years before being traded to N.Y. Rangers 6/4/63 in seven-man deal. Sent to Baltimore for 17 games in 1964–65. Retired. Lured back in 1968 by expansion St. L. Blues, who kept him two seasons, then traded to Leafs 5/25/70 for "future considerations." Traded to Bos. Bruins 3/3/73 by Leafs for draft choice. Mask has been integral part of career. Began wearing it on full-time basis 11/1/59 after nose was broken in nets in N.Y.; he refused to return to ice without it. Got idea for face protection from welder's mask which fan sent him, and now has factory which manufactures face guards in Magog, Que. Overcame asthma to make it in NHL. One of instigators of rules limiting curved sticks, pointing out that shots off hooked blade can be lethal to goalies. Won seven Vezina Trophies, including five straight while at Montreal, getting seventh in comeback year at St. Louis. Won Hart MVP Trophy in 1962. After 1972–73 season, signed 10-year contract to coach, be GM of Quebec Nordiques.

NHL record: allowed 1965 goals in 837 games for 2.33 average, 82 shutouts; gave up 240 goals in 112 playoff games for 2.14 average, 14 shutouts.

PLEAU, LAWRENCE WILSON (Larry) B. 1/29/47, Lynn, Mass. Forward. 6'1", 190. Mont. Canadien left wing put in first nearly full season in NHL in 1971–72 with 55 games, then signed three-year contract with World Hockey Assn. 4/19/72 to play for New England Whalers. Played as amateur for Jersey Devils of EHL, turned pro in 1969 with Montreal of AHL, called up at end of season.

NHL record: 9 goals, 15 assists in 94 games; no goals, no assists in 4 playoff games.

POILE, NORMAN ROBERT (Bud) B. 2/10/24, Fort William, Ont. Forward. Ex-Van. Canucks' GM, served as player on five of teams in then six-team NHL from 1942 to 1950, with Tor. Maple Leafs, Chi. Black Hawks, Det. Red Wings, N.Y. Rangers and Bos. Bruins. After playing career took over as coach of Tulsa in USHL, and in 1952 became coach of Edmonton Flyers of WHL. Held manager-coach position until 1962, heading western Canada farm system for Red Wings. Took over as GM at San Francisco of WHL from 1962 to 1967, then headed Phila. Flyers in first expansion year. Left in 1969–70 to become GM at Vancouver, still in WHL, and remained when club joined NHL. Resigned 12/15/72 on doctor's orders.

NHL record: 107 goals, 122 assists in 311 games; 4 goals, 5 assists in 23 playoff games.

POLIS, GREGORY LINN (Greg) B. 8/8/50, Westlock, Alta. Forward, 6', 195. Pitt. Penguins' left wing bounced back from March 1971 bout with mononucleosis to score 30 goals in 1971–72, second full one with Pittsburgh after coming up from junior hockey. Scored 107 points in final junior year at Estevan, Sask., drafted by Penguins in first round. Picked for All-Star game in first season. Lives with wife in Dapp, Alta.

NHL record: 74 goals, 57 assists in 215 games; no goals, 2 assists in 4 playoff games.

POLLACK, SAM B. 12/15/25, Montreal, Que. Mont. Canadiens' GM directed club's farm system for 10 seasons, was named to GM post in 1964 after Frank Selke, Sr. stepped down. Played minor league hockey, then became coach of Junior Canadiens from 1947–53. Named GM of Hull-Ottawa when EPHL was formed in 1959, and held post until going to Canadiens.

POPIEL, POUL PETER B. 2/28/43, Sollested, Denmark. Defenseman. 5'8", 170. Started in Chi. Black Hawks' organization. Played minor league hockey at Buffalo, St. Louis, Hershey, and Springfield. Briefly with Bos. Bruins and L. A. Kings before making Det. Red Wings as regular in 1968–69. Got first NHL goal 1/15/69 in Montreal. Split next season between Wings and Cleveland, then was acquired by Vancouver. Jumped to Houston of WHA for 1972–73. Shared American League Rookie of Year honors in Buffalo in 1964. Canucks' coach Hal Laycoe says attitude makes up for physical shortcomings.

NHL record: 13 goals, 41 assists in 214 games; 1 goal, no assists in 4 playoff games.

POTVIN, JEAN RENE   B. 3/25/49, Ottawa, Ont. Defenseman. 5'11", 188. Went to Phila. Flyers from L.A. Kings eight-man deal 1/28/72 and played first full NHL campaign. Traded to N.Y. Islanders mid-1972–73. Started with Hull-Ottawa in OHA as junior and turned pro with Springfield in 1969–70, playing there two seasons after rejecting chance to join Mont. Canadiens' organization with Junior Canadiens. Holds blue belt in karate, starred in teenage baseball, and is better-than-average golfer. Wears helmet, fortunately, because he has questionable distinction of once having scored goal which went into net off back of head. Attends Ottawa U. in summer.

NHL record: 9 goals, 30 assists in 118 games.

PRATT, WALTER (Babe)   B. 1/7/16, Stony Mountain, Man. Defenseman. Hall of Famer had 26-year playing career. Played amateur in Winnipeg and Kenora, Ont., turning pro with Philadelphia before joining N.Y. Rangers in 1936. Traded to Tor. Maple Leafs in mid-1942–43, and finished NHL career with Bos. Bruins in 1946–47. Won Hart MVP Trophy in 1944. Expelled briefly from hockey 1/29/46 for gambling; on plea of Red Dutton, was reinstated 2/14/46. Played with Hershey, New Westminster, B.C., and Tacoma after leaving NHL. Serves as assistant to president of Van. Canucks.

NHL record: 83 goals, 209 assists in 517 games; 12 goals, 17 assists in 64 playoff games.

PRENTICE, DEAN SUTHERLAND   B. 10/5/32, Schumacher, Ont. Forward. 5'11", 180. Minn. North Stars' left wing passed 350-goal mark in 1971–72, his 20th in NHL. Went to Minnesota from Pitt. Penguins in 1970–71. Played junior hockey at Guelph in N.Y. Ranger organization, making Rangers in 1952, never played minor league hockey. Went to Bos. Bruins 2/4/63 in Don McKenney deal, then to Det. Red Wings 2/17/66 for Ron Murphy and Gary Doak. Claimed by Penguins in 1969. Threatens to retire from time to time, blaming long schedule and traveling. Broke back in 1964 when hauled down from behind on breakaway by Stan Mikita. Lives in Guelph, works in summer as hockey school director.

NHL record: 389 goals, 466 assists in 1354 league games; 13 goals, 17 assists in 54 playoff games.

PRIMEAU, A. JOSEPH (Joe) B. 1/29/06, Lindsay, Ont. Forward. Hall of Famer played eight seasons with Tor. Maple Leafs, but also was known as outstanding coach. Was a "late beginner," not learning to skate until he was 12. Turned pro in 1927 with Ravinias of Canadian Pro League and joined Maple Leafs next season sent to London, Ont., to finish season, but returned in 1929–30 to stay until retirement in 1936. Won Lady Byng Trophy in 1932. Coached Memorial and Allan Cup winners, and in 1951 coached Leafs to Stanley Cup. Now represents cement block manufacturer in Toronto and Islington, Ont.

NHL record: 66 goals, 177 assists in 8 seasons; 5 goals, 18 assists in 3 playoff series.

PRONOVOST, JOSEPH JEAN DENIS B. 12/18/45, Shawinigan Falls, Que. Forward. 5'11", 170. Pitt. Penguins' right wing is brother of Marcel Pronovost, former NHL defenseman. Played two seasons with Oklahoma City before joining Penguins in 1968 after being acquired from Boston when Bruins had plethora of good players. Lives in Beauharnois, Que., in off-season. Considered one of league's fastest skaters.

NHL record: 108 goals, 115 assists in 360 games; 4 goals, 5 assists in 14 playoff games.

PRONOVOST, RENE MARCEL B. 6/15/30, Lac la Tortue, Que. Defenseman. 6', 190. Played junior hockey for Windsor Spitfires. Turned pro 1949 with Omaha of USHL, went to Indianapolis next year, called up to Det. Red Wings 1950–51, stayed until traded 5/20/65 to Tor. Maple Leafs in eight-man deal. Left NHL during 1969–70 to coach and play for Tulsa in CHL; stayed until named coach of Chi. Cougars in WHA for 1972–73. Replaced at end of season when Cougars signed Pat Stapleton. Offered job elsewhere in Cougar organization. Seven-time All-Star.

NHL record: 88 goals, 257 assists in 1206 games; 8 goals, 23 assists in 134 playoff games.

PROVOST, CLAUDE B. 9/17/33, Montreal, Que. Forward. Mont, Canadiens' right wing retired in 1970 after 15 years in NHL, all with Canadiens. Played on nine Stanley Cup champs at Montreal, five in row beginning in 1955–56, his rookie year. Played for Junior Canadiens, turned pro in 1954–55 with 61 games at Shawinigan of QHL, then was called up to Canadiens in 1955–56. Offered bonus of $100 for every goal over 15 in 1961–62, and cashed in with 33, for $1800. Credited Jacques Plante with tipping him to use back hand. Charged by police along with Montreal coach Toe Blake with attacking fan with stick 11/19/67 in L.A., was acquitted 8/8/68. First winner of Bill Masterton Trophy for perseverance. Offered position of player and assistant coach with Montreal Voyageurs in 1970.

NHL record: 254 goals, 335 assists in 1005 games; 25 goals, 38 assists in 130 playoff games.

PULFORD, HARVEY B. 1875, Toronto, Ont. D. 10/31/40, Ottawa, Ont. Defenseman. Hall of Famer spent most of life in Ottawa. In addition to hockey, he starred in football, boxing, rowing, lacrosse, and squash, winning championship in all sports during career which lasted until he was almost 50. Was defenseman on Ottawa Silver Sevens from 1893 to 1908 as team won three Stanley Cups. Also starred with Ottawa squash Rough Riders in football and topped off career with Ottawa title in 1924.

PULFORD, ROBERT JESSE (Bob) B. 3/31/36, Newton Robinson, Ont. Forward. 5′11″, 188. L.A. Kings' center, passed 1000-game NHL mark in 1971. Was named coach of Kings for 1972–73 season, replacing Larry Regan, who continued in front office. Led Toronto Marlboros to Memorial Cup before turning pro in 1956 with Tor. Maple Leafs, spending 14 seasons in Toronto before being sent to L.A. for Brian Murphy and Garry Monahan 9/1/70. Hampered by knee injury next season. Studied at three colleges before finally getting degree from McMaster U. through night courses.

NHL record: 281 goals, 362 assists in 1079 games; 25 goals, 26 assists in 89 playoff games.

QUINN, JOHN BRIAN PATRICK (Pat)   B. 1/29/43, Hamilton, Ont. Defenseman. 6'3", 215. Atlanta Flames' player is considered one of league's roughest, but admits he needs work on awkward skating. Roughness attested to by incident 4/2/68, when he was playing for Tor. Maple Leafs—needed nine policemen to escort him to dressing room in Boston Garden after brawl with Bobby Orr. Turned pro in 1964 with Tulsa of CPHL, played with Memphis, Houston, and Seattle in minors, as well as parts of two seasons with Leafs before being drafted by Van. Canucks. Sent to Flames in expansion draft.

NHL record: 8 goals, 44 assists in 310 games; no goals, no assists in 4 playoff games.

RANKIN, FRANK B. 4/1/89, Stratford, Ont. Hall of Famer was outstanding player from 1906 to 1915, playing with Stratford, Eaton Athletic Assn. (Toronto), and Toronto St. Michael's. Later coached Toronto Granites to Olympic title in 1924 in France.

RATELLE, JOSEPH GILBERT YVON JEAN B. 10/3/40, St. Jean, Que. Forward. 6'1", 175. N.Y. Rangers' center. Boyhood pal of Rod Gilbert and came up to Rangers at about same time. Became first N.Y. player to score 100 points, with 109 in 1971–72. Played as junior with Guelph Royals. Turned pro with Rangers in 1961–62, playing half of season at Kitchener, then bounced between N.Y. and Baltimore until he made club to stay in 1964–65. Team Canada 1972. Participated in 1970 salary holdout, which resulted in temporary suspension. Won Masterton Trophy in 1971, and in 1972 won Lady Byng and was voted most valuable player in East Division. Broke ankle 2/1/72, damaging Rangers' playoff hopes. Like Gilbert, had spinal fusion operation, in 1966. Golf pro in off-season.

NHL record: 267 goals, 377 assists in 702 league games; 6 goals, 24 assists in 49 playoff games.

RAYMOND, SEN. DONAT B. 1/3/80, St. Stanislas de Kostka, Que. D. 6/5/63. Hall of Fame builder served as president of company that built Montreal Forum and formed Mont. Maroons and became chairman of board of company in 1955. During Depression this industrialist supported Canadiens financially, also holding posts as director of Canada Cement Co., Dominion Glass Co., and Canadian International Paper Co. Appointed senator in Dec., 1926.

RAYNER, CLAUDE EARL (Chuck) B. 8/11/20, Sutherland, Sask. Goalie. Hall of Famer. Played 10 NHL seasons, eight with N.Y. Rangers. Son of butcher. One of six children. Played juvenile hockey in Sutherland. Junior for Saskatoon Wesleys. Then with Kenora Thistles and Springfield Indians. Joined N.Y. Americans in 1940–41 for 12 games to replace injured Earl Robinson, and played 36 next year for Brooklyn before going into service with Royal Navy until 1945. On return was selected by Rangers and stayed until retirement in 1953, winning Hart MVP Trophy in 1950. Selected for three All-Star games.

NHL record: allowed 1295 goals in 425 league games for 3.05 average, 25 shutouts; gave up 46 goals in 118 playoff games for 2.56 average, 1 shutout.

REARDON, KENNETH JOSEPH B. 4/1/21, Winnipeg, Man. Defenseman. Hall of Famer did not limit his fighting to opponents, also taking on fans and officials. Moved to British Columbia at young age to live with uncle after parents died, playing junior hockey in Edmonton. Joined Mont. Canadiens in 1940, staying in Montreal until retirement in 1950, missing 1942–43, 1943–44, and 1944–45 while in service. Got Field Marshal Montgomery's Certificate of Merit while overseas. In 1950 was fined $1000 for threatening to give Cal Gardner 14 stitches, number Gardner had given him in altercation. Charged, along with teammate, as result of brawl with fans 11/2/49 in Chicago Stadium, which ended up with Reardon in jail. After retirement served Canadiens as vice president until quitting for "personal and business reasons" in May 1964. Lives in Westmount, Quebec.

NHL record: 26 goals, 96 assists in 341 games; 2 goals, 5 assists in 6 playoff series.

REAY, WILLIAM TULIP (Billy) B. 8/21/18, Winnipeg, Man. Forward. Chi. Black Hawks' mentor is dean of NHL coaches, serving since 1963. Reay was player-coach with Quebec Aces in Quebec Senior League in 1943–45, also playing two games with Det. Red Wings each season. Joined Mont. Canadiens as center in 1945. Retired as player 1953. Coached Victoria and Seattle in WHL after retirement; then Rochester in AHL before coaching Tor. Maple Leafs for one year (1957–58). Joined Hawks' organization next season, coaching Sault Ste. Marie in EPHL and Buffalo in AHL before moving up to Hawks in 1963. Lives in Chicago.

NHL record: 105 goals, 162 assists in 479 games; 13 goals, 16 assists in 63 playoff games.

REDMOND, MICHAEL EDWARD (Mickey) B. 12/27/47, Kirkland Lake, Ont. Forward. 5'11", 185. Det. Red Wing right wing scored 136 goals, averaging better than point a game, as junior with Peterborough Petes. Turned pro in 1967–68 in Mont. Canadiens' organization, starting at Houston in CPHL and joining Canadiens for 41 games in first pro season. Played two more years with Canadiens, getting 27 goals and 27 assists in 1969–70. Traded to Wings 1/13/71 as part of Frank Mahovlich deal. Team Canada 1972. Son of Ed Redmond, outstanding Canadian amateur star. Brother Dick is NHL defenseman. Lives in Peterborough, Ont., in off-season.

NHL record: 156 goals, 140 assists in 396 games; 2 goals, 3 assists in 16 playoff games.

REDMOND, RICHARD (Dick) B. 8/14/49, Kirkland Lake, Ont. Defenseman. 5'11", 170. Chi. Black Hawk player is known as attacker on defense. Brother of Mickey, he played amateur hockey with St. Catharines TeePees before turning pro with Minn. North Stars in 1969–70. Played at Waterloo (Iowa) and Cleveland, sent by Stars to Calif. Seals to complete Ted Hampson deal in 1970. To Hawks mid-1972–73.

NHL record: 24 goals, 74 assists in 177 games; 4 goals, 2 assists in 13 playoff games.

REID, ALLAN THOMAS (Tom) B. 6/24/46, Fort Erie, Ont. Defenseman. 6'1", 195. Now with Minn. North Stars. Played junior hockey at St. Catharines, turned pro at Dallas in Chi. Black Hawks' system in 1967, played two years for Hawks, sent to Minnesota 3/14/69 for Mike McMahon and Andre Boudrias. Played at Waterloo briefly next year, then made North Stars. Made mark in record book by scoring on penalty shot in 1971 against Ken Dryden of Canadiens, first penalty shot goal by defenseman in 4000 NHL games. Lives in Fort Erie, and is partner with brother in sporting goods store.

NHL record: 11 goals, 60 assists in 381 games; 1 goal, 13 assists in 40 playoff games.

RICHARD, HENRI B. 2/29/36, Montreal, Que. Forward. 5'7", 160. Allegedly went to Mont. Canadiens' training camp in 1955 to humor his older (by almost 15 years) brother Maurice, ended up making team, and has been with Canadiens ever since. Played for Junior Canadiens and one game with Montreal in QHL in 1952–53 before going to Canadiens' camp. Ended 17th season in 1971–72, serving as appointed captain, position his brother also held. Twice led league in assists. Remembered for remarks made during 1971 playoffs against Hawks in which he called coach Al MacNeil the worst coach he had ever played for, is credited with helping to get MacNeil fired although team made comeback to win Cup in seven games. Called "Pocket Rocket," partly after brother "Rocket" and partly due to small size.

NHL record: 336 goals, 642 assists in 1165 league games; 46 goals, 76 assists in 168 playoff games.

RICHARD, JOSEPH HENRI MAURICE (Rocket) B. 8/4/21, Montreal, Que. Forward. Hall of Famer played forward with Mont. Canadiens from 1942 to 1960 and was installed in Hall of Fame only nine months after retirement. On 12/28/44, scored eight points—three goals and five assists—after having spent day moving furniture. Career was marred by injuries, including broken ankle in first season after he joined Canadiens from junior and senior play around Montreal. Playing career was ended by slashed Achilles tendon. Often involved in fights, was suspended in 1955 playoffs for hitting linesman. Suspension started riot in Montreal Forum which resulted in game being forfeited. However, was hailed by NHL president Clarence Campbell as "completely dedicated." Opponents called him "terrifying." Still lives in Montreal, has several business interests, including fishing equipment sales. Coach, Quebec, WHA; resigned 10/18/72 because of "nervous condition."

NHL record: 544 goals, 421 assists in 978 games; 82 games, 44 assists in 133 playoff games.

RICHARDSON, GEORGE B. 1880s, Kingston, Ont. D. 2/9/16, France, while commanding company in Canadian army in World War I. Hall of Famer. Never turned professional. Played for Queen's U., which won amateur title in 1909, and for 14th Regiment in Kingston.

ROBERTO, PHILLIP B. 1/1/49, Niagara Falls, Ont. Forward. 6'1", 190. St. L. Blues' center, was acquired 12/13/71 from Mont. Canadiens in trade in which St. Louis gave up Jim Roberts, team captain. Played as junior with Niagara Falls Flyers, joined Canadiens in 1969–70 for eight games, then spent rest of season and part of next with Montreal Voyageurs of AHL, playing 39 games with Canadiens in 1970–71. Involved in brawl with fans and police in Jan. 1972, in Philadelphia Spectrum in which coach Al Arbour and other players were charged with assault and battery on police officers. Cleared of criminal charges later.

NHL record: 49 goals, 45 assists in 200 league games; 9 goals, 8 assists in 31 playoff games.

ROBERTS, DR. GORDON B. 9/5/91. D. 9/2/66. Hall of Famer scored 203 goals in 166 professional games, at same time getting medical degree at McGill University. Played for Ottawa in 1910, then with Montreal Wanderers until 1916, when he graduated. Practiced medicine in Vancouver after 1916, playing with Vancouver Millionaires, scoring 43 goals in 23 games in PCL in 1917 for league record. Played one year in Seattle, then ended playing career in Vancouver 1920.

ROBERTS, JAMES WILFRED (Jim) B. 4/9/40, Toronto, Ont. Defenseman-forward. 5'10", 185. Started 1971–72 season as St. L. Blues' captain but was traded 12/31/71 to Mont. Canadiens for Phil Roberto. Played as junior at Peterborough, turned pro in 1960 with Montreal Royals, played two seasons at Hull-Ottawa, then at Omaha, Cleveland, and Quebec before making Canadiens in 1964. Stayed in Montreal until 6/6/67, when Blues grabbed him in expansion draft. Considered handy-man in hockey, has played all positions but goal, and there has been speculation he would try that if asked.

    NHL record: 91 goals, 133 assists in 666 games; 12 goals, 13 assists in 109 playoff games.

ROBERTSON, JOHN ROSS B. ca. 1850. D. 1918. Hall of Fame builder. Newspaperman and philanthropist who served six years as president of Ontario Hockey Assn., beginning in 1898. Donated three trophies for amateur hockey. Operator of *Toronto Telegram* and founder of Hospital for Sick Children in Toronto, he turned down knighthood.

ROBINSON, CLAUDE C. B. 12/17/81, Wellington, Ont. Hall of Fame builder. First secretary of Canadian Amateur Hockey Assn. when it was organized in 1914. Later made life member. Played and was executive with Winnipeg Victorias, which won both Allan and Stanley cups. Managed Canadian team in 1932 Olympics. Lives in Vancouver.

ROBITAILLE, MICHAEL JAMES DAVID (Mike) B. 2/12/48, Midland, Ont. Defenseman, 5'11" 195. Acquired by Buffalo Sabres when Det. Red Wings got into severe goaltending trouble and sent him to Buffalo in exchange for Joe Daley. Broke in with Omaha of CHL, then next season played four games with N.Y. Rangers, but made mark in CHL where he won best defenseman award with Omaha. Joined Rangers at beginning of 1970–71, but was traded to Det. Red Wings as Rangers sought veterans to beef up their Stanley Cup bid.

    NHL record: 11 goals, 36 assists in 134 games; no goals, no assists in 6 playoff games.

ROCHEFORT, LEON JOSEPH FERNAND B. 5/4/39, Cap de la Madeleine. Que. Forward. 6', 175. Ex-Det. Red Wing right wing started career in 1959 with Three Rivers of EPHL. Played in Kitchener-Waterloo, Baltimore, and Quebec as well as with N.Y. Rangers, Mont. Canadiens, Phila. Flyers and L.A. Kings before he joined Wings. Played junior hockey with Guelph Biltmores before turning pro. Career has been marked by abrasion at times. In Oct. 1968 left Flyers briefly as result of contract fight, and arrival in Detroit in 1971 was prompted by sharp words with Montreal coach Al MacNeil during Cup playoffs while he was Canadien. Rochefort then was dealt to Wings 5/25 for minor leaguer Kerry Ketter and cash. Lives in off-season with wife and family in Cap de la Madeleine. To Atlanta Flames mid-1972–73.

NHL record: 93 goals, 121 assists in 477 games; 4 goals, 2 assists in 34 playoff games.

RODDEN, MICHAEL J. (Mike) B. 4/24/91, Mattawa, Ont. Was named to Hall of Fame in 1962 as referee. Played hockey for Queen's U., Haileybury, and Toronto St. Pats, and coached college hockey. He also guided 27 championship football teams during coaching career. Rodden officiated 2864 hockey games, with 1187 of them in the NHL. After leaving college he joined sports staff of *Toronto Globe*, became sports editor in 1928. In 1944 he became sports editor of *Kingston Whig Standard*, retiring in 1959. Still writes column for Kingston paper.

ROLFE, DALE B. 4/30/40, Timmins, Ont. Defenseman. 6'4", 205. N.Y. Rangers' player one of biggest men in NHL. Played as junior with Barrie Flyers, and eight seasons in minors before making majors. Turned pro at Portland of WHL in 1960, then two seasons later spent year at Hershey. Joined Springfield Indians in 1963, staying 4 years, and was involved in 1966 players' strike against owner-coach Eddie Shore after he and two other players were suspended for "indifferent play." In 1967 ran second in voting for AHL's top defenseman. Made L.A. Kings in 1968, and in 1969 was fined $500 as result of fight with Bill Hicke of Oakland. Peddled to Det. Red Wings in mid-1969–70 after Jack Kent Cooke called him troublemaker, then to Rangers 3/3/71 for Jim Krulicki.

NHL record: 21 goals, 105 assists in 419 games; 4 goals, 16 assists in 52 playoff games.

ROMNES, ELWIN N. (Doc) B. 1/1/09, White Bear, Minn. Forward. Played 10 years in NHL, eight with Chi. Black Hawks. Got nickname because he studied premed at St. Thomas (Minn.) College before pursuing hockey career. Moved at early age to Togo, Minn., where father was mayor, justice of peace, and general municipal official. Began organized hockey in Copper Country League, spent three years at St. Paul, joined Hawks in 1930, stayed until being traded to Tor. Maple Leafs in Dec. 1938, for Bill Thoms, and finished career in 1939–40 with N.Y. Americans. Threatened to quit after trade to Toronto, but was given $1000 to soothe feelings. Won Lady Byng Trophy in 1936, serving just three minor penalties. Coached Michigan School of Mines from 1939–45, then took over as Kansas City coach. Hired by U. of Minnesota as hockey coach 6/11/47, resigned in May 1952 after blast at Minnesota athletic director Ike Armstrong. Accepted post in recreation department of Broadmoor Hotel in Colorado.

NHL record: 68 goals, 136 assists in 10 seasons; 7 goals, 18 assists in 7 playoff series.

ROSS, ARTHUR HOWIE (Art)   B. 1/13/86, Naughton, Ont. D. 8/5/64, Boston. Defenseman. Hall of Famer. Although a good player, made mark as innovator and promoter. Played for 14 years with Brandon, Man., Kenora, Ont., Montreal Wanderers, and Ottawa, as well as minor teams, scoring 85 goals in 167 games. Credited with bringing hockey permanently to Boston, coaching Bruins to three Stanley Cups; also refereed, and managed Hamilton Tigers. Invented type of nets and puck in use in NHL and in 1947 presented Art Ross Trophy to league to be awarded to leading scorer.

ROUSSEAU, JOSEPH JEAN-PAUL ROBERT (Bobby)   B. 7/26/40, Montreal, Que. Forward. 5'10", 178. Now with N.Y. Rangers. Plays either right wing or center, wearing helmet. Played for Junior Canadiens. Turned pro at Hull-Ottawa in 1960–61. Came up to Mont. Canadiens at end of season. Didn't leave until 1970, winning Calder Trophy as Rookie of Year in 1961–62 and finishing second in points in 1966. Sent to Minnesota 6/11/70 for Claude Larose, managed only four goals for North Stars. Peddled to Rangers May 1971 for Bob Nevin. On 2/1/64, scored five goals for Canadiens against Red Wings. Got 200th goal 3/25/70 in Montreal. Plays pro golf in off-season, and won 1971 players' tournament from Dale Tallon in sudden-death playoff.

NHL record: 233 goals, 415 assists in 862 games; 26 goals, 49 assists in 116 games.

RUPP, DUANE EDWARD FRANKLIN   B. 3/29/38, MacNutt, Sask. Defenseman. 6'1", 195. Pitt. Penguins' veteran turned pro in 1960 after playing for two Canadian junior champions. Played at Kitchener-Waterloo, Springfield, Vancouver, Baltimore, Rochester, and Cleveland in minors as well as briefly with N.Y. Rangers, Tor. Maple Leafs and

Minn. North Stars before going to Penguins in 1969 trade for Leo Boivin. Operates sporting goods store in Pittsburgh.

NHL record: 24 goals, 93 assists in 374 games; 2 goals, 2 assists in 10 playoff games.

RUSSELL, BLAIR B. 9/17/80. D. 12/7/61, Montreal, Que. Forward. Hall of Famer refused offers to play professional hockey, spending entire career with Montreal Victorias of Eastern Canada Amateur Hockey Assn. Scored 110 goals in 67 games, scoring seven in one game in 1904. Refused an offer from Wanderers in 1909 when amateur league became professional and retired.

RUSSELL, ERNEST (Ernie) B. 10/21/83, Montreal, Que. D. 2/23/63, Montreal, Que. Forward. Hall of Famer. Weighed just 140 lbs., spending most of career with Montreal Wanderers as center or rover. Excelled at football as captain of Montreal AAA team, which won junior championship. Joined Wanderers in 1905 and team won Stanley Cup 1905–08, 10. He won Eastern Canada League scoring championship in 1906–07 and 1911–12.

RUTTAN, J. D. (Jack) B. 4/5/89, Winnipeg, Man. Hall of Famer made name largely in college hockey, both as player and coach. Played for St. John's College team, which won title in Manitoba University Hockey League; Manitoba Varsity team; and Winnipeg Hockey Club. In 1919–20 coached Winnipeg seniors, and coached U. of Manitoba team in 1923. Lives in Charleswood, Man.

SABOURIN, GARY BRUCE (Gaye) B. 12/4/43, Parry Sound, Ont. Forward. 5'11", 180. St. L. Blues' right wing played as junior at Kitchener, brought up through N.Y. Rangers' organization, played in minors at St. Paul, Minnesota, Omaha, and Kansas City. Traded 6/6/67 to Blues in four-player deal for Rod Seiling. Made club that season. Scored two goals in 16 seconds 3/11/70 against North Stars. Suspended for six games 11/27/69 for stick duel with Montreal's John Ferguson. Broke leg 3/5/71; came back to score 28 goals in 1971–72.

NHL record: 129 goals, 108 assists in 409 games; 19 goals, 11 assists in 62 playoff games.

ST. MARSEILLE, FRANCIS LEO (Frank) B. 12/14/39, Levack, Ont. Forward. 5'11", 170. St. L. Blues' right wing played as amateur with Port Huron Flags of International League for four seasons, averaging 40 goals a year, then turned pro in 1967–68, playing 11 games for Kansas City before moving up to Blues in that season. Wears helmet.

NHL record: 93 goals, 175 assists in 432 games; 19 goals, 24 goals in 62 playoff games.

SALOMON, SIDNEY, JR. B. 4/20/10, New York, N.Y. President and chairman of St. Louis Blues is insurance executive who once was executive vice president of old St. Louis Browns baseball team. Onetime sports writer for now defunct *St. Louis Times*. Lives in Frontenac, Mo., and Florida. Founder of Miami Marlins' nine in International League.

153

SANDERSON, DEREK MICHAEL   B. 6/16/46, Niagara Falls, Ont. Forward. 6', 170. Bos. Bruin center jumped to Phila. Blazers of World Hockey Assn. for 1972–73 season, signing $2,500,000 pact, but played little because of injury. In Jan. 1973 Blazers settled contract for $1,000,000 and released him. He then returned to Bruins at higher salary than before. Has been own man through pro career, writing book, appearing in movies and on TV panel shows, wearing bristling mustache and claiming he likes to play dirty hockey. Played for Niagara Falls Flyers as junior, and played just two minor league games before joining Bruins in 1967–68, winning Calder Trophy as Rookie of Year. Had only one NHL season with less than 100 penalty minutes, and piled up 146 in 1968–69. Associated with Joe Namath in Boston version of Bachelor's III saloon. Appeared in X-rated movie *Laughing and Loving*; had his part deleted after movie became hit in Montreal. Hospitalized with colitis 4/4/72. Has aided state of Massachusetts with drug addiction program.

NHL record: 127 goals, 147 assists in 360 games; 17 goals, 12 assists in 50 playoff games.

SATHER, GLEN CAMERON   B. 9/2/43, High River, Alta. Forward, 5'11", 175. N.Y. Rangers' left wing, made deal with Red Wings when he turned pro in 1964 that they would pay for his college education, but never did play for his benefactors. Played as junior with Edmonton Oil Kings, joined Memphis in 1964, then moved up in Bos. Bruins organization to Oklahoma City, spending two years there, then two years with Bruins before being drafted by Pitt. Penguins in June 1969. Went to Rangers in Jan. 1971 for Syl Apps, Jr. Runs hockey school at Banff, Alta., in off-season and exercises by skiing and mountain climbing.

NHL record: 50 goals, 64 assists in 452 games; no goals, 4 assists in 61 playoff games.

SAVARD, SERGE A.   B. 1/22/46, Montreal, Que. Defenseman. 6'2", 200. Has been hampered by injuries in NHL career with Mont. Canadiens, which began in 1967, including two broken legs and gash suffered saving coach Scotty Bowman from a fire. Played with Junior Canadiens, then went to Houston in Central League in 1966, winning Rookie of Year award. Joined Canadiens next season. Won Smythe Trophy as outstanding player of 1969 playoffs, then broke leg next season. Had bone graft in 1971, but broke leg again during 1971–72 season, getting into only 23 games. Also suffered four-inch gash above right ankle 3/10/72 when he kicked in window to help rescue Bowman, who was trapped by fire on ledge of St. Louis hotel in which team was staying. Team Canada 1972.

NHL record: 35 goals, 105 assists in 341 games; 9 goals, 14 assists in 43 games.

SAWCHUK, TERRANCE GORDON (Terry)   B. 12/28/29, Winnipeg, Man. D. 5/31/70, Mineola, N.Y., of injuries suffered in scuffle with N.Y. Ranger teammate Ron Stewart. Goalie. Hall of Famer had checkered career that ended in tragedy. Won Rookie of Year award in three leagues—USHL, American, and NHL. Broke into NHL in 1949 with Det. Red Wings. Bos. Bruins 1955 to 1957. Detroit through 1964. Played two seasons with Tor. Maple Leafs and one with L.A. Kings. Rejoined Red Wings in 1968. Finished career with Rangers in 1969–70. Played more than 20 seasons. In 1952 Stanley Cup allowed only five goals, with four shutouts, as Wings won Cup in eight games. Won Vezina Trophy three times and shared it once. Made first All-Stars three times and second team four. Tormented by attacks of nerves throughout career; prompted several premature retirements.

NHL record: allowed 2401 goals in 956 games for a 2.50 average, 103 shutouts; gave up 267 goals in 102 games for 2.63 average, 12 shutouts.

SCANLAN, FRED   B. ca. 1880. Forward. Hall of Famer is credited by Frank Selke with being member of forward line, also including Harry Trihey and Arthur Farrell, which originated combination passing plays. Scanlan joined Montreal Shamrocks in 1897 and stayed with team until 1901, when he shifted to Winnipeg Victorias, retiring in 1903.

SCHELLA, JOHN EDWARD   B. 5/9/47, Port Arthur, Ont. Defenseman. 6', 180. Van. Canucks kept him on roster in 1971–72 largely because of early injury to Gary Doak, then he went on to play 77 games after Doak was traded to N.Y. Rangers. In first full NHL season, scored two goals and 13 assists. Used as penalty killer. Jumped to Houston Aeros of WHA for 1972–73. Played three seasons with Ft. William Canadiens (1963–66), then with Peterborough in Ontario Hockey Assn. before joining Houston of CPHL, going on to Denver of WHL and Rochester of AHL in minor league travels.

NHL record: 2 goals, 18 assists in 115 games.

SCHINKEL, KENNETH (Ken)   B. 11/27/32, Jansen, Sask. Forward. 5'10", 172. Pitt. Penguins' right wing turned pro in 1953 with Springfield, also playing at Syracuse that season. Sat out 1954–55, but returned to spend four years with Springfield before making NHL with N.Y. Rangers in 1959–60. Stayed with Rangers for two seasons, then went to Baltimore until joining Penguins in 1967 draft. Broke collarbone 12/30/70 in Montreal, missing most of second half of that season. Lives with family in Fonthill, Ont. Named Penguin coach Jan. 1973.

NHL record: 127 goals, 198 assists in 636 games; 7 goals, 2 assists in 19 playoff games.

SCHMAUTZ, ROBERT JAMES (Bob)   B. 3/28/45, Saskatoon, Sask. Forward. 5'9", 155. Van. Canucks' right wing had tough assignment in first full NHL season, 1968–69 with Chi. Black Hawks as one of replacements for injured Bobby Hull. Turned pro in 1964–65 with L.A. in WHL. Was on L.A. roster three seasons, then moved to Dallas, then to Hawks in 1967–68, winning one playoff game for Chicago with goal in N.Y. 4/14/68. Played 68 games for Hawks next season, then went to Seattle in 1969–70 and most of 1970–71. Bud Poile, on scouting trip to see two other players, decided to acquire Schmautz from minor league club, and Schmautz scored 10 points at end of season for Canucks. Got 12 goals and 13 assists in 60 games in 1971–72 for coach Hal Laycoe, who also coached his brothers Cliff and Arnie at Portland.

NHL record: 67 goals, 60 assists in 239 games; 2 goals, 3 assists in 11 playoff games.

SCHMIDT, MILTON CONRAD (Milt)   B. 3/5/18, Kitchener, Ont. Forward. Now executive director of Bos. Bruins. Played way into Hall of Fame with Bruins as member of Kraut Line with Woody Dumart and Bobby Bauer. With Bruins from 1936 through 1955, when he became their coach. Later became GM. Missed three seasons serving in RCAF during World War II. Played amateur hockey with London Juniors, then briefly with Providence before joining Bruins. From 1938 to 1941 Bruins won four NHL titles and Stanley Cup in 1939. Schmidt led league in scoring in 1939–40. Won Hart MVP Trophy in 1951–52. Was first All-Star three times and second once.

NHL record: 229 goals, 346 assists in 16 seasons; 24 goals, 25 assists in 86 playoff games.

SCHOCK, RONALD LAWRENCE (Ron)   B. 12/19/43, Chapleau, Ont. Forward. 5'10", 165. Pitt. Penguins' center turned pro in Bos. Bruins' organization in 1963, making club in 1966–67 after play at San Francisco. Sent to St. L. Blues next season, then to Penguins in 1969. His 1968–69 season was marred when he was involved in Dec. auto crash near St. Louis in which two persons were killed. Lives with wife and children in Niagara Falls, Ont.

NHL record: 90 goals, 179 assists in 552 games; 4 goals, 10 assists in 38 playoff games.

SCHRINER, DAVID (Sweeney)   B. 11/30/11, Calgary, Alta. Forward.

Hall of Famer played amateur hockey in hometown and turned pro with Syracuse in 1933. Joined N.Y. Americans next year, staying there until going to Tor. Maple Leafs in 1939, ending career in 1946 after sitting out the 1943–44 season. Won scoring championship in 1935–36 and 1936–37. Rookie of Year in 1935. Named to first All-Stars once and second All-Stars once. Lives in Calgary.

NHL record: 201 goals, 204 assists in 11 seasons; 18 goals, 11 assists in 57 playoff games.

SEIBERT, EARL WALTER   B. 12/7/11, Kitchener, Ont. Defenseman. Hall of Famer is son of Oliver L. Seibert, also in Hall of Fame. Won prizes in skating carnivals, turned pro in 1929 with Springfield Indians. Joined N.Y. Rangers in 1931, traded to Chi. Black Hawks in 1935–36 season, then to Det. Red Wings in 1944–45, where he finished career in 1946. Named All-Star 10 straight years, making first team four times. Lives in Agawam, Mass.

NHL record: 89 goals, 187 assists in 15 seasons; 11 goals, 8 assists in 66 playoff games.

SEIBERT, OLIVER L.   B. 3/18/81, Berlin, Ont. D 5/15/44. Hall of Famer once won match race on skates against a trotting horse. After playing for Berlin Rangers of Western Ontario Hockey Assn. for six years, turned pro with Houghton, Mich. Also played with London and Guelph. Son Earl also made Hall of Fame.

SEILING, RODNEY ALBERT (Rod)   B. 11/14/44, Elmira, Ont. Defenseman. 6', 180, N.Y. Rangers' player is former Olympian. Played with Toronto Marlboros, who loaned him to Canadian Olympic team in 1964. Traded into N.Y. Ranger organization in Feb. 1964 with Bob Nevin, Dick Duff, Arnie Brown, and Bill Collins for Andy Bathgate and Don McKenney. Made club next season, though he spent 46 games in Baltimore in 1966–67. Taken by St. L. Blues in 1967 draft. Rangers immediately traded four players to get him back. Team Canada 1972.

NHL record: 43 goals, 175 assists in 580 games; 4 goals, 5 assists in 41 playoff games.

SELKE, FRANK, JR.   B. 9/7/29, Toronto, Ont. Ex-GM of Calif. Seals, son of veteran Montreal exec Frank Selke, Sr. Advanced from maintenance man to front office without ever playing as pro. Started with Canadiens' rink crew in Oct. 1946, moved into PR department and became director. Named VP for sales and promotion for club in 1964, and in 1967 was named president of Seals. Named GM on sale of club in 1968. Handled microphone for seven years with Montreal TV crew, and served two years as radio commentator. Resigned as GM fall 1970.

SELKE, FRANK J. B. 5/7/93, Kitchener, Ont. Hall of Fame builder. Became manager of team in hometown before he was 14, and went on to Toronto where he helped Conn Smythe build Tor. Maple Leafs, leaving in 1946 as asst. GM to become GM of Mont. Canadiens. Held position until retiring in 1964, guiding team to six Stanley Cups. Lives near Montreal, is member of Hall of Fame governing committee.

SELWOOD, BRADLEY WAYNE (Brad) B. 3/18/48, Leamington, Ont. Defenseman. 6'1", 186. Played full year in NHL with Tor. Maple Leafs in 1971–72, then 5/5/72 signed three-year contract with New England Whalers of World Hockey Assn. Played as junior with Niagara Falls Flyers. Turned pro in 1968, playing season at Tulsa, then another at Vancouver. Started 1970–71 at Tulsa, but was called up to play 28 games with Toronto and added 72 more in 1971–72.

NHL record: 6 goals, 27 assists in 100 games; no goals, no assists in 5 playoff games.

SHACK, EDWARD STEVEN PHILLIP (Eddie) B. 2/11/37, Sudbury, Ont. Forward, 6'1", 195. Pitt. Penguins' right wing, broke in with Providence of AHL in 1957 after early career as butcher, in whose union he still holds card. Only other minor league experience was briefly with Springfield in 1959–60 and Rochester in 1965–66. Played two seasons with N.Y. Rangers (1958–60), seven with Tor. Maple Leafs (1960–1961 to 1967), two with Bos. Bruins (1967–69), and in 1969–70 with L.A. Kings before joining Buffalo Sabres. Traded to Penguins 3/4/72. Nicknamed "Entertainer" for style of skating in which he admits he often doesn't know which way he will go. Also admits to semiilliteracy, saying his children "passed him in school." Estimated salary—$35,000 annually, anyway.

NHL record: 230 goals, 217 assists in 962 games; 5 goals, 7 assists in 70 playoff games.

SHEEHAN, ROBERT RICHARD (Bob) B. 1/11/49, Weymouth, Mass. Forward. 5'7", 155. Calif. Seals' center, until he jumped to N.Y. Raiders of WHA for 1972–73. Product of Mont. Canadiens' organization, which he joined after amateur play at St. Catharines, getting 44 goals and 41 assists. Played briefly with Canadiens from 1969 to 1971, but spent most of time with Montreal Voyageurs of AHL before moving to Seals.

NHL record: 28 goals, 32 assists in 123 games; no goals, no assists in 6 playoff games.

SHERO, FREDERICK ALEXANDER B. 10/23/25, Winnipeg, Man. Defenseman-coach of Phila. Flyers, played three years for Rangers (1947–50). Made mark as coach, starting in 1957 with Shawinigan of Quebec League, leaving hockey for the 1958–59 season, then returning to coach St. Paul (1959–65), Minnesota of CPHL (1965–66), Omaha in next season, Buffalo of AHL (1967–70) and Omaha of CHL in 1970–71. Has coached six first-place winners and six playoff champions.

NHL record: 6 goals, 14 assists in 145 games; no goals, 2 assists in 13 playoff games.

SHMYR, PAUL B. 1/18/46, Cudworth, Sask. Defenseman. 5'11", 170. Calif. Seals' defenseman was part of controversial deal involving Chi. Black Hawks and goalie Gary Smith, which finally was consummated just before 1971–72 season began. Stayed that one season with Seals, then jumped to Cleve. Crusaders of WHA for 1972–73. Turned pro in 1966–67 with Vancouver of WHL after amateur play with Fort Wayne Komets, and played for Dallas and Portland in minors as well as Hawks.

NHL record: 8 goals, 37 assists in 153 games; no goals, no assists in 16 playoff games.

SHORE, EDWARD WILLIAM (Eddie) B. 11/25/02, Fort Qu' Appelle, Sask. Defenseman. Hall of Famer was known for explosive temper which created problems even after career ended. Played amateur hockey and turned pro in Western Canada League with Regina, then played with Edmonton. Started 14-year NHL career with Bos. Bruins 1926, remained with Boston until mid-season of 1939–40 when he went to N.Y. Americans. Won Hart MVP Trophy 1933, 35, 36, 38. First All-Star seven times, second All-Star once. Career marred Dec. 1933 when shoulder block on Ace Bailey, Tor. Maple Leaf star, injured Toronto player so seriously he never played hockey again. After retiring as player, Shore entered management level. In 1967, Springfield (Mass.) Indians struck rather than play for owner-coach Shore, and he sold club, though retaining Springfield Arena.

NHL record: 105 goals, 179 assists in 14 seasons; 6 goals, 13 assists in 11 playoff series.

SIEBERT, ALBERT C. (Babe) B. 1/14/04, Plattsville, Ont. D. 8/25/39, St. Joseph, Ont. Defenseman-forward. Hall of Famer. Played minor hockey in Zurich, Ont., for Kitchener in OHA junior league, for Niagara Falls seniors. Joined Mont. Maroons of NHL in 1925 to begin 14-year career. N.Y. Rangers 1932–33. To Bos. Bruins middle of next season. Finally Mont. Canadiens 1936–39. Started as left winger, later became defenseman, winning Hart MVP Trophy in 1937. First All-Stars three straight years. Drowned at height of career.

NHL record: 140 goals, 156 assists in 14 seasons; 8 goals, 7 assists in 54 playoff games.

SINDEN, HARRY   B. 9/14/32, Collins Bay, Ont. Rejoined Bos. Bruins' organization 10/5/72 when he was named managing director, with Milt Schmidt moving up to executive director. Had left as team's coach in 1970 in money dispute after winning Stanley Cup. Played five years in Ontario Hockey Assn. seniors, including 1958 with world champ Whitby Dunlops-as defenseman. Also held job with General Motors. Turned pro at 28 after playing on Canada Olympic team. Coached in minors in EPHL and CPHL, then coached Oklahoma City Blazers to Jack Adams Trophy in 1966. Named Bruin coach 5/10/66, quit 5/14/70 to take job with home building firm after dispute with Boston management over money. Coached Team Canada to series victory over Russians in 1972.

SITTLER, DARRYL GLEN   B. 9/18/50, Kitchener, Ont. Forward. 6', 190. Tor. Maple Leafs' first pick in 1970 amateur draft. Played as junior with London Knights, getting 42 goals and 48 assists in last amateur season. Joined Leafs in 1970 with no minor league experience, playing 49 games and being out for 21/2 months with broken wrist. Hit stride in 1971–72, with 15 goals and 17 assists in 74 games.

NHL record: 54 goals, 73 assists in 199 games; 2 goals, 1 assist in 9 playoff games.

SLOAN, ALOYSIUS MARTIN (Tod)   B. 11/30/27, Vinton, Que. Forward. Played 12 years as NHL center, then regained amateur status, saying pro hockey was "no fun." Played as amateur at St. Michael's College in Tor. Maple Leafs' organization, went to Cleveland Barons, joined Leafs for 29 games in 1948–49, and made club on full-time basis next season. Stayed until summer of 1958, when he was sold to Chi. Black Hawks for $25,000. Played through 1961, then quit to play with Galt Terriers in world amateur tournament of 1962. Played in three All-Star games.

NHL record: 220 goals, 262 assists in 745 games; 9 goals, 12 assists in 47 playoff games.

SMEATON, J. COOPER   B. 1890, Carleton Place, Ont. Started as referee in NHA in 1913, and work in that field won him selection to Hall of Fame for referees. Grew up in Montreal, serving overseas in World War I, won Military Medal. Managed Philadelphia Quakers of NHL in 1930–31, but returned to refereeing when Quakers quit league next year. Named referee-in-chief of NHL and held post until retiring in 1937.

Appointed trustee of Stanley Cup in 1946 and still holds position.

SMITH, ALFRED B. 6/3/73, Ottawa, Ont. D. 8/21/53, Ottawa, Ont. Hall of Famer was instrumental in establishment of Senators in 1906 after breaking up of Silver Sevens. After early play in Ottawa he moved to Pittsburgh, then returned to Ottawa in 1905. Dropped out in 1899, but unretired in 1903. After establishment of Senators, Smith played with Kenora, then in 1907–08 with Ottawa, and finished playing career in 1908 in city league. Smith also coached Renfrew, Ottawa, Moncton and North Bay, as well as N.Y. Americans.

SMITH, ALLAN ROBERT (Al) B. 11/10/45, Toronto, Ont. Goalie. 6'1", 200. Now with New England Whalers of WHA after jumping from Det. Red Wings who had drafted him from Pitt. Penguins 6/8/71. Played one season of junior "A" competition with Toronto Marlboros of Ontario Hockey Association. Turned pro in Tor. Maple Leafs' organization in 1966, playing two games with big club. Played next season in Victoria of WHL, then moved to Tulsa, Rochester, and Baltimore before being drafted 6/11/69 by Penguins, where he stayed two seasons. Surprisingly warlike for goalie, he accumulated 47 penalty minutes in 1970–71, 23 in 1971–72. Posted $1000 bond with league headquarters in 1970–71 as guarantee to stay out of fights. In off-season, lives with wife and children in Lion's Head, Ont.

NHL record: allowed 415 goals in 145 games for 3.12 average, 8 shutouts; gave up 10 goals in 3 playoff games for 3.33 average, no shutouts.

SMITH, CLINTON JAMES (Snuffy) B. 12/12/13, Assiniboia, Sask. Forward. Played 11 years in NHL, seven with N.Y. Rangers and four with Chi. Black Hawks. Moved to Saskatoon in 1929, playing with Wesley juniors, where he was leading scorer. Turned pro with Rangers at 18, and was sent to Springfield in Canadian American League. When league folded, was sent to Saskatoon Crescents, then played with Vancouver for three years. Played with Philadelphia Ramblers for season, finally made Rangers in 1936. Sold to Hawks in 1943, and retired in 1947. Won Lady Byng Trophy in 1939 and 1944. After leaving NHL became playing coach of Tulsa Oilers in USHL, and was named league's MVP. Coached St. Paul of USHL for three seasons, and accompanied club when it was transferred to Cincinnati. Lives in Vancouver, where he has been active in British Columbia Benevolent Hockey Assn.

NHL record: 161 goals, 236 assists in 483 games; 10 goals, 14 assists in 44 playoff games.

SMITH, DALLAS EARL   B. 10/10/41, Hamiota, Man. Defenseman. 5'11", 180. Came up through Bos. Bruins' organization. Quiet. Spends summers on farm in Crandall, Man. Played as junior with Estevan Bruins. Graduated to Bruins in 1960. Stayed two seasons, then spent six years in minors with Hull-Ottawa, Pittsburgh, Portland, San Francisco, Oklahoma City. Split 1966–67 between Oklahoma City and Boston before making Bruins to stay in 1967–68.

NHL record: 36 goals, 162 assists in 570 games; no goals, 17 assists in 55 playoff games.

SMITH, FRANK D.   B. 6/1/94. D. 6/11/64. Hall of Fame builder was one of founders of Metropolitan Toronto Hockey League 12/29/11, and served as secretary from its beginning as Beaches Hockey League until resigning in 1962. Received gold stick of Ontario Hockey Assn. in 1947, and award of merit from city of Toronto in 1961.

SMITH, GARY EDWARD   B. 2/4/44, Ottawa, Ont. Goalie. 6'4", 215. As Chi. Black Hawks goalie shared in Vezina Cup with Tony Esposito in 1971–72. Contribution was 62 goals-allowed in 28 games, with 5 shutouts, for 2.41 average. Spotted by scout at age 13 and given scholarship to St. Michael's School in Toronto by Tor. Maple Leafs. Played for Toronto Marlboros, then with Rochester, Tulsa, Victoria, and very briefly for Maple Leafs (less than five games over two seasons) before being drafted by Oakland Seals (later Calif. Seals) 6/6/67. Stayed there four seasons, playing in 71 games in 1970–71, then was shipped to Hawks 9/9/71 in confused deal in which Gerry Desjardins went to Seals, was ruled unfit to play, and sent back. Hawks were allowed to keep Smith. Attack of nerves put him on back for two months in summer of 1971, and he smashed finger in Sept. before bouncing back to share in trophy. Father Des played with Bos. Bruins. Traded to Van. Canucks 5/17/73 with Jerry Korab for Dale Tallon.

NHL record: allowed 814 goals in 267 games for 3.06 average, 14 shutouts; gave up 44 goals in 15 playoff games for 3.14 average, 1 shutout.

SMITH, REGINALD JOSEPH (Hooley)   B. 1/7/05, Toronto, Ont. D. 8/24/63, Montreal, Que. Forward-defenseman. Hall of Famer had 17-year NHL career with four clubs. Nicknamed Hooley by father after Happy Hooligan cartoon character. Played amateur hockey in Toronto, including appearance with Toronto Granites in Olympics. Also was outstanding oarsman, Rugby player, and amateur boxer. Started in NHL with Ottawa Senators in 1924. Went to Mont. Maroons in 1927 for Punch Broadbent and $22,500. Stayed until 1936–37, going to Bos.

Bruins for one year, then was sold 11/4/37 to N.Y. Americans, where he ended career in 1940–41 season. Started out as left wing, but moved to center as career progressed. Also played defense.

NHL record: 200 goals, 215 assists in 17 seasons. 11 goals, 8 assists in 14 playoff series.

SMITH, RICHARD ALLAN (Rick) B. 6/29/48, Kingston, Ont. Defenseman. 5'11". 200. Was traded by Bos. Bruins 2/23/72 with Reggie Leach to Calif. Seals for Carol Vadnais. Played with Hamilton Red Wings as junior, turned pro in 1968 with Oklahoma City, came up to Bruins same year. Travels in off-season, having spent time in Barbados and Mexico, as well as extended visits to Europe. Attended Queens U. in Kingston. Lives in Kingston.

NHL record: 18 goals, 72 assists in 326 games; 1 goal, 3 assists in 29 playoff games.

SMYTHE, CONN B. 2/1/95, Toronto, Ont. Hall of Fame builder. Led amateur team to Ontario championship in 1915 and in 1928 Varsity team won Olympic hockey title. Assembled team for N.Y. Rangers that won 1928 Stanley Cup. Released before playoffs, he bought Toronto St. Pats, changing name to Maple Leafs. Was driving force behind building of Maple Leaf Gardens; served as managing director and president of Gardens; retired in 1961. Had paving business and horse-racing interests and served with Ontario Society for Crippled Children; also served in both world wars; resigned from Hall of Fame committee in June 1971 in anger over selection of Busher Jackson.

STACKHOUSE, RONALD LORNE (Ron) B. 8/26/49, Haliburton, Ont. Defenseman. 6'3", 185. Started 1971–72 season with Calif. Seals, but traded to Det. Red Wings. "There's one guy who hasn't let me down," said Seals' coach Fred Glover near end of 1970–71, Stackhouse's rookie season, and Stackhouse was on his way to Detroit 10/22/71 in deal for Tom Webster. Played amateur hockey with Peterborough Petes juniors, spent just one season in minors (with Providence of AHL and in playoff with Seattle of WHL) before moving up to Seals in 1970. Lives in West Guilford, Ont., in off-season.

NHL record: 19 goals, 81 assists in 235 games.

STANFIELD, FREDERIC WILLIAM (Fred) B. 5/4/44, Toronto, Ont. Forward. 5'10", 185. Bos. Bruins' center, was one of players shipped to Bruins by Chi. Black Hawks in Phil Esposito deal 5/15/67, after Hawks complained he was not aggressive enough. Played as junior with St. Catharines, joined Hawks in 1964. Sent down to St. Louis of CPHL in middle of next season, and still was there when traded to Bruins, where he became 20-goal and 50-assist man immediately. Lives in Wakefield, Mass., and has served as hockey school instructor in off-season.

NHL record: 145 goals, 286 assists in 555 games; 19 goals, 30 assists in 75 playoff games.

STANLEY, ALLAN HERBERT B. 3/1/26, Timmins, Ont. Defenseman. Spent 21 years in NHL from 1948 until retirement 9/24/69. Served in navy and played with Boston Olympic senior club. Sold by Bos. Bruins' organization to Providence 2/10/47 before joining N.Y. Rangers in 1948. Shipped to Vancouver in 1953–54, then went to Chi. Black Hawks in mid-1954–55. Hawks sold him to Bruins 10/14/56. Spent two seasons there before going to Tor. Maple Leafs in 1958 for Jim Morrison. Taken by Quebec 6/13/68, and was picked up by expansion Phila. Flyers in 1968, playing full 1968–69 season before retiring. Object of fans' wrath at various times during career. Ran unsuccessfully for parliament in 1957. After retirement started hockey school in Finelon Falls, Ont.

NHL record: 100 goals, 333 assists in 1244 games; 7 goals, 36 assists in 110 playoff games.

STANLEY, FREDERICK ARTHUR, 16th Earl of Derby B. 1/15/1841, England. D. 6/14/08, England. Hall of Fame builder. Governor-general of Canada from 1888–93, presented Stanley Cup (worth 10 pounds, or $48.67, at that time) in 1893, then returned to England before ever seeing a Cup game. Served in England as lord mayor of Liverpool and mayor of Preston after leaving Canada.

STANLEY, RUSSELL (Barney) B. 6/1/93, Paisley, Ont. Hall of Famer came up through amateurs to play 15 years as pro. As amateur was with Paisley and three Edmonton clubs from 1909–15, then joined Vancouver Millionaires who won Stanley Cup. Became amateur again in 1919 with Edmonton Eskimos, then pro with Calgary Tigers, where he also coached. Then went to Regina Capitals, played two years with Eskimos, and spent 1926–27 as player-coach with Winnipeg Maroons. In 1927–28 coached and managed Chi. Black Hawks, played next year with Minneapolis Millers, then coached Edmonton Pooler juniors for three years. Played every position except goalie. Lives in Edmonton.

STAPLETON, PATRICK JAMES B. 7/4/40, Sarnia, Ont. Defenseman. 5'8", 185. Ex-Chi. Black Hawks' veteran, played as junior with St. Catharines Hawks, then was spirited away and ended up in Bos. Bruins' organization. Played minor league hockey at Sault Ste. Marie. Went to Bruins in 1961–62. Split next season between Kingston and Bruins.

Played two seasons at Portland and was at St. Louis of CPHL when drafted by Hawks in 1965–66. Served as captain of Hawks during one season, only team captain ever elected by teammates. Injured ligaments in knee 2/7/70, putting him out for rest of season. In 1971 playoffs, sustained 50-stitch facial cut when struck by Montreal's Rejean Houle, but returned to play in next game. Team Canada 1972. Signed million-dollar five-year contract 7/24/73 to be player-coach of Chi. Cougars in WHA. Owns farm in western Ontario, on which he lives during off-season with wife and five children.

NHL record: 43 goals, 294 assists in 635 games; 10 goals, 39 assists in 65 playoff games.

STASIUK, VICTOR JOHN (Vic) B. 5/23/29, Lethbridge, Alta. Forward. 6′1″, 190. Played junior hockey for Edmonton-Wetaskiwin Canadiens in Chi. Black Hawk organization. Turned pro with Kansas City Pla-Mors of USHL in 1948. Went up to Hawks, traded next year to Det. Red Wings, sent to Bos. Bruins in 1955, played on Uke Line. Sent back to Wings in mid-1960–61. Left NHL as player after 1962–63 season. Coached and played in Detroit farm system for two years, then coached EHL Jersey City Devils and AHL Quebec Aces in Phila. Flyer system. Named AHL coach of year 1968. Moved up to coach Flyers in 1968–69; when fired two years later, moved to Calif. Golden Seals. Fired April 1972. Hired 5/2/72 by Van. Canucks. Fired 5/10/73 and replaced by Bill McCreary.

NHL record: 183 goals, 254 assists in 745 games; 16 goals, 18 assists in 69 playoff games.

STEMKOWSKI, PETER DAVID (Pete) B. 8/25/43, Winnipeg, Man. Forward. 6′1″, 205. Was acquired by N.Y. Rangers as result of front office feuding which made it impossible for him to stay with Det. Red Wings, where he had been successful. Played as junior for Toronto Marlboros. Rochester 1964–65, spending half season with Tor. Maple Leafs; made club next year. Went to Detroit 3/4/68, then to Rangers 10/31/70 for Larry Brown. Goal in triple overtime 4/29/71, playoffs against Black Hawks, ended longest game in Ranger history. Works summers as disc jockey.

NHL record: 129 goals, 210 assists in 596 games; 17 goals, 23 assists in 65 playoff games.

STEWART, JAMES GAYE B. 6/28/23, Fort William, Ont. Forward. Played nine seasons in NHL for five teams. Started with Toronto Marlboros seniors and Hershey. Came up with Tor. Maple Leafs in 1943, scoring 24 goals and 23 assists to win Calder Trophy as Rookie of Year.

Went to Chi. Black Hawks in 1947 in multiplayer deal that sent Max Bentley to Toronto. To Det. Red Wings in 1950 in nine-man trade. N.Y. Rangers next season. Finally to Mont. Canadiens in mid-1952–53, last season in league—got into only 23 games. Scored 37 goals in 1946 after return from service, and had 20-or-more years 1948–50.

NHL record: 185 goals, 159 assists in 502 games; 2 goals, 9 assists in 22 playoff games.

STEWART, JOHN SHERRATT (Black Jack) B. 5/6/17, Pilot Mound, Man. Defenseman. Hall of Famer played 12 years in NHL, with time out during World War II. Ten seasons were with Det. Red Wings (1938–39 to 1949–50), last two with Chi. Black Hawks (1950–52). Played junior hockey in Portage la Prairie, then signed with Wings, who sent him to Pittsburgh in 1938, recalling him same season. Known for hard hitting and not infrequent fighting, coached in Ontario, and Pittsburgh of AHL until retiring from hockey in 1963. Lives in Detroit, where he is connected with horse racing.

NHL record: 31 goals, 84 assists in 566 games; 5 goals, 14 assists in 80 playoff games.

STEWART, NELSON ROBERT (Old Poison) B. 12/29/02, Montreal, Que. D. 8/21/57, Toronto, Ont. Forward. Hall of Famer played 15 seasons in NHL. First man to score more than 300 goals, moved to Toronto as boy and played first amateur hockey there. Joined Mont. Maroons of NHL in 1925, was traded to Bos. Bruins in 1932 and then to N.Y. Americans in 1935. In next season played for both Americans and Bruins before finishing career with Americans in 1940. Won Hart MVP Trophy in 1926 and 1930, and played with Stanley Cup winner in 1925–26. Member of Maroons' famed "S" line with Babe Siebert and Hooley Smith.

NHL record: 324 goals, 191 assists in 15 seasons; 15 goals, 11 assists in 12 playoff series.

STEWART, RONALD GEORGE (Ron) B. 7/11/32, Calgary, Alta. Defenseman-forward. 6'1", 197. Ex-N.Y. Ranger veteran made quick turnaround to Van. Canucks and back to N. Y. during 1971–72 season. Involved in scuffle with Terry Sawchuck in May 1970 in New York home which two shared and as result Sawchuck died of internal injuries. Stewart was absolved of blame by investigating officials, and served as honorary pallbearer at Sawchuck's funeral. Played as junior with Barrie Flyers, made Tor. Maple Leafs in 1952 and stayed there for 13 seasons. Traded to Bos. Bruins 6/8/65 for Pat Stapleton, Orland Kurtenbach, and Andy Hebenton, spent two seasons there, grabbed by St. L. Blues in

1967 and sent to Rangers in mid-1967–68. Sent to Vancouver to begin 1971–72 campaign, then bought back by N.Y. 3/6/72. NHL player for more than 20 years. To N.Y. Islanders mid-1972–73.

NHL record: 276 goals, 253 assists in 1353 games; 14 goals, 21 assists in 119 playoff games.

STOREY, ROY ALVIN (Red) B. 1918, Barrie, Ont. Hall of Fame referee starred as football player and was football and lacrosse referee in addition to nine-year career as NHL official. Scored three touchdowns in one game to lead Toronto Aurgonauts to Grey Cup victory in 1938. Joined NHL officiating staff in 1951 and remained until 4/11/59, when he quit. Leaving was marked by blast at NHL president Clarence Campbell, who, Storey said, refused to back league officials. Storey especially angered by furor touched off by call he made in Stanley Cup game in Chicago which resulted in near riot among fans. Lives in Montreal and works in public relations for distillery, also serving as vice president of Montreal Old Times hockey team, which plays benefits for charitable groups. Is referee-in-chief at all team's games.

STUART, BRUCE B. 1882, Ottawa, Ont. D. 10/28/61, Ottawa, Ont. Hall of Famer played in 45 scheduled games during career, scoring 63 goals, six of them in one game. Started with Silver Seven in 1898, then played with Quebec Bulldogs. In 1901 he rejoined Ottawa, then played for Pittsburgh, Houghton, Mich., and Portage Lakes in International League. Played with Montreal Wanderers, then returned to Ottawa with Senators, where team won Stanley Cup in 1909 and 1911. Wanderers also won Cup in 1908.

STUART, HORACE HODGSON (Hod) B. 1880, Ottawa, Ont. D. 6/23/07, Belleville, Ont. in drowning accident. Defenseman. Hall of Famer started with Silver Seven in 1898, then joined Quebec Bulldogs and in 1901 joined Calumet of International League. Left team in 1906 when he refused to take ice at Sault Ste. Marie, Mich., in dispute over referee he disliked. Joined Wanderers in time to regain Stanley Cup from Kenora in March 1907. During 33 games in recorded career, scored 16 goals.

SULLIVAN, GEORGE JAMES (Red) B. 12/24/29, Peterborough, Ont. Forward. Now head scout for Bos. Bruins, played junior hockey with St. Catharines TeePees. Broke into NHL with Bruins in 1949–50, then shuttled to Hershey Bears of AHL, playing with Bruins in 1951–52 and 1952–53. In 1953–54 set league scoring record with Hershey, and was sold to Chi. Black Hawks for $25,000. Played two years with Hawks, then went to N.Y. Rangers in 1956, retiring in 1961. Coached Baltimore Clippers for season, then became coach of Rangers in 1962–63, being fired in 12/5/65 and replaced by Emile Francis.

NHL record: 107 goals, 239 assists in 557 games; 1 goal, 2 assists in 18 playoff games.

SUTHERLAND, CAPT. JAMES T.   B. late 1880s, Kingston, Ont. D. 9/30/55, Kingston, Ont. Hall of Fame builder coached amateur hockey in Kingston and became president of Ontario Hockey Assn., 1915. Served in World War I, then became president of CAHA in 1919.

TALLON, MICHAEL DALE LEE B. 10/19/50, Noranda, Que. Defenseman. 6'1", 200. Van. Canucks' defenseman, scored 14 goals and 42 assists in 78 games in 1970-71 as rookie, better than the 13 goals and 28 assists registered by Bobby Orr in his rookie season. Also has played at forward for Canucks. Is represented in negotiations by Al Eagleson, Orr's lawyer, who says Tallon got much the same rookie contract as Boston star. Outstanding golfer, once losing players' tournament championship by one stroke to Bobby Rousseau of N.Y. Rangers in sudden-death playoff. Traded to Chi. Black Hawks 5/17/73.

    NHL record: 44 goals, 93 assists in 225 games.

TARDIF, MARC B. 6/12/49, Granby, Que. Forward. 6', 180. Mont. Canadiens' left wing, has been criticized for "needing an explosion to get him started," but still has been a productive scorer, getting 19 goals in 1970–71 rookie season and 31 the next. Played with Junior Canadiens, turned pro with Montreal team in AHL in 1969, also getting into 18 games with Canadiens. Came up to NHL next season.

    NHL record: 78 goals, 79 assists in 247 league games; 11 goals, 10 assists in 40 playoff games.

TAYLOR, EDWARD WRAY (Ted) B. 2/25/42, Brandon, Man. Forward. 6', 175. Van. Canucks' left wing walked out of training camp in huff in 1970 in dispute over conditions, then walked back in to become a regular and get 11 goals and 16 assists in 56 games. Jumped to Houston

Aeros of WHA for 1972–73. Started pro career with game at Vancouver, in WHL, in 1960–61. Did minor league duty at Sudbury, Baltimore, St. Paul, and Pittsburgh of AHL, and was with Vancouver when it got NHL franchise. Also had major league tryouts with N.Y. Rangers twice, Det. Red Wings and Minn. North Stars. Lives in Oak Lake, Man.

NHL record: 23 goals, 35 assists in 166 games.

TAYLOR, FRED (Cyclone) B. 6/23/83, Tara, Ont. Forward-defenseman. Hall of Famer started career in Ontario, turned pro with Houghton, Mich., in 1906. Played at Ottawa and Renfrew, joined Vancouver in 1912 and retired as player there in 1921. In 186 games scored 194 goals, getting 32 goals in 18 games in 1917–18. Holds Order of British Empire bestowed for World War II services. Lives in Vancouver and is member of Hall of Fame selection committee.

THOMPSON, CECIL (Tiny) B. 5/31/05, Sandon, B.C. Goalie. Hall of Famer won Vezina Trophy four times in 12-year NHL career. Played amateur hockey in hometown and in Calgary, Bellevue, Duluth, and Minneapolis. When Minneapolis team turned pro in 1926, so did Thompson. Joined Bos. Bruins in 1928, playing 10 years in Boston and two more with Det. Red Wings before retiring in 1940. In 1933, lost game to Toronto, 1–0, which went 1 hour, 44 minutes, and 46 seconds. Now serves as one of chief scouts for Chi. Black Hawks.

NHL record: alloved 1183 goals in 553 games for 2.14 average, 80 shutouts; gave up 73 goals in 44 playoff games for 1.66 average, 7 shutouts.

THOMPSON, PAUL IVAN B. 11/2/06, Calgary, Alta. Forward. Brother of goalie Tiny Thompson. Spent 13 years in NHL with N.Y. Rangers and Chi. Black Hawks, and served as Hawks' coach from 1939 to 1944. Joined Rangers in 1928. Went to Hawks in 1931 for Art Somers and Vic Desjardins. Named assistant coach to Bill Stewart in 1938, and took over club next season, stepping down as player after 1938–39. Quit to accept post with Vancouver; resigned job in 1947. After retirement, entered hotel business in western Canada.

NHL record: 153 goals, 179 assists in 13 seasons; 11 goals, 11 assists in 48 playoff games.

THOMS, WILLIAM D. B. 3/5/10, Newmarket, Ont. D. 12/26/64, Toronto, Ont. Forward. Played 13 years in NHL until forced out by poor health. Played for Toronto Marlboros, joined Leafs in 1932, staying until traded to Chi. Black Hawks in Dec. 1938, for Doc Romnes, then went to Bos. Bruins in mid-1944–45, ending his career there the same season.

Career hampered by ulcers, which almost killed him in Chicago in 1943. Often finished among top scorers, getting 24 goals in 1938, 30 in 1942, and 28 in 1943.

NHL record: 135 goals, 206 assists in 13 seasons; 6 goals, 10 assists in 10 playoff series.

THOMSON, JAMES RICHARD   B. 2/23/27, Winnipeg, Man. Defenseman. Spent 13 seaons with Tor. Maple Leafs, his only team in NHL until 1957–58, when he wound up career with one year with Chi. Black Hawks. Learned to skate at six, played as bantam and midget for Winnipeg Excelsiors, tried high school football but gave it up because of continual injuries. Went to Leafs' camp in 1943, and was sent to Toronto Marlboros, then to St. Michael's juniors. Turned pro in 1945, playing five games with Leafs before going to Pittsburgh, but made big club in 1946. Played in seven All-Star games.

NHL record: 19 goals, 215 assists in 787 games; 2 goals, 13 assists in 63 playoff games.

TKACZUK, WALTER ROBERT (Walt)   B. 9/29/47, Emsdetten, Germany. Foward. 6', 185. N.Y. Rangers' center was voted most popular player on and off ice by Ranger fans in 1970, but not by Ranger management, which suspended him in September of that year for participating in contract rebellion along with several teammates. Born in Germany, where his parents had been taken as forced laborers during World War II from Ukraine. Moved to Northern Ontario, where father worked in mines. Played as junior with Kitchener Rangers, made brief appearances at Omaha and Buffalo of AHL before making Rangers in 1968–69. Worked briefly with father in mines in off-season until ordered to quit by Rangers.

NHL record: 116 goals, 204 assists in 378 games; 14 goals, 15 assists in 49 playoff games.

TOPPAZZINI, GERALD   B. 7/29/31, Copper Cliff, Ont. Forward. Played 12 years as forward in NHL, mostly with Bos. Bruins. Started as junior with Barrie Flyers. Joined Bruins in 1952, was peddled to Chi. Black Hawks 2/17/54 for Gus Bodnar, then sent on to Det. Red Wings in 1955, who shipped him back to Bruins in midseason. Bruins sent him to Hawks again 6/9/64, after 8 years, for Murray Balfour, and Hawks sent him on to Pittsburgh Hornets Oct. 12 of that year. Never returned to NHL. Scored eight goals in 1957 Cup semifinals.

NHL record: 163 goals, 244 assists in 783 games; 13 goals, 9 assists in 40 playoff games.

TREMBLAY, GILLES B. 12/18/38, Montmorency, Que. Forward. Spent nine seasons with Mont. Canadiens as high-scoring forward despite asthma which troubled him constantly. Played for Hull-Ottawa Juniors. Three games at Rochester. Joined Canadiens in 1960, left NHL after 1968–69 season. Had 32-goal season in 1961–62, and scored 20 or more goals in four other seasons. Lives in Montreal, works in radio and television.

NHL record: 168 goals, 162 assists in 509 games; 9 goals, 14 assists in 48 playoff games.

TREMBLAY, JEAN CLAUDE (J.C.) B. 1/22/39, Bagotville, Que. Defenseman. 5'11", 178. Spent entire NHL career, which began in 1959–60, with Mont. Canadiens, then jumped to Quebec Nordiques for 1972–73. Played as junior at Hull-Ottawa, and with Hull-Ottawa in EPHL for two seasons, winning MVP award in 1959–60, same year he appeared in 11 games with Canadiens. Made comeback in 1970–71 after warming bench much of previous season. Always has contributed more than share of assists, going over 50 on two occasions.

NHL record: 57 goals, 306 assists in 794 games; 14 goals, 51 assists in 108 playoff games.

TRIHEY, HENRY JUDAH (Harry) B. 12/25/77. D. 12/9/42, Montreal, Que. Hall of Famer starred in football and lacrosse as well as hockey. Played hockey with McGill University and Montreal Shamrocks, and for Winnipeg Vics. Later was president of Eastern Canada Hockey League. Also was known for military activity, organizing regiment from which came 199th Battalion, Duchess of Connaught's own Irish Canadian Rangers, of which he was commanding officer with rank of colonel.

TROTTIER, DAVID B. 6/25/06, Pembroke, Ont. D. 11/13/56, Halifax, N.S. Played 11 years in NHL, 10 with Mont. Maroons and his last year briefly with Det. Red Wings, after outstanding amateur career. Joined Maroons in 1928, going to Wings in 1938–39, where he scored just one goal and one assist. Best year was in 1931–32 when he scored 26 goals and 18 assists for 44 points. One of few ever to play on Canadian world and Olympic championship teams.

NHL record: 121 goals, 113 assists in 11 seasons; 4 goals, 3 assists in 8 playoff series.

TROTTIER, GUY B. 4/1/41, Hull, Que. Forward. 5'8", 165. Jumped to Ottawa Nationals of WHA for 1972–73 after two years in NHL. Was excellent scorer in minor leagues, getting 55 goals for Buffalo of AHL in 1969–70. Played as amateur with Dayton Gems of IHL before turning pro with N.Y. Ranger organization at Buffalo in 1967. Played there three seasons, traded to Tor. Maple Leafs 6/10/70 in deal involving Tim Horton. Lives in Englewood, Ohio.

NHL record: 28 goals, 17 assists in 115 games; 1 goal, no assists in 9 playoff games.

TURNER, LLOYD   B. 1884, Elmvale, Ont. Hall of Fame builder. Pioneer in western Canada hockey. Moved to Calgary in 1909, organized league and team which played on old roller rink, and in 1924 team challenged for Stanley Cup. After living in Seattle and Minneapolis, went back to Calgary to reorganize Western Canada League. Organized Indian tribes of Alberta into hockey tournament competition. In younger days, played and coached in Sault Ste. Marie and Fort William, Ont.

ULLMAN, NORMAN VICTOR ALEXANDER (Norm) B. 12/26/35, Provost, Alta. Forward. 5'10", 185. Tor. Maple Leafs' center. Has been NHL regular since 1955 and spent only one season in minors. Played as junior with Edmonton Oil Kings, turned pro in 1954 with Edmonton of WHL, then made Det. Red Wings next season at 18. Stayed in Detroit until being traded to Leafs 3/4/68 in Frank Mahovlich deal. Consistent goal scorer has missed 20 goals in only three seasons, and usually has led Leafs in points. Led league in goals in 1965 with 42, finishing second to Bobby Hull in Hart Trophy voting, 96 votes to 103. During playoffs that season, scored goals five seconds apart against Chi. Black Hawks. Got 300th goal against Montreal 11/12/67, and now is one of only six players to score more than 400 goals. Elected for term to head players Assn., 1968. Lives outside Toronto, going into city only for professional reasons due to allergy to city's pollution, for which he has sought medical treatment.

NHL record: 439 goals, 631 assists in 1187 games; 29 goals, 52 assists in 95 playoff games.

UNGER, GARRY DOUGLAS B. 12/7/47, Edmonton, Alta. Forward. 5'11", 170. St. L. Blue center led club in scoring in 1971–72 with 36 goals and 34 assists for 70 points, Career has been marked by disputes over life style, which includes long blond hair and motorcycle riding. Played as junior with London Nationals, made token appearances at Tulsa and Rochester before joining Tor. Maple Leafs in 1967–68. Traded to Det.

Red Wings 3/3/68 in six-man deal that sent Frank Mahovlich to Red Wings. Battles with Detroit management over long hair and other fringe activities ended with trade 2/6/71 to Blues for Red Berenson and Tim Ecclestone. In summer of 1971 traveled through Europe with knapsack, visiting Russia. Lives on farm 40 miles from St. Louis during season. "I just want to be myself," he says of dress, motorcycles, and dates, which have included a Miss America. Performance in 1971–72 earned him All-Star berth.

NHL record: 177 goals, 156 assists in 415 games; 8 goals, 10 assists in 26 playoff games.

VACHON, ROGATIEN ROSAIRE (Roggie) B. 9/8/45, Palmarolle, Que. Goalie. 5'7", 160. L.A. King goalie had to overcame skepticism over size when he first arrived in NHL with Mont. Canadiens. But shared Vezina Trophy with Gump Worsley in 1968, playing in 37 games in which he had 2.48 goals-against average. Ken Dryden's heroics in 1971 Stanley Cup playoffs obscured him again, and Vachon was traded 11/4/71 to L.A. for Denis DeJordy, Dale Hoganson, Noel Price and Doug Robinson. Played junior hockey with Thetford Mines before turning pro in 1965–66 with Quebec. Also played at Houston in 1966–67 before making Canadiens later in season.

NHL record: allowed 776 goals in 287 games for a 2.70 average, 17 shutouts; gave up 38 goals in 19 playoff games for 1.94 average, 1 shutout.

VAN IMPE, EDWARD CHARLES (Ed) B. 5/27/40, Saskatoon, Sask. Defenseman. 5'11", 200. Was first choice of Phila. Flyers in 1967 expansion draft and has played regularly on team since. Played junior hockey with Saskatoon Quakers, turned pro in 1960 with Calgary. Spent five years at Buffalo in AHL before joining Chi. Black Hawks for 1966–67, then being drafted by Flyers. Suffered serious injury in 1969 when he stopped puck with his mouth, required surgery. Picked up more than 100 penalty minutes in several pro seasons. Captain of Flyers.

NHL record: 24 goals, 77 assists in 483 games; no goals, 5 assists in 29 playoff games.

VASKO, ELMER (Moose) B. 12/11/35, Duparquet, Que. Defense-man. Spent 13 years in NHL, 10 with Chi. Black Hawks and three with Minn. North Stars. Played as amateur at St. Catharines. Joined Hawks in 1956, going to North Stars in 1967, after sitting out 1966–67 season. Stars sent him to Salt Lake City for most of the 1969–70 season when he retired. Picked three times for All-Star competition.

NHL record: 34 goals, 166 assists in 783 games; 2 goals, 7 assists in 78 playoff games.

VEZINA, GEORGES B. Jan. 1887, Chicoutimi Que. D. 3/26/26 of tuberculosis. Goalie. Hall of Famer for whom Vezina Trophy for goaltending is named. Did not miss a scheduled game in 15 years with Mont. Canadiens from 1910 to 1925. Played 328 straight, 39 more in playoffs, allowing 1267 goals. Last game was 11/28/25 against Pitts-burgh. Forced to withdraw with severe chest pains and bleeding from mouth. Never was well again. Father of 22 children, was known as Chicoutimi Cucumber.

VILLEMURE, GILLES B. 5/30/40, Three Rivers, Que. Goalie, 5'8", 170. N.Y. Rangers' goalie shared Vezina Trophy with Ed Giacomin in 1970–71 after long climb up through minors. Played as amateur with Charlotte of Eastern League, turned pro in 1962 with Vancouver of WHL in N.Y. Rangers' organization. Also put in time at Baltimore and Buffalo of AHL, winning AHL MVP award twice, before sticking with Rangers in 1970–71. Drives trotting horses in off-season.

NHL record: allowed 265 goals in 118 games for 2.25 average, 11 shutouts; gave up 26 goals in 11 playoff games for 2.60 average, no shutouts.

VOSS, CARL B. 1/6/07, Chelsea, Mass. Forward. Played with seven NHL clubs in six-year career. Went on to become official, serving as referee-in-chief of NHL. Played at Queens U. Signed with London in 1928. Led International League with Buffalo in 1931–32 with 41 points. Joined N.Y. Rangers in 1932, then played with Det. Red Wings (1933–34), Ottawa (1934), St. Louis Eagles (1934–35), N.Y. Americans (1935–36), Mont. Maroons (1936–37), and Chi. Black Hawks. Retired, lives in Florida.

NHL record: 34 goals, 70 assists in 6 seasons; 5 goals, 3 assists in 24 playoff games.

WAGHORNE, FRED C. B. 1886, Tunbridge Wells, England. D. 1956. Hall of Fame builder was outstanding referee of hockey and lacrosse. First to drop puck for face-off, rather than laying it on ice, and to use whistle rather than bell to stop play. Referee in more than 2000 games, and one of pioneers of Toronto Hockey League in 1911.

WAKELY, ERNEST ALFRED LINTON (Ernie) B. 11/27/40, Flin Flon, Man. Goalie. 5′11″, 160. Was with St. L. Blues before jumping to WHA's Winnipeg Jets in 1972–73. Played as junior with Winnipeg Braves. Spent 10 years in minors with Winnipeg, Hull-Ottawa, Kingston, North Bay, Spokane, Quebec, Omaha, Seattle, Cleveland, and Houston before traded by Mont. Canadiens to Blues 6/27/69. Won EPHL goaltender awards in 1962–63 and 1963–64.

NHL record: allowed 290 goals in 113 games for 2.79 average, 8 shutouts; gave up 37 goals in 10 playoff games for 4.36 average, 1 shutout.

WALKER, JOHN PHILLIP B. 11/28/88, Silver Mountain, Ont. D. 2/16/50. Hall of Famer played on three Stanley Cup winners during career from 1906 to 1932. Started in Port Arthur, played for Moncton and then for Toronto Arenas, Also played for Seattle and Victoria Cougars. Played two seasons in NHL with Detroit, then the Cougars, in 1926–27 and 1927–28, scoring five goals and eight assists. In three playoff years, all in PCL, he scored eight goals and three assists. After NHL years, returned west to Edmonton, went to Hollywood Stars in

1931–32 and then to Oakland, retiring in 1934 as active player. Continued to coach and manage in PCL.

NHL record: 5 goals, 8 assists in 2 seasons.

WALL, ROBERT JAMES ALBERT (Bob) B. 12/1/42, Richmond Hill, Ont. Defenseman-forward. 5'10", 175. Det. Red Wings' veteran played more than 300 NHL games before jumping to Alberta Oilers for 1972–73. Played amateur hockey with Hamilton Red Wings, and in minor leagues at Pittsburgh, Edmonton, Cincinnati, Omaha and Quebec. Came up with Wings, but was drafted by L.A. Kings, playing three seasons as regular and captain from 1967 through 1970. Traded to St. L. Blues in 1970, then went back to Wings in Carl Brewer–Ab McDonald deal 2/19/71. Lives with wife and children in King City, Ont., during off-season.

NHL record: 30 goals, 55 assists in 322 games; no goals, 3 assists in 22 playoff games.

WALTON, MICHAEL ROBERT (Mike) B. 1/3/45, Kirkland Lake, Ont. Forward. 5'9", 170. Traded to Bos. Bruins 2/1/71 by Tor. Maple Leafs as result of psychiatrist's diagnosis after treatment for depression in Toronto. Played with Toronto Marlboros as junior, turned pro in 1964 at Tulsa, winning CPHL Rookie of Year award. Played a season and a half at Rochester, then joined Maple Leafs for 31 games in 1966–67, and next season scored 30 goals for them. Troubles began in Feb. 1969, when he walked out on club. Returned, but was suspended 12/11/70 when he said he was run down and unfit to play. Doctor examined him and suggested "geographical relocation," which came in three-corner deal with Phila. Flyers involving Bruce Gamble, Bernie Parent, Rich MacLeish, and Danny Schock, with Walton going to Flyers, then immediately to Boston without ever donning Philly uniform. Bounced back in 1971–72 to play 78 games and score 28 goals. Partner with Bobby Orr in sports camp.

NHL record: 137 goals, 162 assists in 411 games; 13 goals, 10 assists in 41 playoff games.

WARD, JAMES B. 9/1/06, Fort William, Ont. Forward. Played 12 seasons as forward for two Montreal teams, 11 with Maroons and one with Canadiens. Joined Maroons in 1927, stayed until going to Canadiens in 1938 when Maroons folded. Played just four games for Canadiens, and stepped out of NHL. Seriously hurt 1/22/35 in Boston when he collided with Eddie Shore, suffering brain concussion. Son Pete became major league baseball player, primarily with Chicago White Sox.

NHL record: 147 goals, 127 assists in 12 seasons; 4 goals, 4 assists in 9 playoff series.

WARD, RONALD LEON (Ron) B. 9/12/44, Cornwall, Ont. Forward. 5'10", 180. Made NHL as regular with Van. Canucks in 1971–72 after admitting he delayed his career with malice aforethought. "I didn't figure I had a chance to make the big club," he says of the 1970–71 season, "and I preferred going to Phoenix to being shipped to Rochester." However, he went to Rochester, where he got 23 goals in 69 games. Drafted by Canucks 6/10/70. Jumped to N.Y. Raiders of WHA for 1972–73. Turned pro with Tulsa in 1965, also played at Phoenix, and Rochester, with 18-game tryout with Maple Leafs in 1969–70.
NHL record: 2 goals, 5 assists in 89 games.

WARWICK, GRANT DAVID (Knobby) B. 10/11/21, Regina, Sask. Forward. Played eight seasons in NHL for N.Y. Rangers, Tor. Bruins and Mont. Canadiens. Played as amateur for Regina Rangers, made Rangers in 1941–42 when 16 goals and 17 assists were enough to win him Calder Trophy as Rookie of Year. Went to Bruins in 1947–48, and to Canadiens in 1949–50, his last year in NHL. Lives in British Columbia.
NHL record: 147 goals, 142 assists in 399 games; 2 goals, 4 assists in 16 playoff games.

WATSON, BYRAN JOSEPH B. 11/14/42, Bancroft, Ont. Defenseman. 5'10", 170. Bounced back from broken leg in 1970–71 to get into 75 games with Pitt. Penguins in 1971–72, scoring three goals, 17 assists, turned pro in Mont. Canadiens organization in 1963, playing with Omaha and Quebec Aces, then going to Det. Red Wings in 1965–66. Bounced back to Canadiens in 1967–68 after play at Memphis, and played with Cleveland and Houston before being sent to Calif. Seals in 1968–69 who sent him to Penguins the same season. Played forward as well as defense, and earned name "Superpest" for activities shadowing stars of other teams, including Chi. Black Hawks' Bobby Hull, with whom he has engaged in fights.
NHL record: 11 goals, 68 assists in 490 games; 2 goals, no assists in 32 playoff games.

WATSON, HARRY E. (Moose) B. 7/14/98, St. John's, Newfoundland. D. 9/11/57, Toronto, Ont. Hall of Famer remained amateur throughout career, turning down $30,000 to play for Mont. Maroons in 1925. Moved to Toronto in 1915, where he started playing hockey. Served in army during World War I, returned to play for Toronto Granites in 1920. Team won Olympic gold medal in 1924, with Watson scoring 13 goals against Czechs. Retired in 1925, returning briefly in 1931 to play and coach Toronto National Sea Fleas to Allan Cup.

WATSON, HARRY PERCIVAL B. 5/6/23, Saskatoon, Sask. Forward. Spent 14 seasons in NHL, mostly at left wing. Played for Saskatoon Juniors, came up with Brooklyn Americans in 1941, went to Det. Red Wings next season, then off to war, returning to Tor. Maple Leafs in 1946 in deal for Billy Taylor, was sold to Chi. Black Hawks 12/11/54. Retired from NHL after 1956–57 season, taking coaching job at Buffalo.

NHL record: 236 goals, 207 assists in 809 games; 16 goals, 9 assists in 62 playoff games.

WATSON, JAMES ARTHUR (Jim) B. 6/28/43, Malartic, Que. Defenseman. 6'2", 195. Was considered one of quietest Buffalo Sabres, but chalked up 248 penalty minutes in first two seasons with team. Broke in with Det. Red Wings' organization in 1963–64, then was shipped to Cincinnati, and bounced back and forth between Wings and minor league teams of Pittsburgh, Memphis, San Diego, Baltimore, Fort Worth and Cleveland before joining Sabres in 1970. Had played only one full NHL season before that, with Wings in 1967–68, where he failed to score. Got first NHL goal on opening night in Pittsburgh in 1970. Jumped to Los Angeles of WHA in 1972–73.

NHL record: 4 goals, 19 assists in 221 games.

WATSON, JOSEPH JOHN (Joe) B. 7/6/43, Smithers, B.C. Defenseman. 5'10", 180. One of original members of Phila. Flyers when team joined NHL in 1967–68. Played junior hockey with Estevan Bruins, turned pro with Minneapolis of CPHL in 1963, went to Oklahoma City in 1965, and made NHL with Bos. Bruins in next season, teaming with Bobby Orr in Orr's rookie season before moving to Flyers.

NHL record: 18 goals, 61 assists in 382 games; 1 goal, 1 assist in 12 playoff games.

WATSON, PHILLIPE HENRI B. 10/24/14, Montreal Que, Forward. Spent 13 seasons in NHL, all but one of them with N.Y. Rangers, then went on to coaching, including head coach jobs of both Rangers and Bos. Bruins. Played for Montreal Royals; turned pro with Philadelphia Ramblers, started with Rangers in 1935, spent a wartime season (1943–44) with Mont. Canadiens, returned to Rangers in 1944–45 and retired from NHL as player in 1948. Always outspoken and a critic of officials, he was hired to coach Rangers 5/2/55 and "promoted" to front office 11/12/59. Replaced Milt Schmidt as Bruins' coach 6/6/61, fired 11/19/62. Pressures of hockey created ulcer, for which he had surgery in 1959. Went on to coach Quebec Aces and threatened lawsuit when he was fired in 1967 with time remaining on three-year contract. In 1971 he was bashed over the head with stick by Johnstown's Blake Ball while coaching Syracuse, and resulting furor ended in forfeit of game to Syracuse. Became interim coach of Phila. Blazers of WHA in Nov. 1972, replacing John McKenzie.

NHL record: 144 goals, 265 assists in 590 games; 10 goals, 25 assists in 54 playoff games.

WEILAND, RALPH (Cooney) B. 11/5/04, Seaforth, Ont. Forward. Retired in 1971 as coach of Harvard hockey team after career that included 11 years as player in NHL. After junior hockey he played for Minneapolis from 1925 to 1928 before joining Bos. Bruins in 1928, went to Ottawa Senators in 1932, Det. Red Wings in mid-1933–34, and returned to Boston in 1935, ending career as player in 1939. Scored 43 goals in 44 games in 1929–30. Made second All-Stars in 1934–35. Coached Bruins 1939–41, leading them to Stanley Cup in 1940–41, then coached Hershey and New Haven in AHL before joining Harvard staff.

NHL record: 173 goals, 160 assists in 11 seasons; 12 goals, 10 assists in 8 playoff series.

WESTFALL, VERNON EDWIN (Eddie) B. 9/19/40, Belleville, Ont. Forward. 6'1", 197. Drafted for 1972–73 season by N.Y. Islanders from Bos. Bruins. Was goalie as boy. Turned into forward whose forte is penalty killing. Played with Niagara Falls Flyers as junior. Turned pro with Bos. Bruins in 1961 and stuck, with short trips to Kingston and Providence only minor league experience. A 25-goal season won him new car on bet with auto dealer. Lives in Pelham, N.H., and does promotional work for brewery in off-season.

NHL record: 141 goals, 244 assists in 794 games; 13 goals, 17 assists in 50 playoff games.

WESTWICK, HARRY (Rat) B. 4/23/76. D. 4/3/57, Ottawa, Ont. Hall of Famer got nickname because of his small size. Started in Ottawa City League and joined Ottawa Silver Seven in 1895. Team won Stanley Cup three straight years starting in 1903. In 1904–05 he scored 24 goals in 13 games. Retired in 1907, continuing to referee in NHA.

WHARRAM, KENNETH MALCOLM B. 7/2/33, Ferris, Ont. Forward. Regular for Chi. Black Hawks from 1958 to 1969, when he was forced out by heart condition. Played as amateur with Galt Juniors and with Buffalo before making Hawks to stay in 1958, although he appeared briefly with club in 1951–52, 1953–54, and 1955–56. Had three 30-goal seasons, four in which he scored 20 or more. Lives in North Bay, Ont.

NHL record: 252 goals, 281 assists in 766 games; 16 goals, 27 assists in 80 playoff games.

WHITCROFT, FREDRICK   B. 1880s, Fort Perry, Ont. D. 1931, Vancouver, B.C. Hall of Famer, developed into outstanding player in seven-man hockey. Played for Peterboro Colts, Midland, Ont., and helped Kenora Thistles to Stanley Cup in Jan. 1907. Moved to Edmonton, scoring 49 goals in 1907–08 season, ended career in 1909–10 with Renfrew Millionaires.

WHITE, WILLIAM EARL (Bill)   B. 8/26/39, Toronto, Ont. Defenseman. 6'2", 190. Chi. Black Hawk considered one of finest strictly defensive defensemen in NHL. Spent eight seasons in minors before making L.A. Kings in 1967. Two seasons were at Rochester and five at Springfield, where, says White, "Eddie Shore owned us outright and could let us go or keep us as he wished." One of many players on L.A. owner Jack Kent Cooke's "trouble" list, sent to Hawks 2/21/70. Team Canada 1972.

NHL record: 40 goals, 152 assists in 425 games; 6 goals, 21 assists in 68 playoff games.

WIDING, JUHA MARKKU (Whitey)   B. 7/4/47, Uleaborg, Finland, Forward. 6'1", 190. L.A. Kings' center led club in scoring in 1971–72 for second straight year, with 27 goals and 28 assists in 78 games. Was imported to Canada by N.Y. Rangers to play junior hockey, scoring 62 goals in 1966–67 for Brandon Wheat Kings. Turned pro with Omaha, getting 41 goals in first season, called up to Rangers two years later and traded to L.A. late in 1969–70 season for Ted Irvine. Spent summer of 1971 in Sweden with Ralph Backstrom organizing hockey school.

NHL record: 75 goals, 131 assists in 281 games.

WILKINS, BARRY JAMES,   B. 2/28/47, Toronto, Ont. Defenseman. 5'11", 180. Van. Canucks' defenseman scored team's first NHL goal, against Los Angeles, on opening night. Played one pro game with Bos. Bruins in 1966–67, then worked way up with Oklahoma City in CPHL averaging 10 goals a season, before being drafted by Canucks.

NHL record: 19 goals, 40 assists in 199 games.

WILLIAMS, THOMAS MARK (Tom)   B. 4/17/40, Duluth, Minn. Forward. 5'11", 180. Calif. Seals center, who jumped to New England Whalers for 1972–73. Starred with U.S. Olympic team in 1960 that upset Russians for gold medal at Squaw Valley, then went on to one of longest NHL careers of any American-born player. Played amateur hockey with Fort William Hurricanes before joining Kingston of EPHL in 1960–61 after Olympics, moved up to Bos. Bruins for eight seasons, then to Minn. North Stars and finally to Seals at end of 1970–71 after being suspended by Minnesota as result of argument with coach Jack Gordon. Hobbled by back and knee injuries, Williams was shocked further during that season by unexpected death of wife. While with Bruins in 1966, took NHL to task for its image, saying it would have trouble attracting American players as long as parents considered players "guys with no teeth and scars all over their faces."

NHL record: 131 goals, 229 assists in 556 games; 2 goals, 5 assists in 10 playoff games.

WILSON, DUNCAN SHEPHERD (Dunc) B. 3/22/48, Toronto, Ont. Goalie. 5'11", 175. Took over as No. 1 Van. Canucks' goalie in 1971–72, third year in pro hockey, after veteran Charlie Hodge stepped down. Turned pro in Phila. Flyers' organization with Quebec Aces in 1968–69, and stayed with Aces next year, though playing one game for Flyers. Talking about Wilson's play with Quebec, Bud Poile, Canuck GM, said: "He put that club in the playoff two years running almost single-handed." Drafted by Canucks from Flyers 6/10/70. Senior lacrosse player in Vancouver, also has worked in off-season as public relations man for Vancouver brewery. Traded to Toronto 5/29/73.

NHL record: allowed 473 goals in 132 games for 3.64 average, 2 shutouts.

WILSON, GORDON ALLAN (Phat) B. 12/29/95, Port Arthur, Ont. Defenseman. Hall of Famer, although remained amateur throughout playing career. Started with Port Arthur War Veterans in 1918. Iroquois Falls 1920. Returned to play with Port Arthur Bearcats. Team won three Allan Cups and toured western Canada. Retired 1937. Coached Bearcats in 1938, 1940. Served on Port Arthur Public Utilities Commission. Lives in Port Arthur.

WILSON, JOHN EDWARD B. 6/14/29, Kincardine, Ont. Forward. Played parts of 12 seasons in NHL, joining Det. Red Wings for one game in 1949–50, then returning for 28 games in 1951–52. NHL career continued until retirement in 1962. Red Wings' coach mid-1971–72 replacing Doug Barkley through 1972–73 when released. Played for Red Wings, Chi. Black Hawks, Tor. Maple Leafs and N.Y. Rangers. Coached Ottawa Montagnards beginning in 1963, then served as Princeton U. coach. Took over Springfield Kings in 1967, taking them to Calder Cup, AHL championship trophy, in 1971. During part of 1969–70, served as interim L.A. coach, then returned to Springfield. Took over Tidewater in Red Wings' farm system in 1971 before being called to major league club. Played in Shawinigan Falls, Que., as youth before signing with Windsor, Ont., junior club. Brother Larry also is pro coach.

NHL record: 161 goals, 171 assists in 688 games; 14 goals, 13 assists in 66 playoff games.

WIRTZ, ARTHUR M. B. 1/23/01, Chicago, Ill. Hall of Fame builder was partner of James Norris Sr. and James D. Norris in ownership of NHL clubs. With them Chicago real estate millionaire acquired Det. Red Wings and Detroit Olympia in 1931, adding Chicago Stadium Corp. in 1933. Also added ownership of Madison Square Garden. With James D. Norris, bought Chi. Black Hawks in 1954 after death of owner Maj. Frederic McLaughlin, and sold Detroit interests. Credited with persuading NHL to give franchise to St. Louis in 1966, where he owned St. Louis Arena.

WORSLEY, LORNE JOHN (Gump) B. 5/14/29, Montreal, Que. Goalie. 5'7", 180. Retired 1/24/73 as Minn. North Star goalie at age 43. Turned pro in 1950 with St. Paul, played in Saskatoon before making N.Y. Rangers in 1952, who rewarded their Rookie of Year by sending him to WHL at Vancouver, where he was MVP. Returned to play nine more seasons for Rangers. Sent to Mont. Canadiens 6/4/63 for Donnie Marshall and Phil Goyette. Went to Quebec, then called back for play from 1964–65 through 1968–69. Traded to Minnesota 2/27/70 after fight with Montreal management which wanted to send him down to Voyageurs to "get into shape." Worsley countered by announcing his retirement New Year's Eve 1969. Feared flying and in Nov. 1968 refused to board plane from Chicago to Los Angeles after bumpy flight from Montreal, returning to Canada by train. Canadiens gave him month off. Wry goalie spent much of career with weakling Ranger team. When asked during that period which team gave him the most trouble, he quickly replied: "The New York Rangers." Shared Vezina Trophy in 1966 and 1968. Lives in Beloeil, Quebec.

NHL record: allowed 2346 goals in 831 games for 2.83 average, 43 shutouts; gave up 192 goals in 70 playoff games for 2.82 average, 5 shutouts.

WORTERS, ROY B. 10/19/1900, Toronto, Ont. D. 11/7/57, Toronto, Ont. Goalie. 5'2", 130. Hall of Famer. Known for toughness, once playing seven games with severe hernia. Broke into NHL with Pittsburgh in 1925, went to N.Y. Americans in 1928–29, played part of 1929–30 with Mont. Canadiens, then went back to Americans in 1930, where he finished career in 1937. Known as "The Shrimp" because of size, he won Hart MVP Trophy in 1929 and Vezina Trophy in 1931. Named twice to second All-Stars.

NHL record: allowed 1154 goals in 484 games for 2.38 average, 66 shutouts; gave up 24 goals in 11 playoff games for 2.18 average, 3 shutouts.

WOYTOWICH, ROBERT IVAN (Bob) B. 8/18/41, Winnipeg, Man. Defenseman, 5'11", 195. Came to L.A. Kings from Pitt. Penguins 1/11/72 for Al McDonough. Played two games for Seattle in WHL in 1960–61, then first full season with Sudbury of EPHL next year. Put in a season with St. Paul, then in 1964–65 divided time between Hershey and Bos. Bruins, staying in Boston until 1967–68, when he went to Minn. North Stars. Went to Penguins next season in exchange for top amateur draft choice. Penguin fans formed "Polish Army" to root for him, although he is not Polish. Jumped to Winnipeg of WHA in 1972–73. Lives with family in Winnipeg in off-season.

NHL record: 32 goals, 126 assists in 503 games; 1 goal, 3 assists in 24 playoff games.

YOUNG, GARRY B. B. 1/2/34, Toronto, Ont. Ex-GM of Calif. Seals. Spent 20 years in Bos. Bruins' organization before taking GM job in 1971. Outstanding amateur in Toronto as defenseman. Joined Marlboros at 13, one of youngest ever to play for them. Serious back injury partially paralyzed him for six months; ended playing career. Joined Bruin organization. Complications from injury in later years required bone grafts to enable him to walk. Named Seals' coach 8/19/72, replacing Vic Stasiuk, but resigned Nov. 1972, severing all connection with club.